THE POLITICS
OF CIVIL LIBERTIES

Harper's American Political Behavior Series

Under the Editorship of David J. Danelski

THE POLITICS
OF CIVIL LIBERTIES

JONATHAN D. CASPER

Stanford University

HARPER & ROW, PUBLISHERS

New York, Evanston, San Francisco, London

THE POLITICS OF CIVIL LIBERTIES

Standard Book Number: 06-041213-5

Library of Congress Catalog Card Number: 72-82899

To Isaac and Miriam and Doug

CONTENTS

PREFACE

CIVIL liberties and civil rights embody values that we all think we cherish. Yet we constantly argue about what rights citizens ought or ought not enjoy. Many of us often adopt a highly moral tone in these arguments because we have been taught to value concepts like *free expression, equality, fair procedure*, and feel there are "right" and "wrong" answers in our disputes about them. Not only do we discuss civil liberties and rights with a strongly moral tone, we often think they are the special province of a particular institution—the legal system—whose job it is to resolve disputes involving rights protected in the Constitution. We may attack the Supreme Court when we think it makes errors—when its decisions seem to protect too much or too little—but still much of our thinking and rhetoric about political and civil rights has at its base a notion that there simply are correct answers to the specific issues that arise. ×

×This book argues that such a view misconstrues both the nature of the issues involved and the operation of the American political system. It traces Supreme Court decisions in a variety of areas of civil liberties, attempting to relate these decisions to attitudes and behavior in the political and social system of which the Court is a member. The Court is in the most fundamental sense a political institution; and issues involving civil liberties and civil rights are also fundamentally political for they affect the allocation of values in our society. Therefore, the discussion will suggest that there are not, in fact, simple right or wrong answers, but a series of answers, many equally plausible, to questions about how much freedom of expression we ought to have, what the value of equality means, and what procedural protections members of our society ought to enjoy. People can and do disagree about these issues in much the same way that we disagree about other issues which we are quite comfortable in acknowledging as "political."

Thus, in examining and evaluating the decisions of courts dealing with such rights, we must keep in mind disagreements in the society about what is good public policy, the activities of participants in political institutions, and the general tenor of social and political life. If we are to understand the decisions that emerge from courts, if we are to understand the nature of the "law" dealing with civil liberties and civil rights, the political context in which disputes over civil liberties are embedded must be acknowledged and understood. This is the major argument of this book.

The book has two purposes. First, it discusses the substance of civil liberties litigation—the doctrine that has emerged from the Supreme Court. Second, it discusses the context of this doctrine—the environment of attitudes and behavior that surrounds the promulgation of doctrine and affects what happens after doctrine is developed. The magnitude of both tasks permits neither to be completed. Not all litigation dealing with civil liberties is discussed (two major omissions are the issue of church and state and the controversy over obscenity). In addition, the growing literature on the relation between the political and legal systems is discussed, but by no means exhausted. However, this is an introduction to the subject, and I hope the reader will be sufficiently interested by the arguments advanced to pursue the subject further.

Another fact should be kept in mind. Because the book's

subject involves a highly dynamic process, writing at any particular time means that the "future" must be ignored. Any discussion in 1971 of Supreme Court decisions must bear in mind that this "future" is only days away. As I write, the Court is itself writing and producing new doctrine about the very same subjects that are covered here. Thus, by the time this book reaches the reader, important additions and modifications may be in order. This is especially true today, for the interaction of the political and legal systems has produced a Supreme Court with several new justices quite differently inclined from those who preceded them. Important doctrinal shifts have begun and probably will continue. Such a difficulty in a sense confirms the argument of the book. I conclude this book by saying that "today's dissent often becomes tomorrow's majority opinion." This statement has been made particularly relevant by the recent interaction of the legal and political systems, for this process is going on nearly every day that the Supreme Court sits.

● ● ●

Several individuals have provided me with support and assistance. Mr. Martin Shukert helped me collect the quantitative data discussed in the text. Isaac and Miriam Kramnick and Douglas Rae provided me with more diffuse but no less important support during the writing of this book. Samuel Krislov was kind enough to read and comment upon a draft of the manuscript. Finally, I am indebted to David J. Danelski for suggesting that I try to write on this subject and offering suggestions about improving my efforts.

J.D.C.

THE POLITICS
OF CIVIL LIBERTIES

ONE
SOME CONCEPTUAL
PERSPECTIVES

AMERICANS are ambivalent about civil liberties and civil rights. Most of us express a strong attachment to the notion of a democratic political system and to such values as freedom of speech, equality, the right to vote, and procedural safeguards that we associate with democracy. By the same token, though, our nation has often gone through periods in which the protection of these valued principles has caused strong dissatisfaction. The current stress upon law and order and dismay expressed over the coddling of criminals; the serious questions being raised about the propriety of various forms of dissent from government policy; the growing polarization of the races, of young and old, and of men and women all suggest the questioning of civil liberties and rights in which our society often engages. These disagreements reflect more than mere technical disputes over the precise meanings of democratic concepts; they bespeak basic conflicts over the nature of a free society and the kinds of behavior to be permitted in it.

In a survey conducted in the spring of 1970, CBS News found that more than 76 percent of 1100 adults sampled believed that, even in the absence of a "clear danger of violence," not all groups should be allowed to organize protests against the government. Fifty-five percent felt that newspapers and other media should *not* enjoy an absolute right to publish articles that the government felt might be harmful to the national interest, even in time of peace. Almost 60 percent believed that the protection against double jeopardy should not be enjoyed by an acquitted defendant if later incriminating evidence against him was uncovered.[1]

The point here is not to argue whether these majorities are "right" or "wrong" in their beliefs. Rather, it is to underscore the fact that these findings indicate a division among people in our society about what rights our citizens should enjoy. The apparent consensus about the value of general principles felt to be important to a democratic system covers rather strong disagreements about particular applications of these principles.

Thus, the process by which civil liberties and rights are protected and expanded in our society is complex and often acrimonious. There are typically three aspects of the process: first, the protection of these rights against attempts by the government—often supported by large majorities of the population—to restrict speech, association, and procedural guarantees; second, the extension of these rights (by legislation, the courts, executive order, etc.) to groups not previously fully enjoying them; third, the development of "new" rights (e.g., the "right to privacy," "symbolic speech") not previously protected against governmental infringement.

During the last decade and a half, most of us have been inclined to associate both the protection and expansion of civil liberties with a particular institution, the Supreme Court of the United States. The so-called Warren Court was both lionized and vilified for its extensive activity in behalf of the protections embodied in the Bill of Rights. Whatever one's

[1] The results of this poll were reported in the broadcast "60 Minutes," Volume II, Number 16, April 14, 1970.

ultimate evaluation of the Warren Court and of the policies it promulgated, it did shape importantly the nature and extent of rights available to American citizens.

The purpose of this book is to trace some recent developments in constitutional policy dealing with democratic rights. In doing so, I will deal not only with the decisions of the Warren Court, but also hark back to previous Courts and earlier decisions to provide a context for understanding and evaluating recent developments. Examining the policies embodied in Supreme Court decisions is not a particularly novel venture, though it can be a rewarding one. However, in attempting to place the decisions in a broader political context, I go somewhat beyond the standard treatment of constitutional law. I will examine some of the social and political conditions that produced the conflicts of interest leading to litigation and surrounding the process by which decisions of the Court were translated (or, in important instances, not translated) into changes in behavior within American society. Combining analysis of constitutional law cases with empirical research, this book provides an introduction to the politics of civil liberties and civil rights in American society.

THREE LEVELS OF LAW

Students of jurisprudence, or the nature and function of law, have long argued about what law is. While the issue is a semantic one, it is obviously of great importance, both for understanding the behavior of members of a society and for the study of legal phenomena.[2]

The framework used here for analyzing recent civil liberties and rights litigation suggests that law can fruitfully be viewed as operating at three levels in a society: the doctrinal, the attitudinal, and the behavioral.

[2]For a useful introduction to various schools of jurisprudence see M. P. Golding, ed., *The Nature of Law: Readings in Legal Philosophy* (New York: Random House, 1966).

Law as doctrine

At the doctrinal level, law consists of the rules or norms about behavior in a society enunciated by certain authoritative and legitimate institutions. This doctrine has many sources in our society, including the provisions of the Constitution, the content of statutes, decisions of the Supreme Court and other courts. Whatever its sources (a subject I will return to later) at the doctrinal level, civil liberties "law" says such things as: "The following kinds of material are defined as 'obscene' and can be suppressed under the following circumstances and with the following procedures"; or, "Though the freedom to speak in our society is an important value, the government may prevent or permit speech dealing with certain subjects or under certain circumstances"; or, "Church and state must remain separate and the following kinds of governmental relationships with organized religion are impermissible."

Obviously, all of the above rules are vague and leave many blanks to be filled. In fact, civil liberties litigation is concerned precisely with asking courts to fill in the blanks, or, rather, to decide whether certain activities fall within the "circumstances" specified in the rules. In any event, law as doctrine consists of the formally promulgated decisions and rules governing what behavior is permissible and what is prohibited in a society. These rules are in a constant state of flux, as new decisions are made by courts, new statutes passed, new administrative rulings promulgated, etc. If one wants to know what "the law" is on a given subject, one way of finding out is to examine what the "doctrine" on the subject is.

Law and attitudes

As soon as you begin to think about what constitutes "law" and, importantly, how it affects the behavior of people in a society, it is clear that more is involved than simply the formal doctrine. People's perceptions of what the law, and its doctrine, is are crucial to how they behave. Moreover, the views of members of a society about what the law *ought* to be are also relevant to how they behave—to the congruence of their behavior with the formal rules in the society. Such views are also important to the content of doctrine itself, for institutions promulgating rules work in the environment of attitudes that characterize their society. Thus, in understanding how people behave and what the formal rules themselves prescribe and proscribe, we must look at the attitudes of the people who make up the society toward what the law is and should be.

Whose attitudes? We might well look to the attitudes of the members of institutions charged with the responsibility of promulgating legal doctrine. We might also examine the attitudes of the average or typical citizen. And, we might look carefully at the attitudes of members of society who are especially concerned with and active in politics.

Attitudes toward what? As suggested above, we first may want to look at attitudes toward what the formal norms contain and what they ought to contain. When dealing with civil liberties and civil rights, we may also want to look particularly at attitudes toward the extension of certain safeguards or rights to particular minority groups, for this is often the issue of much of the conflict in a society over civil liberties and rights. And, more generally, we might well want to look at some more generalized attitudes of the people: How tolerant are they? How do they react to political or social behavior at variance with societal norms of "proper" behavior? How open- or closed-minded are they? Again, the "they" in each of these questions might be specified in many of the ways suggested above—doctrinal decision-makers, the man in the street, the political stratum.

In any case, law is not only doctrine, but it is also integrally tied to the attitudes of members of a society. An understanding of what the law "is," how it came to be, and how it is likely to change, requires attention to the attitudinal dimension.

Law and behavior

Law is not only formal rules and attitudes about what rules are or ought to be; law is also behavior. Jurisprudents who have talked about "the living law" are associated with this view, for they have stressed that what the law about any subject "is" in a society involves not only formal rules dealing with the subject, but also behavior. What was "the law" during the 1920s about the consumption of alcoholic beverages or today about use of marijuana? In one sense "the law" prohibited such activity. But in trying to understand what occurs in American society, law in the doctrinal sense seems largely irrelevant. Thus, to understand the existing law in a society requires attention to how people in the society actually behave. In a sense, this is by far the most significant level of law, for presumably the purpose of passing laws, and thereby establishing formal norms and rules, is to affect the behavior of citizens in a society.

This discussion illustrates the kinds of conflicts and debates in which students of jurisprudence have engaged. Many jurisprudents have argued, and quite plausibly, that "the" law is in fact one level or another: doctrine, attitudes or morality, behavior. But to define the law as any one of the three levels ignores the rest. Thus, what I want to do here is not to "answer" the question of what constitutes law, but simply to suggest that it is many things and that attention to all is required.

To give one more example, consider the question "What is the law dealing with freedom of speech in American society today?" At the doctrinal level, we might seek an answer by looking at the Constitution and find that, according to the First Amendment, "Congress shall pass no law abridging freedom of speech." This appears unambiguous, though the definition of what constitutes "speech" or "freedom of speech" suggests some complexities. Then, we might look for statutes that appear to qualify the prohibition of the First Amendment. We would find laws, for example, making it a crime to advocate the violent overthrow of the government and prohibiting conspiracy to commit a number of crimes, with speech presumably being an integral part of conspiracy. Furthermore, the recent trial of the Boston Five for, among other things, "counselling" violations of the Selective Service laws suggests that another form of speech is prohibited by legal doctrine.

We could go further in examining doctrine and look at the decisions of the Supreme Court and other courts dealing with freedom of speech. In addition to their interpretation of statutes, these decisions also embody attempts to specify conditions in which speech is permitted and in which it is not. In any event, even at the doctrinal level, the question about what constitutes "the" law is both complex and confusing.

In examining "the" law about freedom of speech, we would also want to look at societal attitudes towards speech. Are certain forms of speech viewed as impermissible (e.g., libel, slander, obscenity)? Are particular groups viewed as having greater or lesser rights to speech (e.g., communists or socialists should enjoy fewer rights; the rich or educated should enjoy more rights than the poor and uneducated, etc.)? The answers to such questions are important, because they may give us important insight into both the formal norms that we have discovered and the translation of the formal norms into behavior—that is, who speaks and who does not.

Finally, we might look at actual behavior in the society. The doctrine about free speech and attitudes toward it are factors that affect the predisposition for certain behavior to occur. The third level, behavior, would involve an exploration of such issues as who speaks and who does not. Are certain groups more or less likely to speak out than others? Are certain kinds of speech more likely to occur than others? Does certain speech result in the application of sanctions and is other speech accepted without hostile reaction?

This brief examination of the law about free speech suggests several important points about the operation of the law at the three levels.

First, examination of the content of the law operative in a particular system at one level may give a distorted picture of the characteristics of its system. In the free speech and Prohibition examples, if one wanted to characterize the "law" on these subjects in American society at any particular time, quite different impressions might be gained by simply looking at the legal doctrine on the subject as opposed to also examining actual behavior in the society.

The second point involves the interrelatedness of the operation of law at the three levels. We might conceive of the three levels as a kind of hierarchy:

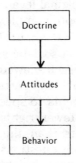

This view of the relationship of the levels is useful when we consider the "impact" of court decisions or legislation—the process by which changes in doctrine are translated into behavioral changes. In this form, the model suggests that doctrinal changes are the "independent" variable and behavioral changes the "dependent" variable, while attitudes act as an "intervening" variable through which doctrinal change influences behavior.[3] This view of the operation of civil liberties suggests that when doctrine changes (e.g., the Supreme Court holds that schools must be desegregated, or that suspects must be afforded certain rights; or Congress

[3]For examples and discussion of the so-called "impact" literature, see Theodore L. Becker, ed., *The Impact of Supreme Court Decisions* (New York: Oxford University Press, 1969); and Stephen L. Wasby, *The Impact of the United States Supreme Court: Some Perspectives* (Homewood, Ill.: Dorsey Press, 1970).

passes a Public Accomodations law), behavior is changed as well, but that attitude structures are important intervening factors in determining the rate and degree of compliance. Doctrinal changes that are generally regarded as embodying "good" public policy will meet with easy acquiescence; those that run counter to the preferences of large segments of the population will produce less behavioral change.

But simply viewing the process as hierarchical misses much of importance in the operation of law in a society. For the relationships between the operation of law at the three levels does not simply operate *down* the system; there is also feedback.

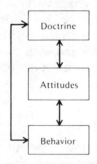

Doctrine not only affects attitudes and behavior but is itself often the product of them. The common view that "the Supreme Court follows the election returns" suggests that doctrine may be a product of attitudes and behavior. The notion that by coercing people to behave in a certain way (e.g., to have social and personal relations with members of other races) we can thereby affect their attitudes suggests that behavior can affect attitudes. Thus, the relationship between the operation of law at the three levels is complex; what goes on at one level affects the others. "The" law in a society at any particular time is the product of these interactions of doctrine, attitudes, and behavior.

Finally, the free speech example suggests the complexity of the notion of what is relevant behavior in the society. In the discussion of free speech above, I stressed "behavior" as exercise of the right of free speech, or who says what in the society. As the relationships of one level to another become clearer, we might well expand the compass of the term "behavior," looking not only at who says what, but at other kinds of legal and political activities that affect this behavior. For example. who in the society supports changes in doctrine or attitudes toward free speech? What kinds of interest group activity or lobbying of courts or legislatures takes place in favor of and in opposition to changes in doctrine and attitudes dealing with freedom of speech? These are important forms of behavior affecting who says what.

Thus, in discussing recent civil liberties and rights litigation, we shall deal not only with the doctrine enunciated in Court decisions, but also with the political and social climate that surrounded these cases and with the societal activity that affected both the development of doctrine and its translation into behavior in our society.

THE ELITE THEORY OF DEMOCRACY

As the statistics cited at the outset of the chapter indicate, support for many civil liberties and civil rights is by no means unanimous in our society. Majorities of our citizens believe that applications of the provisions of the Bill of Rights to dissenting groups or accused criminals is not always good public policy. This finding is not simply an artifact of the particular conditions of 1970. Survey research dealing with public attitudes toward the extension of various civil liberties to unpopular groups has been conducted for the past 30 years and has consistently found a lack of public support for various civil liberties. These studies have suggested that most Americans agree upon the value of *general* democratic norms: that the majority ought to rule, that freedom of speech and the press ought to be protected, that people accused of crimes ought to enjoy procedural rights to insure that they receive fair trials, to name some examples. But this consensus about general principles overlays a broad dissensus about *specific applications* of these principles: consensus on the value of free speech is combined with grave reservations about extending this right to political radicals; consensus about the value of a fair trial is combined with belief that many procedural protections (e.g., protection against double jeopardy or self-incrimination) go too far in protecting the criminal and hamstringing effective law enforcement.

These findings suggest a perplexing question: How can a society maintain such basic liberties when most of the people don't accept them as good public policy? One explanation offered by students of the American political system fixes upon a difference in support for civil liberties between the average citizen and those people who are active in politics. The latter group, which Robert Dahl calls the "political stratum," is, in general, more supportive of extending civil liberties and rights to minority and unpopular groups.[4] Members of the political stratum, because of their educational and socioeconomic backgrounds and their socialization into the process of politics with its give and take, compromise, and toleration of various points of view, generally

---

[4]The following data, dealing with freedom of speech and press, gathered by Herbert McClosky, are illustrative of (1) the consensus among both mass and political stratum on general democratic norms and (2) the greater support for application of these norms among those active in politics:

	Percent agree	
	Political stratum	Mass
People who hate our way of life should still have a chance to talk and be heard.	86.9	81.8
I believe in free speech for all no matter what their views might be.	89.4	88.9
Nobody has a right to tell another person what he should and should not read.	81.4	80.7
A man oughtn't to be allowed to speak if he doesn't know what he's talking about.	17.3	36.7
A book that contains wrong political views cannot be a good book and does not deserve to be published.	17.9	50.3

are more amenable to the applications of the "rules of the game" of the democratic political system.

In addition to being somewhat more attached to civil liberties and civil rights than most citizens, members of the political stratum are also in a position to be influential in decisions dealing with the protection and extension of these rights. Because they possess both the interest and the resources necessary to active and effective political participation, the political stratum is able to promote and protect democratic values in the face of a broader public that is not so attached to these values. As Dahl argues:

> Ordinarily, then, it is not difficult for a stable system of rights and privileges to exist that, at least in important details, does not have widespread public support and occasionally even lacks majority approval. As long as the matter is not a salient public issue—and whether it is or not depends partly on how the political stratum handles it—the question is substantially determined within the political stratum itself. When disagreements arise, these are adjudicated by officials who share the beliefs of the political stratum rather than those of the populace; and even when these officials adopt positions that do not command the undivided support of the political stratum, members of the political stratum, and particularly the professionals, tend to accept a decision as binding until and

Herbert McClosky, "Consensus and Ideology in American Politics," *American Political Science Review*, 58 (1964), pp. 361-382, 366-367. Other research which suggests the same result includes Samuel A. Stouffer, *Communism, Conformity and Civil Liberties* (New York: Doubleday, 1955); Raymond W. Mack, "Do We Really Believe in the Bill of Rights?" *Social Problems*, 3(1956), pp. 264-269; James W. Prothro and C. W. Grigg, "Fundamental Principles of Democracy: Bases of Agreement and Disagreement," *Journal of Politics*, 22 (1960), pp. 276-294. A detailed exploration of the political ideology of a small group of Americans, including a discussion of their attitudes toward civil liberties and rights, can be found in Robert Lane, *Political Ideology* (Glencoe, Ill.: Free Press, 1962).

unless it can be changed through the accepted procedures. This is the essence of their code of democratic legitimism.[5]

Dealing with the same point, Herbert McClosky says:

Democratic viability is, to begin with, saved by the fact that those who are most confused about democratic ideas are also likely to be politically apathetic and without significant influence. Their role in the nation's decision process is so small that their 'misguided' opinions or nonopinions have little practical consequence for stability. If they contribute little to the vitality of the system, neither are they likely to do much harm.[6]

Thus, this argument goes, in a sense "democracy" is a value preserved in our society by an elite more accepting of the implications of democracy than is the majority. There has been a good deal of debate as to whether the general "pluralist" theory of politics is an adequate account of the American political system. Critics have attacked the view as being too elitist, as well as for implying an openness to participation by minority groups in political decision-making that is illusory. Whatever the merits of the theory, prescriptively or descriptively, there seems little doubt that applications of civil liberties and civil rights are more highly valued by those active in politics than by the average man in our society.

The elite theory suggests one explanation for the fact that much policy about civil liberties and civil rights—rules of the game about who is permitted to speak and who is not, procedural rights available to persons accused of crime, applications of the principle of equality in support of minority groups not previously enjoying access to political

[5]Robert A. Dahl, *Who Governs?* (New Haven: Yale University Press, 1961), p. 321.

[6]Herbert McClosky, *op. cit.*, p. 376.

arenas—may be pursued by the government in a society in which large groups of the citizens oppose (though perhaps often without great intensity) these policies.

But the theory also suggests that governmental policy (whether court decisions or legislation) increasing civil liberties and civil rights is also fertile ground for political dispute. Dispute may center around such policy simply because it can be highly allocative, affecting who gets what in the society. Thus, application of the principle of equality to permit new groups like blacks or Chicanos to participate more fully in the political arena, or to force reapportionment of legislatures, may affect governmental policy and hence the distribution of costs and benefits in the society. The application of the principle of "equality" thus can be a bread-and-butter issue much like other political choices and be fought over because people feel their own interests are at stake. Moreover, the lack of consensus about the wisdom of many of the applications themselves, regardless of their direct allocative effects, makes the politics of civil liberties and civil rights an area in which there are likely to be grave disagreements.

The major crises in the system, the periods in which the rules of the game are most likely to be questioned, would appear to come when these principles themselves become the subject of intense public debate, when decisions normally made within the political stratum are "taken" to the people. These periods may be very dangerous for the system, for the general populace is likely to become aware of (and often aroused about) decisions taken by the political stratum that are normally not much noticed, and is perhaps forced to face the implications of their generalized belief in democratic norms. For example, the man who believes quite sincerely in a principle like freedom of speech may discover that this principle implies that communists, atheists, socialists, or others with whom he is not in sympathy must be permitted to speak in public. One possible response, in addition to some withdrawal of support for the institution that implements the principle, may be to begin to question his own belief in the principle itself. Thus, the crises in which the rules of the game themselves become the subject for debate include both questioning of the normal operation of the political system, as well as the institutions that make political decisions, and also, sometimes, of the basic principles of the system as well. The experience with "McCarthyism" during the 1950s, the law-and-order issue today, and recent attacks upon dissent by government officials are examples of the process by which civil liberties and rights can become salient political issues.

The discussion thus far suggests that the protection of civil liberties and rights is both complex and often acrimonious. It is complex because understanding the content and meaning of liberties involves looking not only at the formal doctrine dealing with them, but also at the attitude structures and activities of many individuals and institutions in our society. The data dealing with the acceptance of these principles by members of American society suggest why the process may be acrimonious, why our attachment to these liberties is always in a state of flux, why they are always to some extent endangered or under attack.

• • •

The bulk of this book deals with three areas of civil liberties and civil rights: freedom of expression, equality, and criminal justice. The chapters discussing these topics trace doctrinal developments—particularly Supreme Court decisions—dealing with each issue area. In discussing each topic, I also explore the political process that surrounded the litigation. This process, involving attitudes in the society and behavior supportive of or opposed to the policy implicit in doctrinal change, is crucial to understanding civil liberties and rights in American society. Because the issues implicit in doctrinal choices are highly allocative and because of the skepticism with which most Americans view civil liberties and rights, decisions about what these liberties protect and who shall enjoy them are fertile ground for political dispute.

These are not questions, even on the doctrinal level, that are peculiarly "legal"—matters to be decided by some mechanical process of applying "the law" or "the Constitution" to a specific dispute. Rather they involve choices that affect the preferences and sometimes the material quality of our lives. Thus, the decisions of the Court—the "doctrine" dealing with civil liberties—are neither the beginning nor the end of the process by which our society makes decisions about civil liberties and rights. The decisions of the Court are themselves the product of political activity in the society; by the same token, they are not the end of the process of collective choice. A Supreme Court decision is often merely the beginning of a complex process by which the doctrine it enunciates is translated into changes in behavior, modified, or ignored.

In the brief compass of a short book, I cannot discuss either the litigation or its surrounding political and social context in the detail that they deserve. But I hope that I can provide an introduction to these issue areas, and a general perspective upon litigation that is lacking if attention is limited solely to the cases themselves.

TWO
FREEDOM OF EXPRESSION AND THE PROBLEM OF LOYALTY-SECURITY

THE freedom to speak, to publish, and to assemble with others for the purpose of expressing a point of view are at the core of what most Americans conceive as a democratic political system. Freedom of expression is a crucial element of a marketplace of ideas in which citizens holding various beliefs and preferences interact with one another and ideas compete for community acceptance. Such interchange is an integral part of the process of selecting public representatives, which most of us identify with the notion of democracy. Another function of such interchange, which was stressed by John Stuart Mill, is seeking truth, for dispute and interchange are important elements of the process by which "good" or "right" ideas win acceptance over "bad" or "false" opinion.[1] In addition to these instrumental aspects of freedom of expression, many also value it simply for itself, believing that such freedom is an essential component of human dignity and is thus a quality of life that every individual, as an individual, simply ought to enjoy.

[1]John Stuart Mill, *On Liberty* (New York: Appleton-Century-Crofts, 1947), Chapter II.

Thus, the freedom to express varying and often opposing ideas is essential to a variety of conceptions of democracy.[2] If democracy is viewed as essentially a process—a way in which collective decisions for a society are made—free expression is crucial to the openness of the process and to such characteristics as elections, representation of interests, and the like. If the outcomes of such collective decisions are stressed as the touchstone of democracy—for example, that alternatives preferred by the majority win out over those preferred by minorities—freedom of expression would seem equally crucial, for it provides the means by which the variety of alternative policies available to the society can be disseminated, placed on the agenda for collective decision, and evaluated by members of the collectivity. Finally, if democracy is thought of as a quality of life, as a political system in which the dignity of its members is protected, the freedom to hold and express beliefs is probably the essential quality that such a free society ought to possess.

The centrality of the notion of protection of expression to the American system is evidenced by the fact that it is the first of the liberties protected in the Bill of Rights. The First Amendment provides that "Congress shall make no law . . . abridging the freedom of speech, or of the press; or the right of the people peaceably to assemble, and to petition the government for a redress of grievances."

To rehearse some of the arguments about why freedom of expression is valuable in a free and democratic society, as I've done very briefly above, is perhaps to belabor the obvious. But even a cursory examination of one's own preferences or of the history of our society makes manifest another equally obvious point: The freedom of expression that we think so

[2]For an introduction to somewhat varying theories of democracy, see Joseph A. Schumpeter, *Capitalism, Socialism and Democracy* (New York: Harper & Row, 1962), especially Part IV; H. B. Mayo, *An Introduction to Democratic Theory* (New York: Oxford University Press, 1960); Robert A. Dahl, *A Preface to Democratic Theory* (Chicago: University of Chicago Press, 1956).

obviously important and valuable is at the same time a very fragile commodity, for there are often intense pressures towards restriction of this freedom. Most members of those majorities of Americans sampled in 1970 who felt that not all groups should be permitted to organize protests against the government or that the press should not have an absolute right, even in peacetime, to publish stories the government felt might endanger the national interest would consider themselves believers in democracy and would no doubt overwhelmingly affirm the necessity of the protection of freedom of expression. Their preferences for some limitations upon this freedom stem, perhaps, from an inevitable desire to restrict the dissemination of ideas believed to be wrong or pernicious. Or, perhaps their view simply reflects their feeling that other values—law and order, patriotism, national unity or security, or whatever—compete with, and take precedence over, the value of free expression in certain circumstances.[3] Whatever their reasons, any large and diverse society will experience strong tendencies toward the restriction of freedom of speech at the same time that it expresses confidence in the necessity for its protection. To put it another way, the operation of the political and social systems of a democratic society will make the exercise of freedom of expression—a commodity valued by most members of the society—itself an issue for discussion and decision, not simply a self-evident value that is inevitably to be protected.

QUESTIONS ABOUT FREEDOM OF EXPRESSION

Viewing freedom of expression not only as a value that ought to be protected and maximized, but as an issue about which

[3]In his discussion of the political beliefs of Americans, Lane suggests that political freedom is not the most important aspect of freedom valued by American. Other kinds of freedom—especially freedom of religion, of movement, of economic opportunity—appear to be more highly valued than political freedom. See Robert E. Lane, *Political Ideology* (Glencoe, Ill.: Free Press, 1962), Chapter 1, especially pp. 22-25.

we have and will always have dispute, suggests several questions. First, assuming that we value free expression and wish to protect it, what falls under its rubric? In other words, what is expression? Looking simply at spoken or printed words, do libel and slander fall in the category of expression? Some would say no, for the connection between the words and the injury is so close that they might want to call such expression not speech, but speech-action, or action itself. Moving away from language, what about expression that is more than just words, as for example, picketing, mass demonstrations, the burning of a draft card? There can be little doubt that such activities are in fact designed to express a point of view, to constitute an argument for one position or another. At the same time, are they to be classified in that category of expression which we value and wish to protect? Thus, one major question that must be dealt with in determining a society's policy toward freedom of expression is simply *what kinds of activities or behavior* do we wish to protect.

A related question is *how much* expression we want to protect. Once we have succeeded in identifying behavior that is in fact expression, the task is not done. The next choice concerns the degree to which we wish to protect this behavior against infringement by the government or private citizens. As soon as it is admitted that not *all* expression is to be protected, some lines must be drawn distinguishing what is to be protected from what is not. How can we draw these lines? We might draw them on the basis of *who* is speaking: That is, it might be suggested that some individuals and groups should enjoy more or less protection than others. These groups might be identified by characteristics like race or religion; or they might be selected by their preferences, intentions or conduct (e.g., revolutionary groups, atheists or socialists should enjoy less freedom than those not sharing such beliefs; convicted felons are not entitled to full participation in the political process). Or, we might draw the lines on the basis of the *character of the expression* itself.

Expression likely to produce consequences the society believes harmful might be restricted. Thus, we might wish to restrict expression which incites listeners to riot or is believed to be morally deleterious. We might wish to protect vigorously expression that seems integrally tied in with the operation of our political system (what has been called "public" speech) and less vigorously expression that is not as important to the work of the democratic process (e.g., commercial advertising, libel, literature).[4]

The two distinctions suggested here—what is expression and how much of it ought to be protected—are related. For the question of whether a certain kind of activity is in fact to be labelled expression may determine whether the second question—should it be protected—has to be answered. If we label an activity (as the Supreme Court has labeled pornography) as not falling within the protected category, then we need not deal with whether it ought to be protected under our test for how much expression should be protected. That is, the second issue—does the expression fall within the protected category?—is avoided, since we have refused to label the activity expression at all.

A third question that must be answered in dealing with freedom of expression involves *who* ought to make the choices. If the government gets into the business of penalizing certain kinds of expression, as it has in our society, which branch of the government ought to make the choice about what expression is to be permitted and what is not? Should the legislature pass laws dealing with certain kinds of expression? Should the courts, by invoking the power of judicial review, decide whether such legislation is permissible or not? Or should the President and the executive branch

---

[4]This view is urged in Alexander Meiklejohn, *Political Freedom* (New York: Oxford University Press, 1965). Meiklejohn suggests that political speech should enjoy absolute protection by the First Amendment; private speech, he urges, is not protected by the First Amendment but by the Due Process Clauses of the Fifth and Fourteenth Amendments, and subject to reasonable governmental regulation.

decide? Obviously all of these institutions are involved in disputes over freedom of expression. When we begin to look at the litigation, we shall see that a good deal of recent controversy in American society has dealt with the question of what roles ought to be played by these various institutions in choosing which speech should be protected and which should not.

These, then, are some of the questions that any society must answer when dealing with freedom of expression. Granted that it is valuable and ought to be protected, a notion agreed upon by most Americans, at least as a general proposition, how ought choices to be made about specific issues arising over such expression? These are not simply abstract questions; they are vital political issues that have confronted and divided our society since its inception. Today, for example, the question of what constitutes expression is raised by such activities as the so-called "symbolic" speech involved in draft-card burning, destruction of draft records, the use of various flags in demonstrations. The question of what expression ought to be protected comes up in the context of laws against certain forms of speech (e.g., counseling evasion of the draft laws), of attacks by public officials upon certain forms of dissent against government policy, of the question of whether the dissemination of allegedly pornographic material ought to be punishable. Thus, we grapple with these issues every day. They are not the domain simply of the lawyer or judge or the democratic theorist. They are disputes that are an integral part of politics in our society.

THE LIMITS OF EXPRESSION

Before turning to a discussion of litigation dealing with freedom of expression, I would like to pursue briefly the question of what kinds of general approaches have been used by the Court to the crucial problem alluded to above: defining the limits upon expression. In dealing with this issue the Court has, during the course of the past fifty years, fashioned a variety of tests to define expression protected by the First Amendment (and the Due Process Clause of the Fourteenth Amendment) against infringement by the federal and state governments. The tests have changed over time, vary in the amount of expression they protect, and to some extent have reflected changes in the nature of the issues coming before the Court and in the complexion of American politics.

At this point, I'd simply like to set forth some of the approaches that the Court has taken. In discussing the litigation in the next section, the applications of these tests and their relationship to other developments in our society are discussed in more detail.[5]

Bad tendency

One of the earliest tests used by the Supreme Court in judging the constitutionality of laws punishing or restricting the exercise of speech is commonly called the "bad tendency" test. Carried over from English doctrines dealing with seditious libel, this approach suggests that though expression is protected by the First Amendment, it is not absolutely protected but may be the subject of restriction when it has a tendency to produce harmful consequences. In terms of the distinctions suggested above, the bad tendency test says that only "pure" expression is protected, and that it is protected only so long as it does not have the tendency to lead to criminal conduct, threat of overthrow of the state, or other evils. The test was expressed succinctly by Justice Sanford, speaking for the majority in *Gitlow* v. *New York*.[6] The case involved a prosecution, under the New York Criminal Anarchy Law, for distributing a document called the "Left Wing Manifesto" which was similar in content to *The*

[5]I am indebted to Professor Samuel Krislov for useful suggestions about the discussion that follows.

[6]268 U.S. 652 (1925).

Communist Manifesto. In upholding the conviction, Sanford said:

> It is a fundamental principle, long established, that freedom of speech and of the press which is secured by the Constitution does not confer an absolute right to speak or publish, without responsibility, whatever one may choose, or an unrestricted and unbridled license that gives immunity for every possible use of language, and prevents the punishment of those who abridge this freedom . . . That utterances inciting to the overthrow of organized government by unlawful means present a sufficient danger of substantive evil to bring their punishment within the range of legislative discretion is clear. Such utterances, by their very nature, involve danger to the public peace and to the security of the State . . . And the immediate danger is none the less real and substantial because the effect of a given utterance cannot be accurately foreseen. The state cannot reasonably be required to measure the danger from every such utterance in the nice balance of a jeweler's scale. *A single revolutionary spark may kindle a fire that, smoldering for a time, may burst into a sweeping and destructive conflagration.* It cannot be said that the state is acting arbitrarily or unreasonably when in the exercise of its judgment as to the measures necessary to protect the public peace and safety, it seeks to extinguish the spark without waiting until it has enkindled the flame or blazed into the conflagration.[7]

Thus, the state may step in to punish or inhibit expression that has a tendency to produce harm, without waiting to see if the harm occurs, and without producing evidence that the particular speech itself produced the harm. The bad tendency test protects only pure speech which does not have a tendency to lead to harmful consequences. Those on the Court who used this approach generally coupled their somewhat restrictive view of permissible expression with a deference to legislative institutions. Thus, the determination

[7]268 U.S. 666, 669. (Emphasis added.)

by the legislature that a given type of speech had a tendency to produce harm was given great weight and the role of the Court was one of legitimating such a finding in the absence of compelling evidence that the legislature had overstepped the bounds of its authority or acted in an unreasonable fashion. In speaking of the New York Criminal Anarchy Law at issue in *Gitlow*, Sanford said:

> By enacting the present statute the state has determined, through its legislative body, that utterances advocating the overthrow of organized government by force, violence, and unlawful means, are so inimical to the general welfare, and involve such danger of substantive evil, that they may be penalized in the exercise of its police power. That determination must be given great weight. Every presumption is to be indulged in favor of the validity of the statute.[8]

Thus, the proponents of the bad tendency test suggested that the answer to the question "who is to decide which speech is permissible" was, within very wide boundaries set by the courts, the legislature.

Clear and present danger

The clear and present danger test was developed, primarily by Justices Holmes and Brandeis, as an alternative to the rather repressive bad tendency test used by majorities of the Court during the 1920s. The clear and present danger test has two basic premises: (1) Freedom of expression, especially the freedom to speak and publish, are important values in a democratic society and are protected against governmental infringement by the First Amendment; but (2) the right to express one's views is not absolutely protected, for speech may sometimes be intimately tied to conduct that the society may wish to prevent. As Holmes put it in *Schenck v. U.S.*:

[8]268 U.S. 668.

The question in every case is whether the words used are used in such circumstances and are of such a nature as to create a clear and present danger that they will bring about the substantive evils that Congress has a right to prevent.[9]

The clear and present danger test thus appears to depend heavily upon the specific character of the expression and the circumstances in which it occurs. Speech that is punishable must be related to action that is prohibited (the danger must be clear) and the connection between the speech and the occurrence of the harmful activity must be direct (the danger must be present). Justice Brandeis suggested these features of the test in *Whitney* v. *California*:

Fear of serious injury cannot alone justify suppression of free speech and assembly. Men feared witches and burnt women. . . . To justify suppression of free speech there must be reasonable ground to fear that serious evil will result if free speech is practiced. There must be reasonable ground to believe that the danger apprehended is imminent. There must be reasonable ground to believe that the evil to be prevented is a serious one . . . . [N]o danger flowing from speech can be deemed clear and present, unless the incidence of the evil apprehended is so imminent that it may befall before there is opportunity for full discussion. If there be time to expose through discussion the falsehoods and fallacies, to avert the evil by the processes of education, the remedy to be applied is more speech, not enforced silence.[10]

Thus, the clear and present danger test resembles the bad tendency test in that both agree on *what* is protected: pure speech, rather than speech that is combined with action. But they differ significantly in answering the question of *how much* speech is to be protected. The clear and present danger test requires a direct nexus between the speech and potential

[9]*Schenck* v. *United States*, 249 U.S. 47 (1919) at 52.
[10]274 U.S. 357 (1927) at 376-377.

harm; the bad tendency test permits the connection to be rather tenuous, and hence justifies suppression of much speech that the clear and present danger test would protect.

The two tests, as applied, also differ on the issue of *who* should decide whether it is permissible to suppress or punish speech. Those espousing the bad tendency test typically granted the legislature great latitude in deciding what kind of speech to punish. Because the clear and present danger test depends greatly upon the circumstances surrounding the speech in question, the burden of decision lies with the judge and jury rather than the legislature.

Thus, the clear and present danger rule, rather than proceeding by categories of speech, examines the circumstances surrounding particular speech. It is a test most appropriate in dealing with face-to-face encounters between a speaker and an audience, for in this context it is most easy (though even here, it is not often in fact easy) to judge the relationship between expression and the possible harmful activity it might produce.

Balancing

Another test that has frequently been used by the Court, and which seemed to replace the clear and present danger test as the predominant approach to issues of free expression during the 1950s, has been called balancing. Unlike the clear and present danger rule, it has never been given an epigrammatic expression by those on the Court who favored its use. Perhaps the lack of a clear definition stems from the fact that it is not a test at all, at least in the sense of providing a set of relatively unambiguous criteria to be applied in making decisions about what is permissible speech and what is not. Essentially, balancing starts from the same two premises as the clear and present danger rule: speech is valued but not absolutely protected. Simply stated, the approach holds that speech must be weighed against competing values (e.g., national security, the state's interest in obtaining certain kinds of information, etc.) and some kind of balance struck.

Balancing is somewhat ambiguous because those using the test do not specify how one goes about achieving it. Presumably every choice made by a judge is a kind of balancing process, and saying that this is how a case is to be decided describes the process but does not specify a set of criteria that are to be taken into account (in the way that the clear and present danger test attempts to do). The balancing test, much used in cases involving loyalty-security programs during the 1950s, typically involved weighing the interest of the government in preserving itself against the individual's interest in expressing himself or in maintaining his associations. Given those two considerations on either side of the balance, the Court typically tended to come out in favor of the government. When some of the cases are discussed in detail, the nature of the balancing test may become more clear. Conceptually, however, all it seems to consist of is a simple statement that the value of expression must be weighed against other and often competing societal values, and that no mechanical (or precise) test is adequate for this delicate task.

In answering the three questions about freedom of speech, the balancing test is silent on the issue of *what* constitutes speech, though its proponents have typically been inclined to restrict their discussion to pure speech rather than speech mixed with action. On the question of *how much* speech is protected, the balancers are also somewhat vague: Speech is protected until its "good" results are outweighed by the "evil" it produces (or may produce). Like the proponents of the bad tendency test, balancers have typically deferred to the legislative and administrative institutions, thereby placing them at the forefront in dealing with the issue of *who* shall decide when infringement of speech is permissible.

Absolutism

The fourth major test that has been applied to problems of expression has never been adopted by a majority of the Court. Long espoused by Justice Hugo Black, absolutism is, on the surface at least, the most simple approach to the limits of expression.[11] Black argues that the "balance" sought by other Justices in dealing with issues of expression was struck by the framers of the First Amendment in the eighteenth century. In saying that "Congress shall make no law . . . ," Black argues, the question of limits upon speech was answered once and for all: No laws infringing upon the right to speak are consonant with the Constitution. Thus, the absolutist position appears to provide a simple answer to the question of how much speech is permissible: All of it is. Thus, laws making it a crime to advocate the overthrow of the government; congressional investigation into the activities of individuals that have the effect of restricting their freedom to speak; even, apparently, laws against libel and slander—all of these are unconstitutional, for they abridge freedom of speech.

Until quite recently, absolutism did appear to provide a simple (if, for many, an unpalatable) answer to the question of defining limits on expression.[12] But recently, the conceptual difficulties of the absolutist position have become more salient. For, though it answers the *how much* speech question easily, it does not, by itself, tell us what is speech (and hence absolutely protected). As suggested before, picketing, mass demonstrations, and the concept of acts constituting "symbolic" speech all raise important questions about the protection of expression in our society. The absolutist approach, especially as employed by Justice Black, appears to restrict the protection of the First Amendment to verbal and written expression. Thus, the absolutist position does protect a tremendous amount of expression. But,

[11]Justice Black has elaborated his position both in Court decisions, discussed in subsequent sections, and off-the-bench writings. See, for example, Hugo L. Black, "The Bill of Rights," *New York University Law Review*, 35 (1960), pp. 865-881.

[12]But, cf., Charles L. Black, Jr., "Mr. Justice Black, The Supreme Court, and the Bill of Rights," *Harper's*, February, 1961, p. 63.

leaving open as it does the question of what in fact is speech (or expression) and hence absolutely protected, it does not provide simple answers to many of the most pressing current issues dealing with freedom of expression. The absolutist test is clear in dealing with the issue of *who* shall decide whether speech is protected or not. It says that this decision was taken by the framers of the Constitution, and hence the Justices of Court should strike down all government activity abridging speech. Judges also will perform the task of deciding what constitutes speech and thus is absolutely protected.

The preceding discussion suggests that freedom of expression is an important value in a democratic political system but that there are likely to be attempts to restrict its exercise. I have sketched briefly some of the general approaches developed by the Court to determine the extent to which government may infringe upon the exercise of the freedom of expression in American society. Now I should like to turn to a discussion of some of the litigation dealing with freedom of expression. The most detailed discussion deals with the past twenty years, though background provided by litigation earlier in this century is discussed briefly. As suggested in Chapter One, the reality of civil liberties and civil rights in this country requires attention to more than simply the decisions of the Court. The doctrine developed by the Court is in part the product of attitudes and behavior in the broader political system; by the same token, the effect of doctrinal change itself depends upon the activities and attitudes of other institutions, groups and individuals.

The discussion of litigation that comprises the bulk of this chapter is roughly chronological, attempting to sketch doctrinal developments since the 1920s and the political context that surrounded the litigation.

EARLY DEVELOPMENTS

The Supreme Court first seriously faced the problem of the limits upon expression in cases beginning around 1920 that arose from state and federal legislative attempts to limit subversive activities by various radical individuals and groups.[13] The first important case, *Schenck* v. *United States*, involved a prosecution for interference with the operation of the armed forces—specifically, the circulation of leaflets urging men not to report for the draft. Schenck was tried under the Espionage Act of 1917 and defended himself upon the ground that his expression was protected by the First Amendment. The Supreme Court, in an opinion by Justice Holmes, affirmed the conviction and introduced the clear and present danger test discussed above. Holmes reasoned that although Schenck's expression might be protected during peacetime, under wartime conditions the state had the right to punish the publication of materials that might interfere with the war effort.

In *Abrams* v. *United States*[14] the Court applied the bad tendency test to uphold a conviction under the Sedition Act of 1918 of a group of Bolsheviks accused of advocating strikes by workers in minitions plants, with the alleged goal of preventing American interference with the Russian Revolution. Holmes and Brandeis dissented from the ruling, relying upon and expanding the clear and present danger test. Noting that the defendants were obviously ineffectual in their efforts, they urged that the prosecution had not demonstrated the connection between the speech and some evil required if punishment was justified under the clear and present danger rule.

In 1927, the Court, in the *Gitlow* opinion, described in the discussion of the bad tendency test above, again faced the problem of limits upon dissent. In rejecting the clear and present danger approach urged by Holmes and Brandeis, the Court embraced the bad tendency test. The majority opinion thus upheld the conviction even though it noted " . . . no evidence of any effect resulting from the publication and

---

[13]The two most important laws were the Espionage Act of 1917 and the Sedition Act of 1918. For a discussion of the provisions of these laws see Zechariah Chaffee, *Free Speech in the United States* (Cambridge, Mass.: Harvard University Press, 1941), Part I.

[14]250 U.S. 616 (1919).

circulation of the Manifesto."[15] This case was important not only because it relied on the bad tendency test and rejected the clear and present danger approach. It was the first case in which the Supreme Court held that a provision of the Bill of Rights was "incorporated" into the Due Process Clause of the Fourteenth Amendment and hence applicable to the activities of state governments. Thus, though Gitlow's conviction was upheld, the Court also held that the protections of the First Amendment did restrict the activities of state governments generally.

It is also worthwhile to note that the arguments of the Gitlow opinion were to reappear later in the loyalty-security opinions of the 1950s. The stress upon the menace of internal subversion, the notion of the potential spark which may produce a revolution and the propriety of the state stepping in to suppress speech that is not itself likely to produce substantive evil directly, and the deference to legislative institutions are all themes in *Gitlow* that would reemerge in the doctrine utilized in the 1950s.

Holmes, joined by Brandeis, dissented, once more urging the use of a clear and present danger test.

> If what I think the correct test is applied, it is manifest that there was no present danger of an attempt to overthrow the government by force on the part of the admittedly small minority who shared the defendant's views. It is said that this Manifesto was more than a theory, that it was an incitement. Every idea is an incitement. It offers itself for belief, and, if believed, it is acted on unless some other belief outweighs it, or some failure of energy stifles the movement at its birth. The only difference between the expression of an opinion and an incitement in the narrower sense is the speaker's enthusiasm for the result. Eloquence may set fire to reason. But whatever may be thought of the redundant discourse before us, it had no chance of starting a present conflagration. If, in the long run, the beliefs expressed in proletarian dictatorship are

[15]268 U.S. 656.

destined to be accepted by the dominant forces of the community, the only meaning of free speech is that they should be given their chance and have their way.[16]

Thus, the Holmes-Brandeis position not only objected to the reliance upon determination by the legislature, but struck at the general classification of certain forms of expression as punishable, regardless of the context in which they were uttered.

The rather restricted role that the majority of the Court seemed to envision for itself in dealing with infringements upon freedom of expression no doubt had a number of sources. The Court was to some extent feeling its way in a new area, for it had not before dealt extensively with the limits that the Constitution might place upon legislation abridging free expression. Thus, perhaps deference to the legislature was natural, for it was a somewhat safer course. Perhaps equally important, the political climate was one in which the kinds of activities being punished were highly unpopular. The fervor of World War I had produced the Espionage and Sedition Acts. The success of the Communist revolution in Russia promoted fear of similar activity in this country and led to the infamous Palmer raids, roundups of alleged Bolsheviks, anarchists, syndicalists, and other radicals. The growth of the labor movement, particularly the Industrial Workers of the World (IWW), also contributed to fears of radical activity. Thus, the Court was operating in a political context in which intervention on behalf of those whose expression was being curbed would have been highly unpopular and perhaps impolitic. As we shall see, the Court faced a similar situation during the 1950s and adopted a similar doctrinal approach to government activities abridging speech. In terms of the attitudes of large segments of the population and the behavior of other branches of government, then, the doctrinal path followed by the Court seems quite congruent, if not particularly appealing.

[16]268 U.S. 655.

From a doctrinal point of view, the first series of important expression cases involved the use of tests that appeared to permit the government fairly wide latitude in attempting to curb speech. The Court's deference to determination by the legislature of abridgeable classes of speech, its recognition that domestic or international upheaval or tension was a valid consideration in legislative determination, its unwillingness to require a direct and demonstrated nexus between the specific expression being prosecuted and any specific acts of harm (rejection of the clear and present danger rule espoused by Holmes and Brandeis)—all of these constituted a doctrinal approach that was not jealously protective of the freedom of expression. And, though little rigorous empirical data are available, the plausible suggestion is that this doctrinal path chosen by the Court was congruent with the general attitudinal structure of the populace and to the activities being pursued by other political institutions and groups.

The thirties

The issues raised in this period included the activities of the growing Communist Party in the United States and expression issues raised by the labor union movement. Especially toward the end of the decade, the Court adopted a much more protective approach toward freedom of expression. This development, in part the result of Roosevelt's appointments to the Court, was accompanied by changes in the complexion of American politics: the depression, the coming to power of the New Deal, the success of the industrial labor union movement. A brief review of some of the landmark cases dealing with freedom of expression suggests the changing approach of the Court.

In *Stromberg* v. *California*[17] the Court overturned the conviction of the defendant under a California statute that made criminal the displaying of "a red flag, banner or

[17]283 U.S. 359 (1931).

badge . . . as a sign, symbol, or emblem of opposition to organized government or as an invitation or stimulus to anarchistic action or as an aid to propaganda that is of a seditious character. . ."[18] Stromberg had displayed, in her children's camp, a Soviet flag. The California Supreme Court construed the provision of the statute dealing with opposition to organized government as including "peaceful and orderly opposition to government by legal means."

The Supreme Court, in an opinion by Chief Justice Hughes, found this clause of the statute unconstitutional. Rather than using a clear and present danger test, the Court argued:

> A statute which upon its face, and as authoritatively construed, is so vague and indefinite as to permit the punishment of the fair use of this opportunity [for free discussion of governmental policy] is repugnant to the guaranty of liberty contained in the Fourteenth Amendment.[19]

This was not a direct application of the clear and present danger test (i.e., the possible harm that might have come from the display of this particular flag). But it foreshadowed a test that would come to be used later, in civil rights and loyalty oath cases in the early 1960s, in which the vagueness of a statute and the possibility of its use against protected activity came to dominate the Court's approach to expression cases. In a sense the vagueness test may be a version of the clear and present danger rule, for subsumed under the notion of "protected activity" is a class of speech that may in fact be expression which does not constitute a clear and present danger.

The *De Jonge* case

In another case, *De Jonge* v. *Oregon*,[20] the defendant was convicted under the Criminal Syndicalism Law of Oregon,

---

[18]283 U.S. 361.
[19]283 U.S. 369.
[20]299 U.S. 353 (1937).

which, among other things, defined criminal syndicalism as "the doctrine which advocates crime, physical violence, sabotage, or any unlawful acts or methods as a means of accomplishing or effecting industrial or political change or revolution."[21] The defendant was charged with assisting in the conduct of a meeting of the Communist Party, an organization alleged by the state to be devoted to advocating criminal syndicalism. He defended against the charge by arguing that the meeting itself was lawful and orderly and that although it was held under the auspices of the Communist Party, no unlawful conduct was taught or advocated at the meeting.

The Supreme Court, again in an opinion by Chief Justice Hughes, overturned the conviction. Admitting that incitement of overthrow or assistance in the organization of a group devoted to such activity might be punishable, the Court stressed that all this defendant was charged with was participation in a meeting. Regardless of the auspices under which the meeting was held, so long as the conduct that occurred there was peaceable, the defendant could not be constitutionally punished: " . . . peaceable assembly for lawful discussion cannot be made a crime. The holding of meetings for peaceable political action cannot be proscribed."[22]

Preferred position

Implicit in these developments in the late 1930s restricting the power of the state to punish expression was the notion of "preferred position." This view, first propounded in a footnote by Justice Stone in an economic regulation case, suggested that legislation dealing with political freedoms did not enjoy the presumptions of constitutional validity enjoyed by other types of legislation:

[21]299 U.S. 357.
[22]299 U.S. 365.

There may be narrower scope for operation of the presumption of constitutionality when legislation appears on its face to be within a specific prohibition of the Constitution, such as those of the first ten amendments, which are deemed equally specific when held to be embraced within the Fourteenth. It is unnecessary to consider now [in the context of this specific case] whether legislation which restricts those political processes which can ordinarily be expected to bring about the repeal of undesirable legislation, is to be subjected to more exacting judicial scrutiny under the general prohibitions of the Fourteenth Amendment than are most other types of legislation.[23]

The opinion went on at this point to discuss litigation dealing with various forms of political freedom, e.g., speech, assembly, voting, religion. It ended with the key justification for this notion of preferred position: " . . . prejudice against discrete and insular minorities may be a special condition, which tends seriously to curtail the operation of those political processes ordinarily to be relied upon to protect minorities, and which may call for a correspondingly more searching judicial inquiry."[24]

The Gobitis case

An early and powerful exposition of the preferred position test appeared in Justice Stone's dissent in the first flag salute case, *Minersville School District* v. *Gobitis*.[25] The majority of the Court upheld the application of a compulsory flag salute program to Jehovah's Witnesses who felt that this practice violated their religious tenets. In 1943, the Court reversed its position in a case discussed below and accepted Stone's argument. Stone suggested in his dissent in *Gobitis:*

The very fact that we have constitutional guarantees of civil liberties and the specificity of their command where freedom of speech and

[23]*United States* v. *Carolene Products,* 304 U.S. 144 (1938) at 152.
[24]304 U.S. 153.
[25]310 U.S. 586 (1940).

of religion are concerned require some accommodation of the powers which government normally exercises, when no question of civil liberty is involved, to the constitutional demand that those liberties be protected against the action of government itself.[26]

Thus, preferred position suggested that the presumption of constitutionality enjoyed by legislation might be modified, or reversed, when dealing with liberties essential to the democratic process and that the Court ought to intervene more actively in support of such liberties. Preferred position was partly an attempt to get around a dilemma faced by political liberals during the 1930s. New Deal legislation had been repeatedly struck down by a Court which broadly construed the Due Process Clause to prevent the restrictions upon individual activities necessary to much economic regulation. Thus, liberals were loudly complaining about the "activist" and "undemocratic" Court that was thwarting the will of the people in dealing with economic problems. At the same time, such liberals *wanted* an activist Court willing to intervene and declare unconstitutional legislation restricting political freedom. There was some difficulty in formulating a theoretical basis for this apparent contradiction, and preferred position provided this justification. By distinguishing between legislation dealing merely with "property" and that dealing with political freedoms—and pointing out that the latter were crucial to the operation of the democratic process—one could advocate "activism" in the latter area and deference in the former. This suggests a more general point: The rhetoric surrounding attacks or defenses of the activities of the Supreme Court in this century have often been more informed by the concept of "whose ox is being gored," that is, by the critic or supporter's agreement or disagreement with the outcomes which have emerged from the Court, than by consistent theories of the role that the Court ought to play in our society. The rhetoric of the "liberal" New Deal

[26]310 U.S. 602-603.

critics of the Supreme Court during the 1930s and of the "conservatives" during the 1950s and 1960s are strikingly similar. Both attacked the Court as an undemocratic, elite institution, bent upon thwarting the more responsive and representative institutions. What they had in common was not a theory of democracy but an intense disagreement with the decisions the respective Courts had been making.

Thus, the trend of the Court's decisions dealing with freedom of expression during the 1930s was much more protective of such rights. Though the Court did not typically revert to the clear and present danger formula, it did, by virtue of focussing upon the vagueness of statutes,[27] manage to expand the area of protected expression. Since Court opinions did not specify precisely what fell within this protected area (rather they provided ostensive definitions by saying in specific cases that the activities did in fact fall in the area of protected speech), the "test" being applied was not really clearly spelled out. The justices, as suggested above, may have been implicitly applying the clear and present danger rule, using it tacitly to distinguish protected speech from that which was not protected. This more liberal approach to expression came at a time of unrest in the society when diverse views gained widespread currency, when the labor movement was using speech, assembly, and picketing as means for successful development both of unions and of organizations potent in the political arena. Legislation restricting freedom of expression was on the books and was passed during this period. Prosecutions were initiated. But, unlike the past decade, the Supreme Court more actively intervened to restrict the application of this legislation. Attitude structures and the behavior both of other institutions of government and growing private interest groups provided a context in which this doctrinal change seems congruent with the changing character of the political process.

[27]In addition to the cases discussed above, see also *Herndon* v. *Lowry*, 301 U.S. 242 (1937) and *Thornhill* v. *Alabama*, 310 U.S. 88 (1940).

The forties

This decade, dominated by World War II, was not notable for the development of a great deal of doctrine touching directly upon freedom of expression. Indeed, some of the most important cases of the decade, dealing with the treatment of Japanese Americans,[28] involved the subverting of almost all liberties of a class of citizens in the name of protection of the national interest. But a few important cases dealing directly with the limits upon expression did emerge from the Court during this decade.

The first case, *Chaplinsky* v. *New Hampshire*,[29] involved an encounter between a Jehovah's Witness and a police officer. In a heated exchange of words, Chaplinsky called the officer a "damned Fascist." He was convicted under a statute which, as interpreted by state courts, forbade words that have a "direct tendency to cause acts of violence by the persons to whom, individually, the remark is addressed." The Supreme Court upheld the conviction, applying the doctrine of "fighting words." The Court, holding that such speech could be punished, asserted: "There are certain well-defined and narrowly limited classes of speech, the prevention and punishment of which have never been thought to raise any constitutional problems. These include the lewd and obscene, the profane, the libelous, and the insulting or 'fighting' words—those which by their very utterance inflict injury or tend to incite an immediate breach of peace."[30] The Court went on to suggest that such speech was not communication useful to a democratic system and was likely to create a clear and present danger of a breach of peace. The significance of the case, in addition to the fact that its rather offhand reference to obscenity as not protected by the First Amendment, was the tendency of the majority to proceed by

[28]See, for example, *Hirabayashi* v. *United States*, 320 U.S. 81 (1943) and *Korematsu* v. *United States*, 323 U.S. 214 (1944).

[29]315 U.S. 568 (1942).

[30]315 U.S. 571-572.

classes of speech, rather than circumstances. There is allusion to the clear and present danger test; however, it is not applied to the specific, but rather to the general type of speech in which the defendant was alleged to have engaged.

Another important case, also involving the activities of Jehovah's Witnesses, dealt with the practice of requiring students in public schools to salute the flag. In 1940, in the *Gobitis* case discussed above, the Court had upheld such a law, arguing that such activity was a valid element of a general educational program designed to promote patriotism and good citizenship. The Court reversed itself in 1943 and overturned a West Virginia law requiring the flag salute.[31] The opinion of the majority did not specify precisely what test was being applied, but did enunciate clearly the preferred position doctrine and expand the notion of what constituted expression protected by the First Amendment. The majority opinion, written by Justice Jackson, asserted:

> There is no doubt that, in connection with the pledges, the flag salute is a form of utterance. Symbolism is a primitive but effective way of communicating ideas. The use of an emblem or flag to symbolize some system, idea, institution, or personality, is a short cut from mind to mind. Causes and nations, political parties, lodges and ecclesiastical groups seek to knit the loyalty of their followings to a flag or banner, a color or design.[32]

Jackson's opinion also enunciated clearly the preferred position doctrine:

> The test of legislation which collides with the Fourteenth Amendment, because it also collides with the principles of the First, is much more definite than the test when only the Fourteenth is involved. . . . The right of a State to regulate, for example, a public

[31] *West Virginia Board of Education* v. *Barnette,* 319 U.S. 624 (1943).
[32] 319 U.S. 632.

utility may well include, so far as the due process clause is concerned, power to impose all of the restrictions which a legislature may have a "rational basis" for adopting. But freedoms of speech and of press, of assembly, and of worship may not be infringed on such slender grounds. They are susceptible of restriction only to prevent a grave and immediate danger to interests which the state may lawfully protect.[33]

The majority concluded that the statute was unconstitutional, for it "transcends constitutional limitations on their power and invades the sphere of intellect and spirit which is the purpose of the First Amendment.[34] The opinion thus did not spell out precisely what doctrinal test it was utilizing, though it clearly relied upon a notion of preferred position and made allusion to the clear and present danger doctrine. However, it stands both as a courageous protection of the political rights of a minority during a time of great patriotic fervor, and is among the most eloquent elaborations of the importance of freedom of expression.

A final case in the 1940s, *Terminello* v. *Chicago*,[35] dealt with the prosecution of a self-avowed fascist for breach of peace. He had been delivering a speech, denouncing Jews and others, in a hired hall surrounded outside by an incensed crowd. The Court overturned his conviction on the ground that the vagueness of the statute (as interpreted by the trial judge in his charge to the jury) might have permitted conviction for simply making remarks that stirred controversy and anger. This case is discussed in more detail in Chapter Three. Again, the Court did not revert to clear and present danger, but relied upon the vagueness doctrine.

Thus, the cases of the late 1930s and 1940s seemed to have established firmly the notion of a preferred position for

[33]319 U.S. 639.
[34]319 U.S. 642.
[35]337 U.S. 1 (1949).

political freedoms. But subsequent experience indicates that shifts in the political and social climates can make such "preference" a sometime thing.

LOYALTY-SECURITY: 1950-1970

Our discussion now turns to the period that is the major focus of this book, the years from 1950 to 1970. The discussion is divided into three sections, in part chronological, in part dealing with the changing character of the issues that have faced our society. The first section deals with the various loyalty-security programs adopted by the government and the issues and litigation they produced. These issues to a large extent dominated litigation before the Court from 1950 to the early 1960s. The second area concerns the rights of blacks, and is the subject of Chapter Three. In addition to the substantive issue of equality of treatment for black people in our society, which has vast social, political and constitutional dimensions, members of the civil rights movement adopted a variety of tactics that raised questions about freedom of expression. In a sense, then, the question of expression during the 1950-1970 period first emerged in the context of attempts to deal with alleged subversive activity by those of supposedly totalitarian ideologies. As concern with these individuals and groups subsided, the activities of advocates of racial equality became the dominant focus of dispute over the limits upon freedom of expression. In the past few years, the focus has again begun to shift, with many of the disputes centering on freedom of expression involving the activities of Viet Nam War opponents and the so-called New Left, and on the question of new forms of expression such as "symbolic" speech, whose constitutional protection is currently the subject of developing doctrine.

An overview

The loyalty-security issue dominated for more than a decade both Court decisions and public controversy surrounding the limits on free expression. As is clear from the previous discussion, concern over internal security, and especially over the activities of Communist Party members and sympathizers, has been an aspect of American life since the early twentieth century. A good deal of the litigation dealing with freedom of expression discussed thus far has involved attempts to restrict the activities of political radicals, often of the left wing. The loyalty-security effort undertaken by federal and state governments after the end of World War II[36] was perhaps the most intensive attack upon freedom of expression and association in the history of our nation. The programs were almost exclusively directed at the beliefs and expression of ideas of a particular ideological group within our society.

People may debate the reason for this focus upon beliefs and expression. Some would maintain that many of the individuals punished for their beliefs and expression had no intention of illegal action in the first place, but merely strong preferences about how our society ought to be changed. Or, it might be argued, those who suffered from the loyalty-security effort may have been intellectually committed to leading a revolution but were never strong enough to do so, the climate in the society being such that their beliefs and expressions simply failed to produce the adherents necessary to effective (and perhaps violent) activity. Or, finally, some may argue that the absence of much measurable violent or illegal activity is itself an indication of the prudence and effectiveness of the government's attacks upon left-wing beliefs and the curtailing of their expression and therefore that the government's preemptive attack to rob the radicals, fellow-travellers, and sympathizers of their potential for fomenting a revolution was right.

[36]The most detailed analysis of the loyalty-security programs by a political scientist is Earl Latham, *The Communist Controversy in Washington* (Cambridge, Mass.: Harvard University Press, 1966). For a critical review of Latham's book, see Frank J. Donner, "Leaving Out the Letter 'E'!" *The Nation*, 203 (1966), pp. 422-425.

Whatever one's evaluation, the fact remains that the loyalty-security programs, in their various manifestations, did focus mainly upon the repression of ideas, expression and association rather than upon behavior. The very concept of "fellow traveller," alluded to above, a common expression during the 1950s, suggests the kinds of notions that informed the loyalty-security effort in this country. For what was a fellow-traveller but an individual lacking organizational ties, but viewed as having beliefs sympathetic to positions espoused by the Communist Party, and who might have contributed money or moral support to causes championed by the Party. Thus, the objects of attack during the loyalty-security era included not only members of organizations that consciously urged change (perhaps violent) in our form of government,[37] but also those who were sympathetic with some of the specific social and political positions espoused by the Party. This is not to deny that such a thing as a fellow-traveller existed; there were, without doubt, individuals who, while not members of the Communist Party, took cues from it about their positions on specific issues. However, the concept does suggest the kinds of "activities" that came to be the subject of scorn, obloquy, and sometimes criminal sanction during the decade of the 1950s.

The loyalty-security effort began to build after the close of World War II. Our erstwhile ally, the Soviet Union, became our enemy. As the Cold War built in intensity, the American public became concerned with the threat of internal subversion by individuals and groups within America whose sympathies lay not with us but with them. This developing concern was led by a group of public and political figures who used the issue of the menace from internal subversion as a platform for initiating political careers or increasing their

[37]Many would argue that even membership in such organizations should not be penalized, but that the government should apply sanctions only to illegal behavior, not membership in organizations that *might* engage in such behavior.

salience and popularity. This is not to say that these men were insincere and were trumping up an issue (though no doubt some were), but simply to point out that the issue of national security, and its concomitant, programs to restrict beliefs and expression, became a very important, if not the dominating, concern of American political life.

The programs developed to deal with internal subversion often involved direct or indirect restrictions upon the freedom to express political views, to join organizations in order to espouse such views, and even to hold views themselves. Examples include the Smith Act, with its penalties for advocating or teaching the necessity of the overthrow of the government of the United States; the provisions of the McCarran Act calling for the registration of organizations declared to be Communist action or Communist front groups, and various penalties (e.g., noneligibility for a passport or for jobs in sensitive industries) for members of such organizations; extensive investigating activities by federal and state legislative committees, aimed not so much at legislation as at the exposure of individuals' beliefs, memberships, and activities; and the proliferation of loyalty oaths as prerequisites to government employment. Whatever one thinks of the propriety of such programs and activities by the government, it is clear that they restricted both directly and indirectly the freedom of individuals in our society to hold opinions and to express them.

These programs had the support of the general public and of important government officials, including the President, the Congress, and, to a large extent, the Court itself. As suggested before, to understand the doctrine emerging from the Court, one must take account of the activities of other individuals and institutions, and of the attitude structures in the society at large. Table 1 suggests the intensity of feeling that characterized American attitudes toward Communists.

The table indicates two things. First, it clearly demonstrates the intensity of popular opposition to members of the Communist Party. Communists were feared and most citizens

	Percent		
Year	Yes	No	Don't Know/No Opinion

1. Should membership in the Communist Party be forbidden by law?

Year	Yes	No	Don't Know/No Opinion
1940	67	22	11
1946	44	38	18
1947	62	23	15
1949	70	21	9
1953	74	20	6
1954	51	34	15

2. Should communists be permitted to hold public office?

Year	Yes	No	Don't Know/No Opinion
1939	16	72	12
1946	17	69	14
1948	19	67	14

3. Should members of the Communist Party be allowed to speak on the radio?

Year	Yes	No	Don't Know/No Opinion
1943	48	40	12
1945	49	39	12
1948	36	57	7
1954	22	73	5
1956	22	76	2
1957	22	75	3

Sources: Hadley Cantril, *Public Opinion 1935-46* (Princeton, N.J.: Princeton University Press, 1951), pp. 130-131 and summaries of responses to polls provided by the Roper Public Opinion Research Center, Williamstown, Mass.

felt they should not enjoy the rights extended to those of more palatable political views. Second, the table suggests, though admittedly imperfectly, the gradual dimunition of the fear of Communists that began to set in during the second half of the 1950s. Unfortunately, survey research to support this proposition is generally lacking. One indirect indication of this gradual loss of salience is indicated by the sharp decline in the number of questions asked by the pollsters about the activities of political extremists. During the 1935-1945 period, the pollsters asked 58 questions dealing with communism, right-wing groups, and congressional investigations. During the 1946-1955 period, this number rose to 143. From 1956-1963 the number fell dramatically to 5. This is admittedly indirect evidence, and requires something of a leap (the inference required is that the questions selected by the pollsters are to some extent representative of the kinds of issues the public finds salient), but it suggests the general reduction of public interest in and concern with the activities of alleged subversives, particularly Communists.[38]

As suggested above, this intense public opposition to Communists was accompanied by the activity of political figures, most notably Senator Joseph McCarthy of Wisconsin, stressing the dangers of internal subversion and the necessity of legislation, screening programs, and investigations to uncover and uproot the internal menace of communism.[39] These activities not only fed upon and helped to generate the anticommunist sentiments sketched above, but also produced legislation designed to restrict the freedoms of alleged radicals. The activities and programs that produced the litigation are of particular interest here, for the doctrine developed by the Court to deal with these issues was itself reflective of the general desire in our society to sacrifice the rights of radicals in the name of national security.

Table 2, a time chart of some of the important decisions, provides a perspective on the discussion of the litigation that follows. It suggests that the Court's posture toward protec-

[38]These data are presented and discussed in Hazel Gaudet Erskine, "The Polls: Some Gauges of Conservatism," *Public Opinion Quarterly*, 28 (1964), pp. 154-168.

[39]For contrasting views about Senator McCarthy's motivations, activities, and impact see the following: Richard Rovere, *Senator Joseph McCarthy* (New York: Harcourt Brace Jovanovich, 1959); William F. Buckley and L. B. Bozell, *McCarthy and His Enemies* (New York: Henry Regnery Company, 1954); Roy Cohn, *McCarthy: His Side of the Story* (New York: New American Library, 1968). Striking visual evocations of McCarthy are found in two films by Emile de Antonio, "Point of Order," and "Charge and Countercharge."

tion of freedom of expression underwent several relatively distinct periods. The doctrinal positions taken by the Court cannot be understood simply by analyzing the types of issues confronting the Court or the changing personnel on the Court (though this is of course important). Rather, as the table suggests, events in the broader political system have a distinct impact upon the doctrinal choices made by the Court.

Table 2 suggests that the Court's treatment of constitutional issues arising out of the loyalty-security programs developed in this country fell into four periods. The first set of cases (A), arising during the developing intensity of the loyalty-security scare, legitimated many activities of government that infringed upon expression in the name of protecting national security. As the fervor of the loyalty-security era began to subside with the demise of Senator McCarthy and an apparent general decline of interest in the problems of internal subversion, the Court stepped in, especially during the 1956-1957 terms, and struck down government activities that were not, manifestly at least, much different in content and constitutional dimension from those it had several years before upheld (B). However, the Court misjudged the temper of the times, for these libertarian decisions were met by a wave of protest, especially within the Congress. Legislation and constitutional amendments aimed at reversing many of the Court's libertarian decisions were introduced, and though most failed of passage, the Court received the intended message. It proceeded to step back in the next three years (C), once more upholding loyalty-security activities. Finally, after about 1961, the Court stepped in once again (D). Since that time, it has to a large extent emasculated the antisubversive statutes of the federal government and severely hampered the efforts of states and municipalities to screen employees on the basis of their loyalty.

Table 2 Important court decisions on freedom of expression, 1950-1967

Year	Case	Issue	Outcome*
A			
1950	American Communications Assn. v. Doud	anticommunist provision of Taft-Hartley Act	—
1950	Bailey v. Richardson	federal employee screening	—
1951	Dennis v. United States	Smith Act prosecution	—
1951	Garner v. Board of Public Works	municipal employee loyalty oath	—
1952	Adler v. Board of Education	state employee screening	+
1952	Wieman v. Updegraff	state loyalty oath	+
1953	United States v. Rumely	legislative investigation	
B			
1956	Pennsylvania v. Nelson	state antisubversive activities statute	+
1957	Yates v. United States	Smith Act prosecution	+
1957	Watkins v. United States	legislative investigation	+
1957	Sweezy v. New Hampshire	legislative investigation	+
1957	Slochower v. Board of Education	municipal employee screening	+
1957	Schware v. Board of Bar Examiners	loyalty test for admission to bar	+
1957	Konigsberg v. State Bar	loyalty test for admission to bar	+
1958	Speiser v. Randall	state loyalty oath	+
C			
1958	Lerner v. Casey	municipal employee screening	—
1958	Beilan v. Board of Education	municipal employee screening	—
1959	Greene v. McElroy	federal employee screening	—
1959	Barenblatt v. United States	legislative investigation	—
1959	Uphaus v. Wieman	legislative investigation	—

Year	Case	Description	
1960	Nelson v. Los Angeles	municipal employee screening	—
1961	Scales v. United States	Smith Act prosecution	—
1961	Noto v. United States	Smith Act prosecution	+
1961	Communist Party v. Subversive Activities Control Board	McCarran Act proceeding	—
1961	Wilkinson v. United States	legislative investigation	—
1961	Braden v. United States	legislative investigation	—
1961	Cafeteria Workers v. McElroy	federal employee screening	—
1961	Koenigsberg v. State Bar	loyalty test for admission to bar	—
1961	Cramp v. Board of Public Instruction	state loyalty oath	+

D

Year	Case	Description	
1963	Gibson v. Florida Investigation Committee	legislative investigation	+
1964	Aptheker v. Secretary of State	passport provisions of McCarran Act	+
1964	Baggett v. Bullitt	state loyalty oath	+
1965	Albertson v. Subversive Activities Control Board	registration provisions of McCarran Act	+
1966	Elfbrandt v. Russell	state loyalty oath	+

Table 2 *(continued)*

Year	Case	Issue	Outcome*
1967	*Keyishian v. Board of Regents*	state loyalty oath	+
1967	*Whitehill v. Elkins*	state loyalty oath	+
1967	*United States v. Robel*	employment provisions of McCarran Act	+

Sources: The cases listed in the table do not include all those dealing with loyalty-security issues decided by the Supreme Court during the 1950-1970 period. Rather the table attempts to include all the significant decisions. "Significance" is obviously a somewhat subjective term. In an attempt to gain some measure of objectivity in selection, several standard case books dealing with constitutional law were consulted, and any case excerpted in at least two of the case books was included in the table. The sources consulted included the following: Edward L. Barrett, Jr., et al., *Constitutional Law: Cases and Materials* (Mineola, N.Y.: The Foundation Press, 1st ed., 1959; 2nd ed., 1963; 3rd ed., 1968); Paul A. Freund, et al., *Constitutional Law Cases and Other Problems* (Boston: Little, Brown, 1st ed., 1954; 2nd ed., 1961; 3rd ed., 1967); Thomas I. Emerson, et al., *Political and Civil Rights in the United States* (Boston: Little, Brown, 1st ed., 1952; 2nd ed., 1958; 3rd ed., 1967); William B. Lockhart, et al., *Case Materials in Constitutional Rights and Liberties* (St. Paul, Minn.: West Publishing Company, 1964; Supplement, 1968; Supplement, 1969); Milton R. Konvitz, *Bill of Rights Reader* (Ithaca, N.Y.: Cornell University Press, 1st ed., 1954; 2nd ed., 1960; 3rd ed., 1965; 4th ed., 1968); Milton R. Konvitz, *First Amendment Freedoms* (Ithaca, N.Y.: Cornell University Press, 1963).

*The sign in the "Outcome" column denotes whether the Supreme Court opinion was favorable (+) or unfavorable (−) to the civil liberties claim involved in the case.

Repression, 1950-1955

To explore the impact of these programs upon freedom of expression and the response of the Court, let us look at some of these cases in more detail. The most notable case of the first period was *Dennis* v. *United States.*[40] The leading figures in the American Communist Party were charged under provisions of the Smith Act[41] that prohibited "knowingly or willfully advocat[ing] . . . or teach[ing] the duty, necessity, desirability or propriety of overthrowing . . . our government in the United States by force or violence"; the dissemination of literature advocating such overthrow with intent to cause such overthrow; the organization of " . . . any society, group or assembly of persons to teach, advocate, or encourage" the overthrow of the government; membership in " . . . any such society, group or assembly" if the individual knew the purposes of such an organization. The statute made it a separate offense to conspire with others to perform any of the acts indicated above. Eleven leaders of the Communist Party were indicted in 1948. Their trial in 1949, lasting eight months, was both highly publicized and acrimonious. The defendants, some of whom chose to conduct their own defense, attempted to use the trial as a forum to express their political views and indignation at what they viewed as political persecution. Their behavior, not dissimilar to that which occurred in the 1969-1970 trial of the Chicago Eight, led to punishment of some of the defense lawyers for contempt and the conviction of the defendants.

The case reached the Supreme Court for decision in 1951, during the period of rising concern over internal subversion. The Court limited its hearing of the case to the issue of the constitutionality of the Smith Act and held that the Smith Act was not in violation of the First Amendment. The

[40] 341 U.S. 494 (1951).

[41] Title 18, Section 2385, United States Code.

Court's limitation of its consideration of the case is of particular interest. First, by considering only the constitutional issues, the Court avoided considering claims about the unfairness of the trial and of error and bias on the part of the trial judge. As suggested above, the *Dennis* trial had been a highly acrimonious affair, with both obstreperous defendants and an apparently hostile judge. In addition to avoiding questions of prejudicial error at the trial, the limited consideration of the Court also relieved it of the burden of considering the character of the evidence against the defendants—the actual behavior that had led to their conviction under a law making it a crime to conspire to advocate the violent overthrow of the government. The Court upheld the constitutionality of the act in terms that indicated it was applying the clear and present danger test—yet they concerned themselves with the statute in the abstract rather than the particular activities of the defendants. In a subsequent case discussed later in this chapter, *Yates* v. *United States*,[42] the Court did choose to examine the evidence presented against defendants in a Smith Act prosecution and overturned the convictions. In any event, the limited consideration given in the *Dennis* case suggests that the Court's power in setting its own agenda is a useful tool in handling issues that are potentially explosive.

The majority opinion, written by Chief Justice Vinson, asserted that it was applying the clear and present danger rule:

In this case we are squarely presented with the application of the 'clear and present danger' test, and must decide what the phrase imports. . . . Overthrow of the Government by force and violence is certainly a substantial enough interest for the Government to limit speech. Indeed, this is the ultimate value of any society, for if a society cannot protect its very structure from armed internal attack,

[42]354 U.S. 298 (1957).

it must follow that no subordinate value can be protected. . . . Obviously the words [clear and present danger] cannot mean that before the Government may act, it must wait until the *putsch* is about to be executed, the plans have been laid and the signal is awaited. If Government is aware that a group aiming at its overthrow is attempting to indoctrinate its members and to commit them to a course whereby they will strike when the leaders feel the circumstances permit, action by the Government is required. . . . Chief Judge Learned Hand, writing for the majority [of the Circuit Court of Appeals, which also upheld the conviction] interpreted the phrase [clear and present danger] as follows: "In each case [courts] must ask whether the gravity of the 'evil,' discounted by its improbability, justifies such invasion of free speech as is necessary to avoid the danger." We adopt this statement of the rule.[43]

This language is very similar to the majority view in the *Gitlow* case, just as the Smith Act was to a large extent modelled upon the New York law upheld in *Gitlow*. Despite their disclaimers, the majority was not in fact applying clear and present danger as developed by Holmes and Brandeis. First, there was nowhere in the majority opinion any detailed examination of the circumstances surrounding the activities of the Communist Party in America in the late 1940s. The possibility of their success, the likelihood that their words or association would produce attempts at overthrow, the context in which they were alleged to have conspired to speak and teach—none of these was the subject of more than very general statements, often prefaced by the adverb "obviously." Moreover, the formulation of Judge Hand—"the gravity of the evil discounted by its improbability"—is quite different from clear and present danger. Clear and present danger requires both that the evil be substantial and that the connection between the speech and the danger be demonstrably clear. The gravity-of-evil test introduces a sliding scale; if the evil is large enough, it does not have

[43]341 U.S. 508, 509, 510.

to be immediately present. Thus, for the Communists, though the probability of success was slight, the potential evil—overthrow of the government—was held to be sufficient to justify restrictions upon their freedom of expression.

Justice Frankfurter concurred in the result, but on somewhat different grounds. After an extensive review of past free speech cases, he first attacked the notion that legislation infringing upon freedom of speech enjoyed any preferred position when under consideration by the Court: "Free speech cases are not an exception to the principle that we are not legislators, that direct policymaking is not our province. How best to reconcile competing interests is the business of legislatures, and the balance they strike is a judgment not to be displaced by ours, but to be respected unless outside the pale of fair judgment."[44] He proceeded then to develop the themes of deference to legislative judgment and the notion of balancing: "A survey of the relevant decisions indicates that the results which we have reached are on the whole those that would ensue from careful weighing of conflicting interests."[45] Then, he suggested that on any scheme for ranking the value of speech, the kind involved in this case—advocacy of overthrow of the government—must rank low. Thus, given the fact that the speech was not very valuable to a free society, given the nature of the Communist party as a revolutionary organization, and given the deference due to the legislature in balancing the interest of speech against that of national survival, he concluded:

Can we then say that the judgment Congress exercised was denied it by the Constitution? Can we establish a constitutional doctrine which forbids the elected representatives of the people to make this

[44]341 U.S. 539-540.
[45]341 U.S. 542.

choice? Can we hold that the First Amendment deprives Congress of what is deemed necessary for the Government's protection?[46]

His answer was no.

Justice Jackson, concurring, argued that the clear-and-present-danger rule was not really applicable. It had been developed, he suggested, for the street-corner situation of a speaker facing an audience, and was not a useful instrument in dealing with the conspiratorial speech of secretive cadres of hardened ideologically committed revolutionaries, not competing in the marketplace of ideas but plotting in private. Given this character of the party and the dangers it presented to our national security, Jackson voted to uphold the conviction.

Black and Douglas dissented. Douglas stressed the fact that there was no evidence of the defendants' activities actually endangering national security, for they were small, relatively powerless, and apparently not gaining many adherents. Black urged the unconstitutionality of the statute on its face.

These petitioners were not charged with an attempt to overthrow the Government. They were not charged with overt acts of any kind designed to overthrow the Government. They were not even charged with saying anything or writing anything designed to overthrow the Government. The charge was that they agreed to assemble and to talk and publish certain ideas at a later date. The indictment is that they conspired to organize the Communist Party and to use speech or newspaper and other publications in the future to teach and advocate the forcible overthrow of the Government. No matter how it is worded, this is a virulent form of prior censorship of speech and press, which I believe the First Amendment forbids.[47]

Alluding to the social and political climate in which the case arose, Black observed:

[46]341 U.S. 551.
[47]341 U.S. 579.

Public opinion being what it now is, few will protest the conviction of these Communist petitioners. There is hope, however, that in calmer times, when present pressures, passions and fears subside, this or some later Court will restore the First Amendment liberties to the high preferred place where they belong in a free society.[48]

During this same period, the Court validated other aspects of the loyalty-security effort. In 1951, the Court upheld, by equally divided vote and without opinion, the dismissal of an employee of the Civil Service Commisssion who was accused of past membership in the Communist Party. The Court, by not issuing an opinion in the case (standard practice when it is evenly divided), permitted the doctrine of the circuit court opinion to become the definitive word about rights of employees in loyalty-security proceedings:

> In terms, the due process clause [of the Fifth Amendment] does not apply to the holding of a Government office ... [t]he plain hard fact is that so far as the Constitution is concerned [here, the First Amendment] there is no prohibition against the dismissal of government employees because of their political beliefs, activities or affiliations.[49]

The Court was eventually to modify, if not deny, this proposition, but in the early 1950s it did not choose to challenge it.

A third case of the early 1950s, *Garner* v. *Board of Public Works*, is worth looking at briefly.[50] A Los Angeles ordinance required municipal employees to swear that they did not and had not for five years previously "advised, advocated or taught, the overthrow by force, violence or other unlawful means, of the Government of the United States or of the

[48]341 U.S. 580.

[49]*Bailey* v. *Richardson*, 182 F. 2d(D.C. Cir.) 46 (1950); affirmed by equally divided vote of Supreme Court, 341 U.S. 918 (1951).

[50]341 U.S. 716 (1951).

State of California"[51] and had not been members of organizations which did so. The program also required execution of an affidavit stating whether the employee had ever been a member of the Communist Party of the United States and if so, when. The Court held that the affidavit was relevant to the employee's competence to hold municipal office, and, reading a requirement of *scienter* (knowledge and intent) into the oath dealing with memberships, the dismissal was upheld.

Thus, the Court validated a statute making it a crime to conspire to advocate the violent overthrow of the government, and accepted a variety of programs designed to screen public employees on the basis of their beliefs and associations. The Court based its decisions upon doctrine which suggested, perhaps not unreasonably, that speech was not the only value to be pursued by our society, and that other values, including self-preservation, might compete and take precedence over the value of free expression. In retrospect, most would probably agree that the Court somewhat overstated the potential danger to our society presented by Communists and fellow-travellers. In so doing, it was simply accepting a judgment (again, in retrospect probably incorrect) by the society at large that it was endangered. As a result of society's fear and the Court's acquiescence to the programs developed as a result of this fear, our society was made less free. As a further result, hindsight suggests that many suffered who were no danger at all to the society: individuals who had innocently in the distant past joined organizations, donated money, attended meetings. Individuals whose only "crime" had been a concern with social justice suffered along with the hard-core radicals and Party members.

The point of this discussion is not simply to belabor an earlier generation, the political figures who led it, or the

[51]341 U.S. 718.

Court itself. What I am trying to suggest is that most members of the Court, being what Dahl has called "inevitably a part of the dominant national alliance,"[52] probably felt themselves in no position to reverse a powerful impulse of the society of which it was a part. To understand the outcomes of these cases, one must not look simply at the issues raised and the constitutional principles involved in them, for subsequent cases raising very similar issues were decided differently. The key to understanding the Court's decisions lies, then, not entirely in the issues and the doctrinal principles, but in the men on the Court and the political climate which surrounds the cases.

In fact, half a decade later, the Court tried to change its constitutional course. As Black had suggested in his *Dennis* dissent, perhaps we had come upon "calmer times" in which the Court could move effectively to "restore the First Amendment liberties to the high preferred place where they belong in a free society." The decisions of the 1956-1957 period, and the reaction they engendered, suggest once more the relation between Court decisions and attitudes and behavior in the broader political system; moreover, they suggest that the Court, like others, can make mistakes in judging the direction in which the political winds are blowing.

The 1956-1957 terms

During the 1956-1957 terms, the Court moved back into the loyalty-security area with a vengeance. What differentiated this period from the one previously discussed?

In part, as suggested above, the level of public attention and concern with internal subversion appears to have waned to some extent. Some of the most salient public leaders of the fight against alleged subversives, particularly Senator McCarthy, had lost the prestige and public support they had

[52]Robert A. Dahl, "The Supreme Court as a National Policy-Maker," *Journal of Public Law*, 6 (1958), pp. 279-295 at 293.

once enjoyed. In addition, there were some changes in the personnel on the Court. Since his election in 1952, President Eisenhower had made four appointments to the Court. Chief Justice Vinson had been replaced by Earl Warren (in 1953); Justice Jackson by John Marshall Harlan (in 1954); Justice Minton by William Brennan (in 1956); and Justice Reed by Charles Whittaker (in 1957). Not all of the new appointees were particularly intense libertarians, but two, Warren and Brennan, were more liberal than their predecessors. These three combined with the old dissenting bloc of Black and Douglas (occasionally supported by some of the remaining four justices) to strike down or modify various activities associated with the loyalty-security programs.

In 1956, a conviction under the Pennsylvania Sedition Act (one of a series of so-called "little Smith Acts" passed by 42 states) was overturned by the Court,[53] basically on the ground that the crime of advocating the violent overthrow of the government had been superseded by federal legislation. Arguing that the federal government's interest in preventing overthrow was great, that the scheme of federal legislation had occupied the field, and that the dangers of interference with enforcement of the federal laws by state prosecutions were great, the Court held the Pennsylvania law to be invalid. The dissenters (Reed, Minton and Burton) made a fairly convincing case that the administration of such state acts did not interfere with federal government prosecutions and that the supersession argument misread the legislative history of the passage of the federal laws, but they did not carry the day.

The year 1957 was the big one for the Court's intervention in behalf of civil liberties. In a series of decisions, they attempted to place restraints upon federal and state legislative investigations, to restrict the application of the Smith Act by tightening the standards of evidence required for conviction, and to place limitations upon the loyalty-security screening programs of federal and municipal governments.

[53]*Pennsylvania* v. *Nelson*, 350 U.S. 497 (1956).

The *Watkins* case

Perhaps the most significant case was *Watkins* v. *U.S.*,[54] the first major confrontation between the Court and the House Committee on Un-American Activities. One of the most potent and publicized weapons in the fight against alleged subversives in this country had been the investigations by legislative committees. These investigations, often televised and the subject of intense publicity, typically involved calling as a witness an individual with alleged subversive connections who was extensively questioned about his own past activities, memberships, associations, and about others he had known. Some witnesses were friendly and willing to testify about their own and other people's activities. Others were hostile and the hearings were often highly acrimonious.[55] Witnesses refusing to answer questions but unwilling or unable to claim the protection of the Fifth Amendment privilege against self-incrimination were often cited for contempt of Congress. The legislative investigations raised serious constitutional issues. Because being called before a committee often produced penalties for the witness—scorn, obloquy, loss of employment, sometimes a citation for contempt—important issues dealing with the defendants' freedom of association and expression were raised. In addition, because the investigations often appeared to be aimed at exposure of the witnesses' activities and beliefs rather than at legislation, the power of Congress to engage in such activities was called into question.

Watkins, a union organizer, was called before HUAC to answer questions about subversive activities within the labor movement. He freely testified about his own past political activities, denying previous testimony of others that he had been a member of the Communist Party, but admitting that

[54]354 U.S. 178 (1957).

[55]For an entertaining account of the activities of the House Committee on Un-American Activities, see Walter Goodman, *The Committee* (New York: Farrar, Straus & Giroux, 1968).

he had cooperated with the Party on a number of occasions. However, he refused to testify about friends who he knew had been members of the Party, but who had since severed their ties. He based his refusal upon the protection of the First Amendment. In so doing, he indicated his belief that questions about others were beyond the proper scope of the committee's activities.

> I do not believe that such questions are relevant to the work of this committee nor do I believe that this committee has the right to undertake the public exposure of persons because of their past activities. I may be wrong, and the committee may have this power, but until and unless a court of law so holds and directs me to answer, I most firmly refuse to discuss the political activities of my past associates.[56]

This appeared to raise squarely the crucial issue in the legislative investigation phase of the loyalty-security effort, for there could be little doubt that exposure was in fact the purpose of most of the investigations.

Watkins' conviction of contempt of Congress was overturned by the Supreme Court. The majority opinion, by Chief Justice Warren, appeared to be a sweeping denunciation of many of the activities of legislative investigating committees. Admitting that the power of Congress to conduct investigation is "inherent in the legislative process," and that such power is "broad," Warren's opinion went on to say, "But broad as is this power of inquiry, it is not unlimited. There is no general authority to expose the private affairs of individuals without justification in terms of the functions of the Congress . . . . Investigations conducted solely for the personal aggrandizement of the investigators or to 'punish' those investigated are indefensible."[57]

Since many observers felt that the investigations were in

[56]354 U.S. 185.
[57]354 U.S. 187.

fact largely devoted to punishment of the witness and that personal aggrandizement was an essential element of the investigations as well, the opinion seemed to strike at the heart of the loyalty-security investigations.

Warren went on to argue that the provisions of the Bill of Rights, including the protections of the First Amendment, applied to such investigations: "The First Amendment may be invoked against infringement of the protected freedoms by law or lawmaking . . . We have no doubt that there is no congressional power to expose for the sake of exposure."[58]

Somewhat ironically, in discussing the Court's role in evaluating constitutional claims made by witnesses who did not wish to testify, Warren indicated that a crucial aspect of this process was balancing.

> The critical element is the existence of, and the weight to be ascribed to, the interest of the Congress in demanding disclosures from an unwilling witness. We cannot simply assume, however, that every congressional investigation is justified by a public need that overbalances any private rights affected. To do so would be to abdicate the responsibilities placed by the Constitution upon the judiciary to insure that the Congress does not unjustifiably encroach upon an individual's right to privacy or abridge his liberty of speech, press, religion or assembly.[59]

This approach—the balancing of interests—was to be adopted by other justices in later cases and used as a justification for upholding activities of legislative investigating committees and other loyalty-security programs.

However, when it came to actually deciding the case, Warren chose somewhat more limited grounds. The contempt statute required that an element of the offense be refusal to answer a question "pertinent to the question under inquiry"[60]

[58]354 U.S. 197, 200.

[59]354 U.S. 178.

[60]Title 2, Section 192, United States Code.

by the committee. The opinion reasoned, therefore, that a question's pertinence to the subject of the investigation must be made clear to the witness, so that he could know whether his refusal put him in jeopardy of violating the contempt provision. The Court cited the vagueness of the resolution authorizing the activities of HUAC:

> The Committee on Un-American Activities, as a whole or by subcommittee, is authorized to make from time to time investigations of (i) the extent, character, and objects of un-American propaganda activities in the United States, (ii) the diffusion within the United States of subversive and anti-American propaganda that is instigated from foreign countries or of a domestic origin and attacks the principle of the form of government as guaranteed by our Constitution, and (iii) all other questions in relation thereto that would aid Congress in any necessary remedial legislation.[61]

In addition to this inherent vagueness in the specification of the committee's mandate, the Court opinion noted the lack of any explicit statements of relevance and pertinence by the chairmen and committee members at the hearing in which Watkins refused to testify. The Court therefore concluded that Watkins' contempt conviction could not withstand the test suggested above:

> Unless the subject matter has been made to appear with indisputable clarity, it is the duty of the investigative body, upon objection of the witness on the grounds of pertinency, to state for the record the subject under inquiry at that time and the manner in which the propounded questions are pertinent thereto.[62]

Thus, the import of *Watkins* was somewhat unclear. It contained some sweeping language that appeared quite restrictive of the activities of investigating committees. But

[61]Rule XI, passed by House of Representatives in 1938.
[62]354 U.S. 214-215.

the actual holding of the case—the ground upon which it was decided—was much narrower. As we will soon see, in the next major HUAC case, the narrow rather than the broad aspect of the opinion was to survive.

The *Yates* opinion

In another of the most significant decisions of the 1957 term,[63] the Court overturned the conviction under the Smith Act of several "second-string" Communist Party leaders. In overturning the conviction and ordering the acquittal of five of the defendants and new trials for the remaining nine, the Supreme Court set forth evidential and constitutional requirements for conviction that to a large extent emasculated the advocacy provisions of the Smith Act. The government did not attempt to reprosecute the nine.

The *Yates* majority opinion, written by Justice Harlan, tightened the requirements for what constituted "advocacy" of overthrow under the Smith Act. The majority opinion held advocacy of the mere doctrine that forcible overthrow was advisable to be insufficient; the statute could constitutionally reach only advocacy of action towards overthrow:

> ... The Smith Act does not denounce advocacy in the sense of preaching abstractly the forcible overthrow of the Government ... the Smith Act reaches only advocacy of action for the overthrow of the government by force and violence. The essential distinction is that those to whom the advocacy is addressed must be urged to *do* something, now or in the future, rather than merely to *believe* in something.[64]

The majority opinion, discussing the evidence against the defendants, found it to be slim:

[63]*Yates* v. *United States, supra,* note 42.
[64]354 U.S. 324-325. (Emphasis in original.)

Instances of speech that could be considered to amount to 'advocacy of action' are so few and far between as to be almost completely overshadowed by the hundreds of instances in the record in which overthrow, if mentioned at all, occurs in the course of doctrinal disputation so remote from action as to be almost wholly lacking in probative value. Vague references to 'revolutionary' or 'militant' action of an unspecified character, which are found in the evidence, might in addition be given too great weight by the jury in the absence of more precise instructions [by the trial judge].[65]

In addition to restricting both the test for advocacy of overthrow and examining the evidence and finding it insufficient to justify conviction (because it generally went to the character of the Party, not to individual acts), the Court also made an important interpretation of the clause of the Smith Act dealing with "organizing" groups to advocate overthrow. The majority held that the term "organize" in the Smith Act applied only to the creation of new organizations. Since the American Communist Party, in its current manifestation, had been organized in 1945 and the indictments against these defendants not returned until 1951, the five-year statute of limitations had tolled and they could not be indicted for "organizing" the Party. Thus the *Yates* opinion greatly curtailed the application of the Smith Act to the Communist Party.

The 1956-1957 terms saw several other Court decisions applying restrictions to government loyalty-security programs. These cases dealt with such diverse areas as state legislative investigating committees,[66] municipal employee screening[67] admission to the bar,[68] access to FBI files dealing

[65]354 U.S. 327.

[66]*Sweezy* v. *New Hampshire*, 354 U.S. 234 (1957).

[67]*Slochower* v. *Board of Education*, 350 U.S. 551 (1956).

[68]*Konigsberg* v. *State Bar of California*, 353 U.S. 252 (1957); *Schware* v. *Board of Bar Examiners of New Mexico*, 353 U.S. 232 (1957).

with information provided by informers,[69] and federal employee security programs.[70]

Thus, the Court had actively stepped in to put the brakes on the antisubversive programs of the federal and state governments. Discontent over these rulings, together with an unpopular decision dealing with the rights of criminal defendants also made in 1957[71] and the smoldering discontent by Southerners over the school desegregation decision of 1954, produced a violent attack upon the Court by the Congress, much of the press, and large segments of the organized bar. This attack, which took the form of proposed legislation, constitutional amendments, and threats of impeachment proceedings, attempted not only to reverse the Court's specific rulings but also threatened to change its very jurisdiction.[72] Though almost all of the anti-Court proposals failed of passage (with the exception of the Jencks bill, modifying the Court's ruling to some extent), the furor was not without its effect.

The retreat of 1958-1961

The Court had apparently misjudged the political climate. Perhaps believing that the "calmer times" Justice Black had longed for in his *Dennis* dissent had come to pass, the Court judged that the time had come to reassert its power in protection of the rights of expression and association which had been sacrificed in the name of national security. The violent reaction to its loyalty-security decisions of the 1956-1957 period, added to discontent over other rulings,

[69] *Jencks* v. *United States*, 353 U.S. 657 (1957).

[70] *Service* v. *Dulles*, 354 U.S. 363 (1957).

[71] *Mallory* v. *United States*, 354 U.S. 449 (1957).

[72] The Constitution specifies classes of cases in which the Supreme Court has original jurisdiction. Congress has the power to establish and modify the appellate jurisdiction of the Court. For an excellent account of the interplay between Congress and the Court in the 1956-1961 period, see Walter Murphy, *Congress and the Court* (Chicago: University of Chicago Press, 1962).

especially that dealing with school segregation, had produced a storm of protest, some of which was directed at the very heart of the Court's power in the political system. A prudent retreat was called for, and the Court obliged in relatively short order.

Returning to many of the issues dealt with in the 1956-1957 period, the Court decided a series of cases differently. In 1958, two municipal loyalty-oath cases came before the Court. Both of them were decided against the petitioner, and municipal employee firings were upheld. in *Lerner* v. *Casey*[73] a subway conductor in New York City had been fired for refusing (on Fifth Amendment grounds) to answer a superior's question dealing with his membership in the Communist Party. In *Beilan* v. *Board of Education*,[74] a teacher in Pennsylvania had been fired for "incompetency" because of failure to answer the school superintendant's questions about past activity in the Communist Party and similar questions asked by a Congressional committee. In both cases, the Supreme Court ruled that the state supreme courts' construction of the concept of "competency" was not so unreasonable as to violate the Constitution. By implication, the Court agreed that such questions were relevant to the employee's fitness for state employment, something they had been unwilling to do in the 1956 *Slochower* opinion. This approach was also followed in *Nelson* v. *Los Angeles*,[75] in which a social worker had been discharged for "insubordination" for failure to obey a superior's instruction to answer questions before HUAC. The Court accepted the argument that the employee was discharged for insubordination, not for exercise of his constitutional privilege against self-incrimination, and held that such a dismissal did not have a built-in inference of guilt as a result of assertion of the privilege. The Court attempted to

[73]357 U.S. 468 (1958).
[74]357 U.S. 299 (1958).
[75]362 U.S. 1 (1960).

distinguish the latter three cases from the *Slochower* ruling of 1956 by asserting that in the later cases the state could demonstrate the relevance of the information sought to fitness for employment and its interest in obtaining such information. Lumping subway conductors, teachers, and social workers together, but excluding college professors, the Court granted the states a good deal of latitude in determining what was relevant and what was not. The coincidence between the reaction to the 1956-1957 decisions and the Court's attempts to distinguish *Lerner, Beilan,* and *Nelson* from *Slochower* suggests both the malleability of the doctrinal principles used by the Court and the retreat from the position taken by the Court in the 1956-1957 terms.

The *Barenblatt* case

The year 1959 brought a retreat in the area of legislative investigations. The sweeping dicta of *Watkins* evaporated in the wake of public and Congressional hostility. Barenblatt, an instructor at Vassar, was called before HUAC and asked about his alleged Communist activities while a graduate student at the University of Michigan. He refused to answer, among others, questions about his own memberships, arguing that the Committee did not possess the power to inquire into such subjects, and refusing to rely upon the self-incrimination privilege. In appealing his contempt conviction to the Supreme Court, he argued that *Watkins* had in effect stripped HUAC of its power to compel this testimony, because of the vagueness of Rule XI. In the majority opinion[76] by Justice Harlan, the Court held that *Watkins* had turned on the question of whether the witness had been adequately apprised of the relevance of the questions to the specific investigation. The Court in *Watkins,* Harlan argued, was not dealing with Rule XI in general, but in the context of that particular hearing. The majority opinion went on to hold that there was nothing in the legislation indicating that the House

[76]*Barenblatt* v. *United States,* 360 U.S. 109 (1959).

of Representatives did not approve of the Committee's investigation of subversion in educational institutions, and that in general Rule XI "cannot be said to be constitutionally infirm on the score of vagueness."[77]

The majority opinion pointed out that Barenblatt had made no objection at the hearing on the ground of pertinency to the questions asked of him, and that in fact members of the Committee had made the relevance of the questions to the subject under investigation quite clear.[78]

In dealing with the First Amendment claim, the majority adopted the balancing approach (mentioned by Warren in *Watkins*). Balancing the individual rights of Mr. Barenblatt in maintaining his associations and thus in remaining silent against what the Congress and the Court felt to be the nature of the menace to national security presented by Communist activity and infiltration, the Court struck the balance in favor of the government's need to compel testimony, and the contempt conviction was upheld.

Chief Justice Warren and Justices Black, Douglas, and Brennan dissented. The major dissenting opinion, by Justice Black, argued that Rule XI was so broad and vague as to void any contempt conviction. He went on to attack the balancing approach to the First Amendment, arguing his absolutist position that when the First Amendment says no law (or governmental activity associated with lawmaking) it simply means that. Even under the balancing test, though, he argued that the case had been wrongly decided. The test should balance not just the interest of the individual witness, he argued, but also the interest of "the people as a whole in being able to join organizations, advocate causes and make political 'mistakes' without later being subject to govern-

---

[77]360 U.S. 122-123.

[78]Another difference between the two cases was not stressed in the *Barenblatt* opinion, but was fixed upon in a later decision as having been crucial: Watkins has freely answered questions about his own activities and memberships; Barenblatt, challenging the very basis for the investigation, refused to answer questions about his own activities.

mental penalties for having dared to think for themselves."[79]
Finally, he argued that the basic, and impermissible, purpose
of such hearings was to punish "by humiliation and
shame."[80]

> Thus if communism is to be made a crime and communists are to be
> subject to 'pains and penalties,' I would still hold this conviction
> bad, for the crime of communism, like all others, can be pun-
> ished only by court and jury after trial and with all judicial safe-
> guards.[81]

In a parallel development dealing with state legislative
investigations, the Court upheld a contempt conviction
arising in New Hampshire.[82] The defendant, Uphaus, was
convicted for contempt after he refused to produce the guest
list of a summer camp he ran that was suspected of being a
"Communist front." Attempting to differentiate Uphaus
from the *Sweezy* case two years earlier, the Court used the
balancing technique and held that the state's interest in
delving into subversive activities outweighed the invasion
of freedom of association involved in production of the
lists.

The McCarran Act
The retreat continued into the early 1960s. In 1961, the
Court upheld the basic constitutionality of the Subversive
Activities Control Act, a major pillar of the government's
antisubversive statutory scheme.[83] This law, commonly called
the McCarran Act, set up the Subversive Activities Control
Board (SACB) and empowered it to hold hearings to

[79] 360 U.S. 144.

[80] 360 U.S. 153.

[81] 360 U.S. 160.

[82] *Uphaus* v. *Wyman* 360 U.S. 72 (1959).

[83] *Communist Party* v. *Subversive Activities Control Board*, 367 U.S. 1
(1961).

determine whether various organizations were either Communist action or Communist front groups. Upon a finding that a group fell in either category, the organization was required to register under the act, providing information about its officers, monies received and spent, names and addresses of members, a list of all printing devices in the possession of the organization. Once an organization had registered, or a final order from the SACB had been filed, the organization and its members had to fulfill certain requirements. For example, any publication of the organization sent through the mails had to be enclosed in an envelope indicating that it was being sent by a "communist organization." Such organizations were not entitled to tax exemptions under the Internal Revenue Code, and contributions were not tax deductible. Employment of members of such organizations by the government or in defense-related industries was restricted, and members could not apply for passports or use those they already possessed. If an organization failed to obey a final order to register, its members were required to register individually.

The Court upheld the basic constitutionality of the act, relying heavily upon legislative findings as to the nature of the menace of international communism and the possibility of internal subversion. Though upholding the provisions of the act against a First Amendment attack, the Court did not decide the Fifth Amendment self-incrimination issue raised by the registration provisions—individuals coerced to register might be placing themselves in jeopardy of prosecution under other statutes, particularly the Smith Act. The Court held that the self-incrimination issue was not ripe for decision, but would be deferred until an individual could claim for himself that he was being forced to register and hence raise the self-incrimination issue.

The Court also returned to the Smith Act in 1961, this time in cases involving the prohibition upon *membership* in organizations that advocated the violent overthrow of the government. The Court upheld the conviction of Scales for violation of the membership provision by virtue of his membership in the Communist Party.[84] In a five-to-four decision, the majority opinion held that the membership clause of the Smith Act applied only to those who were "active" members of the Party and who had "guilty knowledge and intent" in relation to such membership. On the same day, the Court overturned another conviction under the membership clause.[85] The cases were distinguished on the ground that the evidence against Noto indicated that the Communist organization of which he was a member had been involved in advocating the "abstract teaching of Communist theory," not the violent overthrow of the government with intent that such advocacy be acted upon. Thus, the distinction in Yates, combined with an examination of the character of the two organizations, was used to differentiate the two cases.

The Court was highly divided in the legislative investigation cases in 1961. A majority held that questions about Communist activity at Cornell University were not pertinent (under the *Watkins* approach) to an investigation of Communist infiltration of the labor movement in New York State.[86] During the same year, the Court, in two 5-4 decisions, upheld the HUAC contempt convictions of two individuals, Wilkinson and Braden.[87] Though there was strong evidence that in fact it was the defendants' public opposition to the activities of HUAC which had sparked their being called as witnesses, the Court held that because the hearings (dealing with Communist infiltration in labor union activities) were valid under the *Barenblatt* rule, the investigations were proper, despite any possible defect in the motives for calling these particular witnesses.

[84]*Scales* v. *United States*, 367 U.S. 203 (1961).

[85]*Noto* v. *United States*, 367 U.S. 290 (1961).

[86]*Deutch* v. *United States*, 367 U.S. 456 (1961).

[87]*Wilkinson* v. *United States*, 365 U.S. 399 (1961); *Braden* v. *United States*, 365 U.S. 431 (1961).

Dealing with the federal government's loyalty-security screening programs in 1961, the Court upheld the firing of a cafeteria worker from her position at the Naval Gun Factory in Washington.[88] The majority argued that this exclusion was justified by Naval Regulations and military history, both of which supported the right of a commander to summarily exclude civilians from his base. Thus, the Court held, there was not constitutional requirement for a hearing and specification of a ground for the discharge.

The period of 1958-1961 saw the Court step back from much of the doctrine it had appeared to be developing in the 1956-1957 period. The relatively small majorities in some of the 1956-1957 cases, coupled with the intense reaction to the allegedly prosubversive decisions of the Court, no doubt were important in these developments. In terms of the issues raised, the constitutional doctrine involved, and the reasoning followed by the Court, it is hard to argue that the shifts we have seen (the original validation in the early 1950s, the break in the 1956-1957 period, the retreat in 1958-1961) can be accounted for simply in terms of concepts like "the law" or the "constitution" or similar doctrinal notions. Rather, the Court, part of the political process, cautious about adverse reaction, guarding its flanks, had engaged in a strategic retreat during the 1958-1961 period. Shortly thereafter, it reentered the battle, and this time seemed to carry the day.

The legal community and loyalty-security cases

Public opinion and the activities of other public institutions are crucial to understanding the somewhat checkered path followed by the Court in the loyalty-security cases. Attitudes and behavior hostile to the protection of freedom of expression created a climate in which it was difficult for the Court to strike out affirmatively to protect this liberty. This climate was not limited to the nonlegal world. Organizations

---

[88]*Cafeteria Workers* v. *McElroy*, 367 U.S. 886 (1961).

we usually think of as bulwarks of civil liberties, those that today conjure up the image of fearless protectors of civil liberties, were themselves somewhat quiescent. The ACLU, today one of the most salient organizations working in behalf of the protection of civil liberties, was, during the 1950s, somewhat reticent about leaping to the defense of those caught in the loyalty-security net. The organization itself indicated a disinclination to have Communists as officers or members.[89] The justification offered for its concern over Communist members and its reticence to become directly involved in loyalty-security cases was based upon the premise that Communists—ideologically hardened, themselves not dedicated to the principles of civil liberties and rights— would not make good members or clients. Because of the tendency on the part of some Communists to want to turn their trials into political forums, the ACLU generally took the position that their cases did not make good vehicles for the protection of civil liberties. This is not to say that lawyers who were members of the ACLU did not participate in loyalty-security litigation—in fact, some members were highly active—but simply to suggest that the organization showed some reticence about taking positions in loyalty-security cases.[90]

[89]For example, in a 1954 statement to the Commission on Government Security, the ACLU asserted:
    ... the policy of the American Civil Liberties Union [is] not to have as an officer, board member, committee member, or staff member, national or local, any person who does not believe in civil liberties or who accepts the discipline of any political party or organization which does not believe in civil liberties or which is under the control or direction of any totalitarian government, either Communist or Fascist, which itself does not believe in civil liberties or in practice crushes civil liberties. (*The New York Times*, February 16, 1954, p. 13.)

[90]Two studies discussing the reticence of lawyers to become involved in loyalty-security cases are Milnor Alexander, "The Right to Counsel for the Politically Unpopular," *Law in Transition Quarterly*, 22 (1962), pp. 19-45; and Jack H. Olender, "Let us Admit Impediments," *University of Pittsburgh Law Review*, 20 (1959), pp. 749-753. For a discussion of the role of ACLU lawyers during the 1950s, see Nathan Hakman, "The

Other organizations did participate in loyalty-security litigation, both in providing counsel and publicly challenging the loyalty-security programs, particularly the Emergency Civil Liberties Committee and the National Lawyers Guild.[91] These organizations themselves came under attack as Communist-dominated. Thus, the defense of the political offenders of the 1950s came into the hands of a small group of lawyers willing to handle such cases and risk being tarred with the same brush as their client as well as the all-too-real personal and professional sanctions.[92] These lawyers typically had personal and sometimes ideological ties with their clients. Because of most lawyers' reticence about becoming involved in loyalty-security cases, these lawyers became specialists in loyalty-security cases, as involvement in one case led to another and then more:

> We left the government [in the mid 1940s]—I had been a trial examiner for the NLRB; my partner had been working [for another government agency]. We were interested in practicing law and generally interested in things. Let me say this—I don't think that if the McCarthyite period hadn't come and people hadn't come to us—I don't think we would have . . . I mean, it's not our personality—it's almost that these cases just came. And we didn't feel in good conscience that we could turn them down, cause they were important cases. I don't mean we struggled over it—we thought they were good cases and we were glad to do them. But the kind of thing happens—more so in those days than today—this business, if you take one or two of these cases you find you're not handling any

---

Supreme Court's Political Environment: The Processing of Noncommercial Litigation," in Joel Grossman and Joseph Tanenhaus, *Frontiers of Judicial Research* (New York: Wiley, (1969), pp. 199-251, especially pp. 226-227; and Jonathan D. Casper, "Lawyers and Loyalty-Security Litigation," *Law and Society Review*, III (1969), pp. 575-596.

[91]A bar association, formed in the 1930s by liberal and radical lawyers as an alternative to the more conservative American Bar Association.

[92]See Casper, *op. cit.*

others. I mean, it's not your choice—it seems to be other people's choice.[93]

Lawyers associated with the ACLU, who were committed more to principles in the abstract than to their specific applications to particular groups, became active later in the loyalty-security cases when the Court after 1961 once more began to move in to protect freedom of expression. Their entry was one sign of the fact that the fear of Communist subversion and the dangers attached to involvement in loyalty-security litigation had eased. But long after the virulent strains of McCarthyism had died, remnants of the reticence about becoming involved with a Communist remained. A lawyer affiliated with the ACLU indicated this reticence when discussing a 1965 case in which he defended a member of the Communist Party:

> He's [the defendant] a cultured, educated man, and he told me that he was afraid that no other lawyer, private lawyer . . . they might fear, they might be afraid to represent him. . . . And I was scared to represent him, but I'd been talking about free speech and the Constitution for 25 years and I either had to take his case or leave town—one of the two. So I took it. I wasn't really happy about it—I was excited about it . . . but, hell, I had to take it.[94]

Thus, the loyalty-security cases arose in a context in which large segments of the bar were somewhat reticent about becoming involved. This is but another indication of the passions which surrounded the protection of freedom of expression of political radicals. This climate, both within and outside the legal community, is crucial to understanding the path taken by the Court. Both on the attitudinal and the behavioral levels, strong pressures militated against the development of doctrine favorable to the rights of Com-

[93]*Ibid.*, pp. 581-582.
[94]*Ibid.*, p. 585.

munists and other radicals. Since the legal community is probably a crucial reference group for judges, the lack of support for protection of the rights of those caught in the loyalty-security programs—combined with the active opposition by political figures and institutions to extension of liberties to such individuals—was an important aspect of the interaction between the Court and the broader society which produced the doctrinal path followed during the 1950s.

Loyalty-security in the 1960s

After the 1958-1961 retreat, the Court moved in again, attacking the remnants of the loyalty-security effort. The Smith Act had been largely curtailed by the interpretation and evidentiary requirements of the *Yates* opinion. The main elements left of the loyalty-security program were the McCarran Act, loyalty oaths, and employee screening programs. The Court moved to strip the McCarran Act of effect, to restrict the use of loyalty oaths, and made some effort to deal with federal employee loyalty-security screening.

As the decade of the 1960s developed, communism became a less salient public issue. With the election of President Kennedy and the rapidly developing civil rights movement, national attention shifted to domestic problems. In a sense, then, the Court during the mid-1960s was faced not with a publicly salient issue and an anxious audience, but with a climate in which loyalty-security programs enjoyed generalized public support, but not a great deal of public attention. As the Court engaged in its mopping-up operations, decisions curtailing loyalty-security activities aroused some outcry from political figures, but not the ferocious response that the 1956-1957 decisions had produced. In part this was attributable to the shift of national attention away from the menace of internal subversion suggested above. In part, it was also the product of the fact that the Court was moving on many other fronts as well—developing protection of the rights of criminal defendants, dealing with freedom of religion, with the rights of the blacks, with the touchy issue of obscenity. During this period, there was by no means a dearth of attacks upon the Court's decisions nor upon the Court as an institution. But, given the political climate and the other issue areas in which the Court was moving, the loyalty-security decisions received relatively little public attention. In fact, as indicated at the outset of this chapter, the major issues dealing with freedom of expression now were arising in the context not of the loyalty-security programs but of the civil rights cases.

Some of the appointments of Presidents Kennedy and Johnson added to the solid liberal bloc previously made up of Warren, Black, Douglas, and Brennan (with sometime support from Stewart). Justice Frankfurter, leader of the conservative faction on the Court, was replaced in 1962 by Arthur Goldberg, one of the most activist-liberal judges ever to occupy a seat on the Court; when Goldberg resigned in 1965, he was replaced by Abe Fortas, also a consistent member of the liberal bloc in civil liberties cases. Justice Whittaker retired in 1962, to be replaced by Byron White, not a consistent liberal, but more prone to vote with the liberal bloc than his predecessor. In 1967, Justice Clark was replaced by Thurgood Marshall who was somewhat more sympathetic to the protection of civil liberties than his predecessor.

The Court moved in the 1960s to strip the McCarran Act of its teeth. In 1964, *Aptheker* v. *Secretary of State*,[95] the Court held unconstitutional the provisions of the McCarran Act that denied the use of passports to members of groups cited by the SACB as Communist organizations. In banning passports to all members, the Court held that the act failed to take into account whether the individual knew and subscribed to the purposes of the organization, whether he was an active member of the organization (shades of the *Yates* opinion), whether the proposed trip was innocent, and whether the individual proposed to visit a security-sensitive area. Without these considerations, the Court held that the

[95]378 U.S. 500 (1964).

act was too restrictive of the right to travel protected by the due process clause of the Fifth Amendment.

In 1965, returning to the self-incrimination question raised by the McCarran Act registration provisions, the Court overturned, on Fifth Amendment grounds, the provision of the act requiring individual members to register if their organizations failed to do so. This decision effectively removed the heart of the Act.[96]

In 1967, the Court overturned the provision of the McCarran Act that made it a crime for a member of an organization under a final order to register as a Communist-action organization to hold employment in any defense facility.[97] Harking back to the language of *Yates* and *Aptheker*, the Court noted that the provisions of the statute did not discriminate between various degrees of membership and knowledge of the illegal purposes of the organization. Thus, the majority opinion held, the statute "contains the fatal defect of overbreadth because it seeks to bar employment both for association which may be proscribed and for association which may not be proscribed consistently with First Amendment rights."[98]

The almost complete inactivity of the SACB since the early 1960s indicates the degree to which its statutory foundation and ability to function has been eroded by this series of Court decisions.

After 1961—when the contempt convictions of Braden and Wilkinson had been upheld—the Court began consistently to overturn contempt convictions produced by legislative investigations. The opinions did not focus upon the basic First Amendment and due process issues discussed in *Watkins* and *Barenblatt*. The Court did not choose to challenge head-on the power of Congressional committees to hold hearings and ask questions. Rather they overturned convictions upon

[96]*Albertson* v. *Subversive Activities Control Board*, 382 U.S. 70 (1965).
[97]*United States* v. *Robel*, 389 U.S. 258 (1967).
[98]389 U.S. 266.

somewhat more technical grounds, including defects in indictments for contempt,[99] failure of committees to act upon requests for executive sessions,[100] and failure of committees to clearly delegate power to subcommittees.[101] Thus, the Court tightened up some of the procedural requirements for investigations without directly confronting the power of committees to conduct them.

The Court also consistently struck down state loyalty oaths, typically stressing the ambiguity or vagueness of the oath and its potential infringement upon protected activity. In *Cramp* v. *Board of Public Instruction*,[102] the Court overturned a Florida oath requiring teachers to swear that they had never aided, supported, or abetted the Communist Party. The Court held the oath to be unconstitutionally vague, since terms like "aided" or "supported" could involve such innocent acts as endorsing candidates for office, or writing in support of the rights of Communists. This vagueness, plus the potential effect of the overbroad scope of the oath upon constitutionally protected activities, rendered it unconstitutional. A similar ruling was made in a 1964 oath case arising out of Washington.[103]

In *Elfbrandt* v. *Russell*,[104] the Court overturned an Arizona oath that proscribed knowing membership in subversive organizations. The interpretation by the Arizona Supreme Court made it clear that the oath was not intended to reach the kind of protected activities alluded to in *Cramp*. The use of the oath and disqualification from employment for inability to complete it were held unconstitutional by the Supreme Court of the United States on the ground that the program required the firing of teachers even if they did not

[99] *Russell* v. *United States*, 369 U.S. 749 (1962).

[100] *Yellin* v. *United States*, 374 U.S. 109 (1963).

[101] *Gojack* v. *United States*, 384 U.S. 702 (1966).

[102] 368 U.S. 278 (1961). Cf. *Wieman* v. *Updegraff*, 344 U.S. 183 (1952).

[103] *Baggett* v. *Bulitt*, 377 U.S. 360 (1964).

[104] 384 U.S. (1966).

subscribe to the unlawful ends of the organization. The *Yates* doctrine was involved, for the Court opinion restricted the permissible scope of the oath to activities of members who joined with the specific intent to further illegal action.

In 1967, the Court overturned a New York law which made Communist Party membership, as such, grounds for firing teachers.[105] Citing the *Elfbrandt* requirement for knowing membership, the Court found that the New York statute, by not permitting rebuttal of the disqualification either on grounds of lack of knowledge of the intent of the organization or nonactive membership, was overbroad and hence unconstitutional. In the course of the majority opinion (by Justice Brennan), the Court also made some rather sweeping statements about the status of public employment. The majority opinion held that the premise of an earlier opinion that "public employment, including academic employment, may be conditioned upon the surrender of constitutional rights which could not be abridged by direct government action"[106] had been discredited by later decisions. Rather, they quoted approvingly from a case involving the right to unemployment compensation for a Seventh Day Adventist who refused work on Saturdays: "It is too late in the day to doubt that the liberties of religion and expression may be infringed by a denial or of placing conditions upon a benefit or privilege."[107] In the same term, the Court overturned a Maryland loyalty oath which required teachers to swear that they were not "engaged in one way or another in the attempt to overthrow the Government of the United States, or the state of Maryland, or any political subdivision of either of them, by force or violence,"[108] again citing the

---

[105]*Keyishian* v. *Board of Regents*, 385 U.S. 589 (1967).

[106]385 U.S. 605.

[107]385 U.S. 606. The quotation is from *Sherbert* v. *Verner*, 374 U.S. 398 (1963) at 404.

[108]*Whitehill* v. *Elkins*, 389 U.S. 43 (1967) at 55.

problem of vagueness and the possible overreach of the statute to constitutionally protected activities.

CONCLUSION

An appraisal of these decisions made in the 1960s does not indicate that the Court finally stepped in and firmly circumscribed government loyalty-security programs which infringed upon freedom of expression, though some forms of control over belief and expression became more difficult. In a sense, as suggested above, the loyalty-security cases of the mid and late 1960s were dealing with a program that itself had run its course. Government screening of employees still exists at the state and federal level; legislative committees still conduct investigations; the Smith and McCarran acts are still on the books. But as the concern over the supposed menace of internal subversion by Communist agents declined, the prominence of the loyalty-security programs also waned. The Smith Act lives but is not applied to Communists; legislative investigations into internal subversion are less publicized and have begun to concentrate upon the New rather than the Old Left. The legacy of the loyalty-security cases has been the development of doctrine making restrictions upon belief and expression more difficult, though by no means impossible, to impose. The current relative lack of concern over communists' freedom of expression is not simply the product of this doctrine, however. It is perhaps at least as much because fewer people in this country are deeply concerned about Communists, or, if they do care, such concern ranks lower on their scale of priorities than it once did.

What, then, is to be said about this extensive litigation dealing with freedom of expression for political dissidents that spanned more than a decade and a half? I don't think we can properly view the Court as a bastion of liberty, holding out against the forces of repression. Rather, the Court—and the doctrine it developed—reflected and interacted with developments on the attitudinal and behavioral level. Some of the 1950-1970 period was characterized by intense fear of and dislike for those on the left and by activities by members of the legislative and executive branches intent upon restricting the freedom of expression, association, and belief of political radicals. The doctrinal tools at the disposal of the Court, especially the balancing test and the notion of deference to legislative determination, proved malleable and were used in ways that legitimated this repressive activity. As the political climate changed and citizens generally, as well as people holding political office, became less concerned with the activities of political dissidents, the doctrine emerging from the Court changed. Doctrine stressing vagueness of statutes, as well as examination of the nature of evidence adduced dealing with defendants' intentions and behavior, emerged and was used to restrict the remnants of the government loyalty-security programs. Thus, doctrine interacted with attitudes and behavior.

To put it another way, members of the Court did what they felt they ought to do and what they felt they could. Some justices, though they might deplore the consequences of the loyalty-security programs, felt it was not proper for the Court to intervene. For some, the loyalty-security programs were simply the proper way of handling an international and domestic emergency. For a few—most notably Justices Black, Douglas, and Chief Justice Warren— the loyalty-security programs were a disaster for democracy. The dominance of these various positions changed over time, as the Court interacted with events in the broader political process (including, importantly, appointment of new justices). Nevertheless, the lesson of the loyalty-security era is that doctrine emerging from the Court is highly related to attitudes and behavior in society at large.

What the future will bring is obviously an open question. In the "Rap Brown" law,[109] the increased use of police

[109]Title 18, Section 2101, United States Code, passed in 1968. This provision, involved in the trial of the Chicago Eight, provides:

informers and gathering of information about the activities of the New Left and militant black organizations, the increased emphasis on wiretapping, and the attacks by high government officials upon dissent, I think one can see the seeds of a new period of repression. The victims would not be members of the Communist Party, but a new generation of "political offenders"—student radicals, members of New Left groups, black militants—and there seem to be striking parallels between the public's and the government's reaction to these new dissidents. What the future will bring is, as I say, an open question. It remains to be seen whether we shall see such a renewal of the loyalty-security programs and what the reactions of groups like the ACLU, the bar in general, and the Court will be. The loyalty-security cases teach us, though, that when broad segments of the polity and its leaders become convinced of the necessity to restrict the expression of those with unpopular views, one cannot simply rest assured that the Court or the Constitution will protect them. The Court, the Constitution, and the law are all very much influenced by the political system in which they live.

Whoever travels in interstate or foreign commerce, including, but not limited to, the mail, telegraph, telephone, radio, or television with intent (A) to incite a riot; or (B) to organize, promote, encourage, participate in, or carry on a riot; or (C) to commit any act of violence in furtherance of a riot; or (D) to aid or abet any person in inciting or participating in or carrying on a riot or committing any act of violence in furtherance of a riot; and who either during the course of any such travel or use or thereafter performs or attempts to perform any other overt act for any purpose specified . . . shall be fined not more than $10,000 or imprisoned not more than five years, or both.

THREE
THE CIVIL RIGHTS MOVEMENT AND OTHER RECENT DEVELOPMENTS IN FREEDOM OF EXPRESSION

THE concern about internal subversion, which produced the various loyalty-security programs that were the major free-expression issues before the Court during the 1950s, involved both public and private speech. The beliefs, associations, and expressions that were censured sometimes involved public demonstrations, speeches to audiences, publications, and the like. But much of the emphasis, especially as the loyalty-security programs were treated by the Court, was upon the conspiratorial nature of disloyal belief and speech. During the 1960s, the civil rights movement grew in dimension and intensity. Activists supporting racial equality engaged in expression on a grandly public scale—speeches, mass demonstrations, picketing, sit-ins, freedom rides. Since many of these activities met with intense resistance from governments in the South, legal proceedings were inevitable—both prosecutions for various forms of expressions and injunctive suits by civil rights advocates attempting to prevent restrictions upon their expression. During the 1960s, as the Court was attacking the vestiges of the loyalty-security programs, it also became increasingly enmeshed in issues of free expression arising from the activities of the civil rights movement.

The Court proved highly sympathetic to the claims of civil rights demonstrators. In fact, one might well argue that the Court itself—beginning with the milestone school desegregation decision of 1954 that placed its imprimatur upon the concept of racial equality—was to some extent responsible for the climate in which the civil rights movement was able to gain momentum and success in the streets, the courts, and the legislature. In part, one might attribute the Court's activism in protecting the right of expression to the nature of the issues presented: the public character of the speech, the relevance of the preferred position doctrine to the special role of the Court in dealing with "prejudice against discrete and insular minorities." But more than this is required, I think, to explain the lengths to which the Court went to protect the rights of expression of civil rights demonstrators. The cases arose in a context in which—outside the South at least—those attempting to express themselves were not, like the political offenders of the 1950s, the subject of fear or hatred. Indeed, civil rights advocates were the subject of a great deal of sympathy and support. Though President Eisenhower appeared at best ambivalent about the wisdom of the Court in urging racial integration, his successors provided support for legislation and federal government activity in behalf of racial equality. The Congress, though to some extent under the sway of leadership dominated by Southern conservatives, did move to pass legislation eliminating racial discrimination. Public opinion also swung in favor of activity in support of racial integration and of the passage of laws to implement it. The data in Table 3, crude though they are, suggest the shift in favor of equality. During 1963, alone, support for federal legislation prohibiting discrimination in public accommodations rose from 49.5 to 61.2 percent.[1]

[1] These data, gathered in a variety of polls, were provided by the Roper Public Opinion Research Center, Williamstown, Massachusetts. For an illuminating survey of changing attitudes towards racial integration, see Paul B. Sheatsley, "White Attitudes Toward the Negro," *Daedalus*, 95 (1966), pp. 217-238.

Table 3 Attitudes toward racial integration

Year	Percent		
	No	Yes	Don't know/No answer
Should the schools be integrated?			
1949	57.8	29.5	12.8
1956	45.7	49.8	4.5
Should federal legislation prohibit racial discrimination in voting?			
1948	49.0	42.5	8.5
1963	8.7	85.8	5.5
Are blacks as intelligent as whites?			
1944	47.2	44.1	8.6
1946	37.1	56.4	6.5
1949	31.1	60.8	7.5
1956	19.2	78.2	3.4

Source: Roper Public Opinion Research Center, Williamstown, Mass.

No doubt the Court itself played a role in the growing acceptance of blacks as human beings entitled to the same rights as others. But the activities of other institutions—political leaders, civil rights groups, labor unions—and the attitudinal structure of broad segments of the population provided a climate in which the Court could and did intervene actively in support of the rights of blacks.

Another important factor was the growth of the direct-action tactics by civil rights proponents in the South. The dominance of figures like Martin Luther King, and the activities of groups like SCLC, SNCC, and CORE in demonstrating in favor of equal rights grew rapidly. A search of *The New York Times Index* for reports of civil rights demonstrations in the South reveals the rapid growth of the civil rights movement. (See Table 4.)

Another indication of the extent of civil rights activity and of the litigation that it developed is suggested by Table 5, indicating the activity of one of the most important litigating

Table 4 Peaceful civil rights demonstrations, 1954-1968

Year	Total	Public accommodations	Voting
1954	0	0	0
1955	0	0	0
1956	18	6	0
1957	44	9	0
1958	19	8	0
1959	7	11	0
1960	173	127	0
1961	198	122	0
1962	77	44	0
1963	272	140	1
1964	271	93	12
1965	387	21	128
1966	171	15	32
1967	93	3	3
1968	97	2	0

Source: This table is drawn from a search of *The New York Times Index* for all references to civil rights demonstrations during the years the table covers. The table should be taken simply as indicative, for the data—news stories in a single paper—are very crude. The classification of the incident as peaceful or violent and the subject area of the demonstration are inferred from the entry in the *Index*, usually the headline from the story. The two subcategories reported here—public accommodations and voting—do not sum to the total because demonstrations dealing with a variety of other issues (e.g., education, employment, police brutality) are included in the total.

interest groups acting in behalf of racial equality, the NAACP Legal Defense and Educational Fund.

What do these figures indicate? First, they suggest that on both the attitudinal and behavioral levels, there was important activity in favor of protection of the rights of blacks. This activity, especially the demonstration phase of it, not only provided the genesis of the legal issues that were to come before the Court; it also was an indication to the Court of the changes that were occurring in our society, of the breadth and intensity of interest in favor of the protection of the rights of blacks. Thus, the demonstrations and the prosecutions that resulted not only provided occasions for

Table 5   Activity of NAACP legal defense and educational fund, 1963-1967

Year	Individuals defended by the LDF	Cases on LDF docket
1963	4,200	107
1964	10,400	145
1965	17,000	225
1966	14,000	375
1967	13,000	420

Source: Report 66, published in 1967 by the NAACP Legal Defense and Educational Fund, New York.

decision by the Court, but also were a means of indicating to the Court when making its doctrinal choices that it was facing a society which urged innovation:

> One of the ways in which pressure to change may be exerted upon the law is through the courts, by the frequent occurrence of litigation. . . To the extent that such disputes are brought before the courts, judges are exposed in various ways to the views of segments of opinion within the community on these issues, a process which presumably facilitates continuous modification of the law to conform with such expression of opinion. When such opportunities for contact with views held by various groups in the community are infrequent, it is to be expected that the law will be less sensitive to changes in the views of the community.[2]

In the next chapter, the changes in doctrine dealing with the substantive aspects of racial discrimination are discussed. I want to concentrate here upon the freedom-of-expression issues raised by civil rights activities. The Court, unlike its treatment of political offenders, rose up to protect the rights of advocates of civil rights. In so doing, it both contributed to and rode the crest of a wave of activity and attitudinal change supporting both this activity and the end to which it was directed.

[2]Julius Cohen et. al., *Parental Authority: The Community and the Law* (New Brunswick, N.J.: Rutgers University Press, 1958), p. 196.

One of the ways in which those hostile to the civil rights movement attempted to attack the proponents of racial equality was by attacking organizations like the NAACP, CORE, and SNCC, that were acting in behalf of integration and supporting litigation designed to test the constitutionality of segregation laws. Attempts were made to force such organizations to divulge their membership and to force individuals to reveal their memberships in them. This technique, commonly used in the congressional investigation phase of the loyalty-security program (and at the heart of the McCarran Act), was designed to make members vulnerable to informal sanctions and thus discourage their memberships and activities.

Chapter Two related how this technique was challenged in litigation dealing with Congressional investigations, with witnesses urging that the requirement of divulging their memberships infringed upon their right to associate with others and their rights of expression as members of groups; similar attacks had been made upon various loyalty-oaths. The Court generally rejected the association argument in the context of legislative investigations, e.g., *Barenblatt*, *Uphaus*, Braden, and Wilkinson, using the balancing formula and arguing that the state's interest in obtaining such information about memberships and activities outweighed the individual's rights of association and expression.

The balancing test in the civil rights context

In dealing with attacks on civil rights groups, the Court came out on the other side. The leading case, coming to Court in 1958, was *NAACP* v. *Alabama*.[3] Alabama attempted to apply to the NAACP a statute requiring foreign corporations doing business in the state to register with the state Attorney General. The Attorney General sought to enjoin the activities of the NAACP on the ground that it had failed to register.

[3]357 U.S. 449 (1958).

The NAACP denied that it fell within the purview of the statute, and the Attorney General moved for the production of information about the organization (including its membership lists) which he urged was essential to the determination of whether the organization was subject to the provisions of the statute. Eventually, the NAACP provided all the information sought (e.g., bank statements, leases, deeds, etc.) but refused to produce its membership lists. The case eventually reached the Supreme Court, and the Court overturned a contempt conviction against the NAACP imposed by state courts.

The Court accepted the argument of the NAACP that production of the lists and the consequent dissemination of the names of its members would produce hardships—e.g., social and economic reprisals, physical coercion and the like—and hence would infringe the members' rights to associate with each other and express their common beliefs.[4] This situation was analogous to that faced by many witnesses who had been and were being called before legislative committees investigating internal subversion. Yet the Court found that the state of Alabama did not have the constitutional power to act in this fashion toward those advocating racial equality. The Court reached this decision with the balancing technique, saying that the crucial question was whether "Alabama has demonstrated an interest in obtaining the disclosures it seeks from petitioner which is sufficient to justify the deterrent effect which we have concluded these disclosures may well have on the free exercise by petitioner's members of the constitutionally protected right of association."[5] Pointing out that the NAACP had complied with almost all requests of the state with the exception of the production of the membership lists, and arguing that the

[4]The Court also alluded to the infringement upon privacy that publication of membership lists would entail. Further developments in the "right to privacy" are discussed later in this chapter and also in Chapter 5.

[5]357 U.S. 463.

membership lists were of dubious utility in determining whether the organization did fall within the purview of the registration act, the Court held that the state had no right to demand their production: "We conclude that Alabama has fallen short of showing a *controlling justification* for the deterrent effect on the free enjoyment of the right to associate which disclosure of membership lists is likely to have."[6]

In loyalty-security cases, the balancing technique used by the Court tended to weigh the national interest in survival against the right of the *individual* to associate and express his point of view. In the NAACP case, the Court balanced somewhat differently. Instead of stressing simply the rights of the individual,[7] the Court's opinion dealt with the importance of the right of association and expression *generally*, with the value in a free society of permitting individuals to form associations to advocate and work for common goals. This is a somewhat different form of balancing, for it takes much more into account in examining the claims of those arguing for their liberty.

On the other hand, it might be argued that there is no inconsistency in the two approaches. It might be pointed out that the *dangers* in the two types of situations were very different: in the one it was held to be the very security of the nation; in the other simply an economic regulation upon which the fate of civil society did not turn. In addition, the character of the association and expression might be differentiated: In the loyalty-security cases, what was alleged to be involved was clandestine association, whereas the civil rights

[6]357 U.S. 446. (Emphasis added.)

[7]One difference, stressed by some members of the Court, was that this case, unlike those involving legislative investigations, dealt with an organization that was attempting to protect itself against hostile activity and that was asserting the right of association of its members. This difference is perhaps crucial, assuming that some groups (e.g., the Communist Party) are less entitled to maintain themselves than others (e.g., civil rights organizations).

cases involved expression in favor of rights that the Court was quickly coming to agree were constitutionally protected.

Thus, one can argue it either way: that the Court was applying a double standard, or that it was perfectly consistent. One cannot escape the suggestion, though, that the political climate surrounding the activities of the two groups—political radicals and civil rights workers—and the degree of public support and sympathy they aroused had something to do with the way in which the Court came out on an issue common to both types of litigation.

The *Shelton* case

In any event, the Court went on to protect consistently the freedom of association of civil rights workers from attack by state governments. In an interesting case in Arkansas, *Shelton* v. *Tucker*,[8] the Court overturned a statute that required every teacher employed by a state school or college to file each year a list of every organization of which he had been a member or to which he had regularly contributed money in the preceding five years. The Court agreed that this situation was not the same as that raised in *NAACP* v. *Alabama*, for Arkansas could demonstrate a strong interest in discovering the associations of its teachers. Indeed, as indicated in the preceding chapter, investigation into such associations had been upheld in the 1958 cases involving loyalty oaths (*Lerner* and *Beilan*). But the majority opinion in *Shelton* noted that disclosure of memberships could impair rights of association and expression should they be made public. The Court overturned the application of the statute by reasoning that though the state could demonstrate a compelling interest in discovering memberships in certain groups of which teachers

[8]364 U.S. 479 (1960). Another case involving an attempt to obtain membership lists of the NAACP in Arkansas was decided the same year. See *Bates* v. *Little Rock*, 361 U.S. 516 (1960). Using the balancing approach, the Court held that the state had not demonstrated a sufficient interest in obtaining the lists to justify the infringement upon associational freedom that would result if the lists were made public.

might be members, or how much time teachers spent on the activities of such organizations, it could not constitutionally compel *all* teachers to disclose *all* their memberships, for many such memberships "could have no possible bearing upon the teacher's occupational competence or fitness. . . The statute's comprehensive interference with associational freedom goes far beyond what might be justified in the exercise of the State's legitimate inquiry into the fitness and the competency of its teachers."[9]

A dissent by Justice Harlan, joined by Justices Frankfurter, Clark and Whittaker, sharply attacked the majority opinion and provided some insight into the nature of the issue and of the balancing test utilized by the majority. First the dissent somewhat sharply noted the problem I have alluded to above: the Court's apparently greater vigilance in protecting the rights of civil rights advocates than of persons whose loyalty was being tested:

> Of course, this decision has a natural tendency to enlist support, involving as it does an unusual statute that touches constitutional rights whose protection in the context of the racial situation in various parts of the country demands the unremitting vigilance of the courts. Yet that very circumstance also serves to remind of the constraints that attend constitutional adjudication. It must be emphasized that neither of these cases actually presents an issue of racial discrimination. The statute on its face applies to *all* Arkansas teachers irrespective of race, and there is no showing that it has been discriminatorily administered.[10]

The dissent, in pointing out the Court's zeal in protecting the rights of proponents of racial equality, was not urging that similar vigilance be exercised in behalf of political radicals; quite the reverse, it argued that the Court ought to be more deferential to legislative determinations. But the dissenters

[9]364 U.S. 488.
[10]364 U.S. 496-497.

did point up the somewhat special treatment accorded civil rights workers by the liberal majority.

The dissent went on to argue that the statute should not in fact have been declared unconstitutional on its face. Harlan rejected the majority view that the statute was overbroad and hence beyond the state's demonstrated interest in obtaining information about its teachers:

> I am unable to subscribe to this view because I believe it impossible to determine *a priori* the place where the line should be drawn between what would be permissible inquiry and overbroad inquiry in a situation like this. Certainly the Court [in the majority opinion] does not point that place out. There can be little doubt that that much of the associational information called for by the statute will be of little or no use whatever to the school authorities, but I do not understand how those authorities can be expected to fix in advance the terms of their inquiry so that it will yield only relevant information.[11]

The dissent argued that, if evidence of abuse of the statute should later be demonstrated, it might be declared unconstitutional in its application. But it should not be declared unconstitutional on its face.

There is more than a little irony in this dissent. The balancing test used by the majority to overturn the Arkansas statute was being used extensively by Frankfurter and his fellow dissenters as a way of justifying various violations of the right of expression in the context of the loyalty-security cases. The more liberal majority, in the civil rights cases discussed here, took the test and applied it as a means of protecting expression rather than justifying its suppression. Indeed, Chief Justice Warren had himself alluded to the balancing test in the *Watkins* case discussed in Chapter Two. It was later used in loyalty-security cases by the conservatives to justify legislative investigations. In the civil rights cases,

[11]364 U.S. 498-499.

much to the dismay of the conservatives, it was used to overturn infringement upon expression and association. This suggests the malleability of the test and its lack of any real criteria.

The dissent criticized the majority for its failure to draw any strict lines, its failure to specify the type of state interest that would be great enough to justify infringements. In fact, in the loyalty-security cases, the conservative majority had never bothered to do this: They had simply referred, as the liberal majority in *Shelton* did, to the nature of the state's interest in relation to that of the individual. This suggests the crucial character of the whole balancing approach: It nowhere encompasses any criteria for judgment. What constitutes a "compelling" state interest is a shibboleth that can be invoked to come out on one side or the other, and not in any sense an objective criterion that can be applied in a rigorous (or, if you will, intersubjectively testable) fashion. As suggested at the outset of Chapter Two, balancing is not in fact a "test" at all, but simply a description of the process by which one makes choices. This is not to imply that other tests (with the possible exception of absolutism) are much more rigorous; but rather to suggest that the proponents of balancing either overstated their claim or were somewhat disingenuous when they decried the use of their own test on the grounds that in the hands of the liberal majority it did not provide any clear standards for judgment. What was its virtue in their hands became, from their point of view, its vice in the hands of more liberal justices.

It is useful to note that the approach which emerged in the association cases involving civil rights groups discussed here—*NAACP* v. *Alabama*, *Bates* v. *Little Rock*, *Shelton* v. *Tucker*—was carried over into some of the loyalty-security cases of the 1960s. The attention to overbreadth—to the state's attempts to obtain information by mechanisms (e.g., loyalty oaths) that might reach protected activity—was combined with the vice of vagueness to become the ground for overturning a series of state loyalty oaths designed to ferret out not civil rights workers but subversives. It seems clear that this doctrinal tool, which was not even a novel invention in the civil rights cases, was available to the Court in its treatment of loyalty-security cases. Their earlier unwillingness to apply it to strike down these infringements upon liberty reflects, then, not simply the nature of the issue nor the doctrine, but the political climate in which those cases arose. When, during the 1960s, it became feasible to intervene in the loyalty-security area, this tool—nurtured in the more hospitable fields of the protection of the rights of blacks—became a potent one for the protection of citizens from loyalty-security programs as well.

The *Gibson* case

A legislative investigation case, *Gibson* v. *Florida Investigation Committee*, intertwining the issue of civil rights activities and communism, further demonstrates the attempts by some members of the Court to differentiate the two issue areas.[12] A committee of the Florida legislature was conducting an investigation in 1957 into Communist activities in the Miami area, and included in its investigation the subject of alleged Communist infiltration of the NAACP. The committee subpoenaed the membership list of the Miami branch of the NAACP. Florida courts held that the committee could not require the production of the lists, but that the local NAACP chapter president could be required to bring the lists with him to the hearing in order to refer to them in connection with questions as to whether specific individuals in whom the committee was interested were members of the NAACP. The president came to the hearing but refused to bring along the lists. He did answer questions about individuals on the basis of his own knowledge of who was and who was not a member of his organization. He was held in contempt for his refusal to bring the lists, and his appeal reached the Supreme Court in 1963.

[12]*Gibson* v. *Florida Investigation Committee*, 372 U.S. 539 (1963).

The Supreme Court overturned the contempt conviction in a five-to-four decision. Justice Goldberg's majority opinion cited both the previous civil rights association cases (which held that the state must demonstrate a compelling interest in order to justify the restriction of rights of association inherent in publication of names of members of organizations) and the prior legislative investigation cases which had generally upheld questions about memberships in Communist organizations. The majority opinion argued that:

> it is an essential prerequisite to the validity of an investigation which intrudes into the area of constitutionally protected rights of speech, press, association, and petition that the State convincingly show a substantial relation between the information sought and a subject of overriding and compelling state interest.[13]

Turning to the loyalty-security investigation cases, Goldberg attempted to distinguish them from the present case. In a curious statement, Goldberg argued that the basis for upholding the convictions of *Barenblatt*, *Wilkinson*, and *Braden* was the fact that each had refused to answer questions concerning his own past or present membership in the Communist Party. Each had in fact refused to answer such questions, but this point had not previously been cited as crucial by the Court. Moreover, the loyalty-security cases were different, Goldberg argued, because they involved membership in the Communist Party—which was "not an ordinary or legitimate political party, as known in this country, and . . . because of its particular nature, membership therein is *itself* a permissible subject of regulation and legislative scrutiny."[14]

However, in the *Gibson* case Goldberg argued that the subject of the investigation was not Communist Party membership but NAACP membership—and the NAACP was a

[13] 372 U.S. 546.
[14] 372 U.S. 547.

"concededly legitimate and nonsubversive organization."
Thus, and here was the crucial statement:

> The prior holdings that government interest in controlling subversion
> and the particular character of the Communist Party and its
> objectives outweigh the right of individual Communists to conceal
> party membership or affiliations by no means require the wholly
> different conclusion that other groups—concededly legitimate—
> automatically forfeit their rights to privacy of association simply
> because the general subject matter of the legislative inquiry is
> Communist subversion or infiltration.[15]

The next hurdle to clear in *Gibson* was the *Uphaus* case,
the New Hampshire legislative investigation case discussed in
Chapter Two, in which the Court had upheld questions
dealing with the guest list at the summer camp run by
Uphaus. Goldberg justified this holding, upon which Florida
had relied heavily in its argument in favor of compelling the
production of NAACP records, by arguing that, in *Uphaus*,
the state had demonstrated the subversive nature of the
summer camp. In the present case, on the contrary, there was
nothing to suggest that the NAACP was a subversive
organization. The difficulty with this argument, though, was
that presumably the *purpose* of the investigation in Florida
was to determine whether the NAACP in fact was or in
danger of becoming dominated by subversives.

> Instead, we rest our result on the fact that the record in this case is
> insufficient to show a substantial connection between the Miami
> branch of the N.A.A.C.P. and Communist *activities* which the
> respondent Committee itself conceded is an essential prerequisite to
> demonstrating the immediate, substantial, and subordinating state
> interest necessary to sustain its right of inquiry into the membership
> lists of the association.[16]

[15]372 U.S. 549.

[16]372 U.S. 551. (Emphasis in original.)

Again, this is a somewhat tortured argument, for it seems to require that the state have prior proof of the subversive nature of the organization it is inquiring into, when this is putatively the purpose for which the investigation was being conducted. My statement, of course, misconstrues the facts of the Florida investigation. Like the Congressional loyalty-security investigations, the real motive of the legislative committee was to expose the names of members of the NAACP and make them subject to informal sanctions in the community. But the argument advanced by Goldberg suggests the lengths to which the majority was forced to go in order to protect civil rights workers under the same doctrinal tool used for legislative investigations. Moreover, the logic of the *Gibson* opinion could equally well have been applied to many of the loyalty-security investigations. If the crucial test was the ability of the state to demonstrate the relationship between the information sought and Communist activities, then the dragnet questioning of many of the loyalty-security investigations (asking about the acquaintances of the witness, his attendance at meetings and activities the "subversive" character of which the Court never bothered to examine, etc.) would likely fail to meet the standards. In any event, the Court, using the balancing approach, overturned the conviction.

Three justices (Clark, Stewart, and White) joined in a dissent written by Justice Harlan. Calling the majority opinion "difficult to grasp," Harlan suggested:

> But, until today, I had never supposed that any of our decisions relating to state or federal power to investigate in the field of Communist subversion could possibly be taken as suggesting any difference in the degree of governmental investigatory interest as between Communist infiltration *of* organizations and Communist activity *by* organizations.[17]

[17]372 U.S. 579. (Emphasis in original.)

He proceeded to cite investigations, validated by previous Court decisions, into Communist infiltration of schools, labor unions, basic industries, and newspapers. Justice White, writing his own dissenting opinion, noted that the majority opinion "fails to articulate why the State's interest is any the more compelling or the associational rights any the less endangered when a known Communist is asked whether he belongs to a protected association than here when the organization is asked to confirm or deny that membership." He added, "Thus to me the decision today represents a marked departure from the principles of *Barenblatt* v. *United States.*"[18] White went on to raise the spectre of the Communist menace: "The net effect of the Court's decision is, of course, to insulate from effective legislative inquiry and preventive legislation the time-proven skills of the Communist Party in subverting and eventually controlling legitimate organizations."[19]

The dissenters had a strong logical point, for many of the investigations of Communist subversion involved in cases like *Barenblatt* and *Wilkinson* and *Braden* appeared in fact aimed at discovering the degree of infiltration by Communists in constitutionally protected areas (e.g., education, labor relations). The Court upheld these investigations, in spite of the fact that many of the questions asked of witnesses appeared to deal with constitutionally protected activities. To be precise, most of the actual questions for which contempt convictions were upheld did deal with specific Communist activities. But the thrust of the investigations and the substance of the questions were aimed, not simply at such activities, but at exposing the witness' associations as well as those of persons whom he could be forced to name as associates. Thus, logically, the attempt by the majority in *Gibson* to differentiate the case from previous investigations was strained at best.

[18] 372 U.S. 583, 584.
[19] 372 U.S. 585.

Their difficulty resulted from their attempt to maintain the balancing doctrine developed in the loyalty-security cases while using it to reach decisions protecting, rather than repressing, freedom of association and expression. The flexibility of the balancing doctrine enabled them to achieve this end, but in the process they had to mangle the older cases to some extent. The unwillingness of the majority in *Gibson* to adopt the approach of Black and Douglas, which was to simply state that such investigations into beliefs, associations, and expression were violative of the provisions of the First Amendment, led them into the contortions of *Gibson*. As suggested before, one cannot escape the notion that it was the Court's different views of civil rights advocates as opposed to Communists that resulted in their attempts to protect the former's freedom of expression while leaving the door open to the repression of the latter. Thus, the association cases arising out of the civil rights movement produced outcomes quite different from cases raising similar issues in the context of loyalty-security investigations.

PUBLIC DEMONSTRATIONS

The civil rights movement acted on a variety of fronts in its attempt to eliminate racial segregation in the South. Litigating interest groups like the Legal Defense Fund pursued litigation; organizations like the NAACP, labor unions, and other liberal groups attempted to lobby for the passage of federal legislation; and, beginning with the sit-ins in the early 1960s, a variety of direct-action tactics—including freedom rides, picketing, mass demonstrations, violation of segregation ordinances through acts of civil disobedience, etc.—became a major focus of civil rights activity. These direct-action tactics had a variety of motives: to place direct pressure upon those discriminating to modify their behavior as a result of economic and moral sanctions; to gain publicity about the types of discrimination being practiced in the South; to rouse national public opinion in favor of racial integration.[20]

These direct-action activities, which were in large part aimed at expressing a viewpoint and gaining adherents both within the locality of the demonstration and in the nation as a whole, generated a good deal of litigation, for they often led to arrests, prosecutions, and eventually appeals to the Supreme Court. Since the demonstrations were in part aimed at the expression of ideas, they raised important First Amendment issues. But the expression involved was often close to the borderline of speech and action. When a civil rights advocate got on a platform and urged that segregation was morally and constitutionally impermissible, there was little doubt that this was simply expression, and thus protected against state infringement by the First and Fourteenth Amendments. When a civil rights demonstration took the form of picketing, it raised, for some, more troubling issues, for the nature of picketing—the emotional baggage that picketing carried from the labor movement, the fact that pickets were usually physically placed at strategic locations around the establishment being picketed—seemed to many to cross the line between pure speech and action. When the civil rights activity involved large numbers of people (often picketing), again this appeared to some to go beyond mere expression, for large groups of demonstrators often interfered with access to establishments and sometimes blocked pedestrian and auto traffic. Finally, when the demonstration involved violation of a law—a segregated seating ordinance, for example—though the demonstrators might characterize their activities as a form of symbolic expression in opposition to an odious practice, the activity clearly moved beyond the realm of pure expression. I have alluded to this problem—the line between speech and action—in discussing the problem of defining the bounds of First Amendment protection. It

---

[20]For an analysis of the tactics of the black protest movement, see James Q. Wilson, "The Strategy of Protest: Problems of Negro Civic Action," *Journal of Conflict Resolution*, 5 (1961), pp. 291-303.

became a salient constitutional issue in the civil rights litigation and even more so in some recent antiwar activity.

The civil rights litigation raised another troublesome question for the Court. The activities alluded to above—the interaction of individuals espousing their point of view, their audience, and state officials—seems quite close to the set of circumstances for which the clear and present danger rule was designed. But application of this type of test contained a difficult problem: collusion between the state and the audience. In the South, many white citizens and government officials were violently hostile to the causes espoused by civil rights demonstrators. If the state wanted to suppress a demonstration, there was little difficulty in finding (or producing) a hostile reaction from the audience that could be used as justification for intervening in the demonstration and breaking it up. The situation in the South was not one in which two sides were vying in the marketplace of ideas, with the state a neutral referee that could be expected to step in only in those extreme situations which held true danger of violence. Rather the state was an active participant in the struggle and hence its judgments about the nature of the situation, and the possibilities for violence, were suspect.

Thus, the Court had to fashion doctrine to meet the problems raised by public demonstrations in behalf of civil rights. As indicated at the outset of this section, there was a great deal of this activity, many arrests resulted, and the Court decided a number of important expression cases. Before turning to these cases, let us look back very briefly at some of the doctrine developed by past Courts to deal with some of the problems raised by public demonstrations.

Prior doctrine dealing with public demonstrations

One area in which a good deal of doctrine had been developed involved picketing, a tactic long used by labor unions. The Court had followed a somewhat checkered path in dealing with picketing. In the first third of this century, the Court—generally hostile to the labor union movement—

had consistently upheld the use of court injunctions which banned picketing. With the growth of the industrial union movement and the passage of the Norris-LaGuardia and Wagner Acts in the 1930s, which were designed to protect the rights of workers to join unions and bargain collectively, the Court's doctrine became more restrictive of the powers of the state to prohibit or limit picketing.

The milestone case in this development was *Thornhill* v. *Alabama*[21] in 1940. The Court held unconstitutional a sweeping state statute banning all picketing that provided no exceptions based upon the number of pickets, the character of the pickets (e.g., whether violent or nonviolent), the nature of the dispute, or whatever. Using a clear and present danger approach, the Court seemed to assimilate peaceful picketing into expression protected by the First and Fourteenth Amendments:

> Abridgement of the liberty of such discussion can be justified only where the clear danger of substantive evils arises under circumstances affording no opportunity to test the merits of ideas by competition for acceptance in the market of public opinion. We hold that the danger of injury to an industrial concern is neither so serious nor so imminent as to justify the sweeping proscription of freedom of discussion embodied in [the Alabama statute proscribing picketing].[22]

Though the Court continued to treat peaceful picketing as protected expression, it gradually loosened restrictions upon the state in controlling such activity, even in the absence of a clear and present danger of violence. The Court validated restrictions upon picketing in situations in which there was no direct connection between the pickets and the establishment being picketed,[23] and restrictions upon picketing, itself

[21] 310 U.S. 88 (1940).

[22] 310 U.S. 104-105.

[23] E.g., *American Federation of Labor* v. *Swing*, 312 U.S. 321 (1941); *Carpenters and Joiners Union* v. *Ritter's Cafe*, 315 U.S. 722 (1942).

not violent but taking place in a context of widespread violence, have been upheld.[24]

The state has been granted powers to restrict picketing in which the object of the picketing was a goal that was in violation of public policy or valid objectives of the state. Thus, for example, in *Giboney* v. *Empire Storage and Ice Company*,[25] the Court upheld an injunction against picketing designed to induce an agreement that would violate the state's anti-trust laws. In *Hughes* v. *Superior Court*,[26] an injunction prohibiting picketing aimed at forcing a business establishment to hire employees in proportion to the racial composition of the community was upheld. Since California public policy forbade employment discrimination on the basis of race—a valid objective of state public policy—the Court held the state was entitled to enjoin picketing to coerce employers to violate this public policy. In *International Brotherhood of Teamsters* v. *Vogt*,[27] in 1957, the Court upheld an injunction against picketing designed to force an employer to require his employees to join a union when state legislation forbade employers to force their employees to become members.

Thus, the Court, though maintaining picketing was protected by the First Amendment, permitted a good deal of state regulation of picketing in the area of labor/management relations. In part, this was probably attributable to changes in the attitude of the society and other institutions of government to the labor movement. As the fervor of the labor union movement in the 1930s diminished, legislation less favorable to unions had been passed (e.g., the Taft-Hartley Law in 1948; the Landrum-Griffin Act in 1959), and some reaction to labor union activity—in the form of right-to-work

[24]*Milk Wagon Drivers Union* v. *Meadowmoor Dairies*, 312 U.S. 287 (1941).

[25]336 U.S. 490 (1949).

[26]339 U.S. 460 (1950).

[27]354 U.S. 284 (1957).

laws, for example—set in. The Court's doctrine was congruent with this trend, validating regulation of union activity, including picketing. In addition, the Court tacitly acknowledged that picketing was something more than mere speech— the history of its use in labor organizing indicated that a line of individuals carrying signs brought with it a kind of emotional baggage that was, perhaps, more than the mere expression of an idea. Generations had grown up thinking there was something special about a picket line; the notion that it was wrong to cross such a line or to fail to adhere to the objective of those participating in such demonstrations was a powerful one for many people in our society. Because of this, one might argue, picketing carries a kind of power to induce compliance beyond the simple expression of a point of view. As suggested before, many believe that picketing lies somewhere beyond "pure" speech, though it is somewhat short of "action," and the Court's treatment of picketing seems to suggest that it does not enjoy the protection that simple speech does.

Thus, as the civil rights era began, the Court's doctrine on picketing was somewhat unclear. It had not returned to the clear and present danger rule, but rather had developed the policy that although states could not ban all picketing, in certain classes of cases (e.g., in the context of violence, or in favor of activities against public policy or valid legislation), picketing could be restricted.

Two other cases, not involving labor relations, are also an important backdrop for the Court's handling of civil rights demonstrations.

The *Terminello* case

In *Terminello* v. *Chicago*,[28] a neofascist speaker had been delivering a speech in a hired hall. Outside, a large group of individuals gathered to protest the speech. His remarks to his audience were antisemitic and the crowd outside threw

[28]337 U.S. 1 (1949).

objects at the hall and attempted to break down the doors. The audience inside the hall was quite sympathetic to Terminello's remarks, moved to cries of "Kill the Jews," "Dirty Kikes," and other social commentary. Terminello was arrested and convicted under a breach of peace statute. The trial court charged the jury that the statute applied to conduct that "stirs the public to anger, invites dispute, brings about a condition of unrest, or creates a disturbance." The majority of the Supreme Court overturned the conviction, arguing that the statute, as interpreted and applied, violated the First and Fourteenth Amendments.

> Accordingly a function of free speech under our system of government is to invite dispute. It may indeed best serve its high purpose when it induces a condition of unrest, creates dissatisfaction with conditions as they are, or even stirs people to anger.[29]

Douglas's majority opinion went on to cite the clear and present danger test and to argue that the statute, as interpreted by the trial court, did not restrict conviction to circumstances which constituted such a clear and present danger.

Justice Jackson, in his dissent, argued that the conviction should have been upheld, for an examination of the facts of the case suggested that the remarks of Terminello did constitute a clear and present danger. His examination of the circumstances of the speech and the words used was informed by a series of rather broad statements about the nature of fascism and communism and the generally troubled times.

Though the majority opinion alluded to clear and present danger, it did not really apply the test, but instead relied upon the construction by the trial court of the statute and upon the fact that it *might* have been applied by the jury in a fashion to permit conviction for activities that did not

[29]337 U.S. 4.

constitute such a clear and present danger. The implicit issue in the case—and the reason why the case is relevant to later civil rights cases—is the fact that it presented a situation in which a crowd hostile to a speaker gathered around him and caused violence. The accounts of Terminello's remarks in the majority and dissenting opinions leave the reader somewhat confused about the facts. But the situation suggests that, at least potentially, it was the objection of the crowd outside to what Terminello stood for, and to the ideas he expressed, that led to violence, not any particular incitement—for the audience inside the hall was quite sympathetic to what he was saying. This was a situation that would recur in civil rights cases—antagonistic whites would threaten or attack speakers and demonstrators, incited to violence not by the speakers, but by the ideas they expressed. *Terminello* certainly cannot be read as standing unequivocally for the proposition that under these circumstances it should be the violent audience rather than the speaker who should be the subject of punishment. But it does point out the difficulty faced by the Court when dealing with an unpopular speaker in a context in which a violent crowd objects to his words.

The *Feiner* case

In *Feiner* v. *New York*,[30] the Court faced this problem more squarely, and came out in favor of punishing the speaker. Again, the facts are somewhat confused, but the situation appears to have been something like this: A student addressed a crowd on a street in Syracuse. In the course of his remarks, he called President Truman a bum and urged that Negroes (a few of whom were in the crowd) should rise up and "fight for their rights." The crowd was generally peaceful, but did fill the sidewalk and spilled out into the street. One individual in the crowd, angered by the speaker's words, approached a policeman and told him that if the police did not make the speaker stop talking, he would. At

[30] 340 U.S. 315 (1951).

this point, an officer approached Feiner and asked him to stop; when Feiner refused, the policeman told him to stop; when he still refused, he was arrested and charged with disorderly conduct. Again, the majority and dissenting opinions presented somewhat different accounts of the facts, but neither alleged that there was actual violence.

The Supreme Court upheld the conviction. Speaking for the majority, Chief Justice Vinson argued:

> [The lower courts] found that the officers in making the arrest were motivated solely by a proper concern for the preservation of order and protection of the general welfare, and that there was no evidence that could lend color to a claim that the acts of the police were a cover for suppression of petitioner's views and opinion. Petitioner was thus neither arrested nor convicted for the making or the content of his speech. Rather, it was the reaction which it actually engendered . . . It is one thing to say that the police cannot be used as an instrument for the suppression of unpopular views, and another to say that, when as here the speaker passes the bounds of argument or persuasion and undertakes incitement to riot, they are powerless to prevent a breach of the peace.[31]

Justice Black, in a dissent, disputed both the factual picture presented by the majority and the reasoning it used.

> As to the existence of a dangerous situation on the street corner, it seems far-fetched to suggest that the 'facts' show any imminent threat of riot or uncontrollable disorder. . . . Moreover, assuming that the facts did indicate a critical situation, I reject the implication of the Court's opinion that the police had no obligation to protect the petitioner's constitutional right to talk. The police of course have power to prevent breaches of the peace. But if, in the name of preserving order, they ever can interfere with a lawful public speaker, they must first make all reasonable efforts to protect him.[32]

[31]340 U.S. 319, 320, 321.
[32]340 U.S. 325, 326.

The evidence suggested in both majority and minority opinions does not support the position that Feiner was inciting a riot. As in *Terminello*, the danger came not from the speaker's words but from the reaction they engendered in a hostile audience. In fact the two cases, two years apart, are somewhat paradoxical. Both in terms of the inflammatory character of the words and the violence that actually occurred, it seems clear that Terminello presented a much more serious situation; yet his conviction was overturned and Feiner's upheld. One potentially important difference lay in the fact that Terminello was speaking inside a hall to an audience that had chosen to come to hear him while Feiner was speaking in the street. Thus, Feiner's audience was in some sense "captive"—though people could, obviously, simply walk past him if they didn't wish to hear his words—because anyone walking on the street was forced into at least some exposure to his ideas. Thus, the cases might be distinguished on the ground that a speaker is in some sense more "liable" for the anger his words will stir if he speaks them to a captive audience than if he speaks them to a self-selected audience. However, this seems a somewhat strained means of distinguishing the cases; moreover, it lays open an unpopular public speaker to organized gatherings of those opposed to his views.

Another potential difference in the cases was the nature of the statutes involved. In *Terminello*, the Court, in overturning the conviction, relied heavily upon the fact that the charge to the jury might have led to conviction for protected speech that "stirred to public anger." The language of the New York statute was not much different from that of the Chicago statute, and held an individual liable to conviction if he "uses offensive, disorderly, threatening, abusive or insulting language, conduct or behavior; acts in such manner as to annoy, disturb, interfere with, obstruct, or be offensive to others; congregates with others on a public street and refuses to move on when ordered by the police."[33] Unlike *Termi-*

[33]340 U.S. 318.

nello, the case was tried before a judge alone, so there was no charge in which the statute was interpreted. The trial judge did say, in making his decision: "The question here, is what was said and what was done. . . . The question is, what did this defendant say and do at that particular time, and the Court must determine whether those facts, concerning what the defendant did or said, are sufficient to support the charge."[34] This isn't much help, but the language of the judge, combined with the words of the statute, suggest that there was little to choose, in terms of the statute, between *Terminello* and *Feiner*.

A final potential explanation for the different ways the two cases were decided lies in changes in the composition of the Court. Four justices who dissented from the 1949 *Terminello* decision, Vinson, Frankfurter, Jackson, and Burton, voted to uphold Feiner's conviction in 1951. They were joined by a new member of the Court, Justice Clark, and by Justice Reed who had voted to overturn Terminello's conviction. Justice Minton, also a Truman appointee joining the Court after the *Terminello*, dissented in the *Feiner* case, joining with Douglas and Black. To put it another way, the *Terminello* case had been decided by the solid four-man liberal bloc of Black, Douglas, Murphy and Rutledge, joined by Reed. Murphy and Rutledge left the Court before *Feiner* was decided, and their successors were, generally, much less liberal. These personnel changes were not only important in the outcomes of *Terminello* and *Feiner* but in the whole tenor of the civil liberties decisions of the 1950s discussed in Chapter Two.

Thus, the two cases were somewhat confusing, at best. What they did illustrate, though, are two problems faced in the civil rights demonstration cases: What should be done when a speaker's ideas produce anger or violence in a hostile audience? What is acceptable evidence of a speech producing enough danger that the state is permitted to step in? The

[34]340 U.S. 321.

second is particularly important. Does a speech present a clear and present danger only when the speaker attempts to rouse his audience to some unlawful acts? Or is hostile reaction sufficient? Or, is the *danger* of hostile reaction sufficient? These questions were crucial in the civil rights demonstration cases.

Civil rights demonstrations

The first major civil rights demonstration case, *Edwards* v. *South Carolina*,[35] reached the Supreme Court in 1963. As black students, desiring to protest discrimination, marched on the state capitol grounds, a crowd of onlookers gathered; however, there was no evidence that violence was in the offing. Pedestrian and auto traffic was not disrupted. The defendants were arrested for breach of the peace, after being told to move on and responding with songs and speeches. The South Carolina Supreme Court held that "breach of the peace" included:

> . . . a violation of public order, a disturbance of the public tranquility, by any act or conduct inciting to violence. . . . It may consist of an act of violence or an act likely to produce violence. It is not necessary that the peace be actually broken to lay the foundation for a prosecution of this offense. If what is done is unjustifiable and unlawful, tending with sufficient directness to break the peace, no more is required.[36]

The Supreme Court, with only Justice Clark dissenting, overturned the conviction. The majority opinion, by Justice Stewart, stressed the generality of the statute, and the lack of the requirement of any clearly defined disruptive conduct. Admitting that a statute designed to prevent disruptions of traffic or regulating the hours during which the capitol grounds were open might meet constitutional standards, the

[35]372 U.S. 229 (1963).
[36]372 U.S. 234.

Court held that this statute did not, for its application here, to peaceful conduct, "infringed the petitioners' constitutionally protected rights of free speech, free assembly, and freedom to petition for redress of their grievances."[37] The majority opinion, discussing *Feiner*, noted that in *Edwards* there was no evidence of a restive crowd or threats of violence. Rather, the Court said, the case was more like *Terminello*, in which a vague statute was used to punish protected activity.

The *Edwards* opinion was somewhat peculiar, for it was not clear upon what grounds the conviction was overturned. There seemed no question that the arrests and convictions were a blatant violation of rights protected under the First Amendment. But the majority opinion used two separate grounds to overturn it: First, it stressed the nonviolent character of the demonstration and the context in which it occurred (the absence of counter-violence, etc.). Thus, it appeared to have a clear and present danger foundation. Second, the conviction was held void on the basis of the vagueness of the statute, a ground which appeared determinative regardless of the degree of violence or danger involved (this was the *Terminello* ground). Thus, it was not clear whether the Court was attempting to return to the clear and present danger approach.

The Cox case

Two years later, in *Cox* v. *Louisiana*,[38] arrests for breach of peace were overturned by the Supreme Court. Here, again, there was a large but peaceful gathering. The opinion overturning the conviction referred to the vagueness point in *Edwards*—the lack of clarity in the statute which permitted conviction for what might be protected conduct. *Cox* also involved prosecution for a statute forbidding obstruction of the sidewalks. Here the Court was faced with what it had said

[37]372 U.S. 235.
[38]379 U.S. 536 (1965); 379 U.S. 559 (1965).

in *Edwards* might be a valid regulation. However, the convictions were overturned on the ground that the police normally (for other demonstrations, parades, conventions and the like) permitted such obstruction, and could not constitutionally enforce such a statute for purposes they did not like simply within their own uncontrolled discretion. In discussing the obstruction convictions, the majority rejected the petitioners' contention that such demonstrations enjoyed the same protection as pure speech:

> We emphatically reject the notion urged by appellant that the First and Fourteenth Amendments afford the same kind of freedom to those who would communicate ideas by conduct such as patrolling, marching, and picketing on streets and highways as these amendments afford to those who communicate ideas by pure speech.[39]

Justice Black concurred in overturning the convictions, but in his opinion, he indicated a view that was to shortly take him (and later the majority of the Court) away from the side of civil rights demonstrators. Black's opinion relied on the vagueness of the statute and the exercise of unfettered discretion in enforcement of the sidewalk obstruction statute. But he made several crucial observations:

> The First and Fourteenth Amendments, I think, take away from government, state and federal, all power to restrict freedom of speech, press, and assembly *where people have a right to be for such purposes.* This does not mean, however, that these amendments also grant a constitutional right to engage in the conduct of picketing or patrolling, whether on publicly owned streets or on private property. . . . Picketing, though it may be utilized to communicate ideas, is not speech, and therefore not itself protected by the First Amendment.[40]

[39]379 U.S. 555.
[40]379 U.S. 578. (Emphasis in original.)

The *Brown* case

A watershed case, *Brown* v. *Louisiana*,[41] occurred in 1966. The case was a watershed because it represented the high point of Court sympathy for civil rights demonstrations. Five demonstrators were arrested in a public library for violation of a breach-of-peace statute which made it criminal to "crowd or congregate with others in a public place or building" and refuse to move on when ordered to do so. The Court overturned the convictions, in a five-to-four decision; not only was the Court as a whole divided over the outcome, but the majority had difficulty in arriving at a common position. The demonstrators, protesting alleged racial discrimination in the library, had come in and asked for a book; the librarian told them that the library did not possess it, but she could order it from the state library. The demonstrators then simply sat down quietly. Later, the sheriff arrived and after requesting they leave, arrested them for breach of peace.

The institutional opinion for the majority, written by Justice Fortas and joined by Chief Justice Warren and Justice Douglas, quickly dismissed the notion that the situation was anything else than a demonstration: "We need not be beguiled by the ritual of the request for a copy of 'The Story of the Negro.' We need not assume that petitioner Brown and his friends were in search of a book for night reading."[42] Rather, this was just a "ceremony," and after it was finished, "the Negroes proceeded to the business in hand. They sat and stood in the room, quietly as monuments of protest against the segregation of the library."[43]

The conviction was overturned on the ground that the demonstrators simply did not violate the terms of the statute.

The statute requires a showing either of 'intent to provoke a breach of the peace,' or of 'circumstances such that a breach of the peace

[41]383 U.S. 131 (1966).
[42]383 U.S. 139.
[43]*Ibid.*

may be occasioned' by the acts in question. There is not the slightest hint of either. . . . We instead rest upon the manifest fact that they intended to and did stage a peaceful and orderly protest demonstration, with no 'intent to provoke a breach of peace.'[44]

Stressing the peaceful nature of the demonstration, the lack of provocative acts or of possible violence from onlookers, the Court held, as it had argued in *Edwards*, that there was no danger of disorder, and hence the statute could not be constitutionally applied.

Fortas went somewhat further:

We are here dealing with an aspect of a basic constitutional right—the right under the First and Fourteenth Amendments guaranteeing freedom of speech and of assembly, and freedom to petition the Government for redress of grievances. . . . As this Court has repeatedly stated, these rights are not confined to verbal expression. They embrace appropriate types of action which certainly include the right in a peaceable and orderly manner to protest by silent and reproachful presence, in a place where the protestant has every right to be, the unconstitutional segregation of public facilities. . . . The statute was deliberately and purposefully applied solely to terminate the reasonable, orderly, and limited exercise of the right to protest the unconstitutional segregation of a public facility. Interference with this right, so exercised, by state action is intolerable under our Constitution. . . . And [the state] may not invoke regulations as to use—whether they are *ad hoc* or general—as a pretext for pursuing those engaged in lawful, constitutionally protected exercise of their fundamental rights.[45]

Thus, not only was the statute applied in circumstances in which there was no threat of violence, but the activity—sitting in a segregated library—was protected by the Constitution.

[44]383 U.S. 139-140.
[45]383 U.S. 141, 142, 143.

Justice Black (joined by Justices Clark, Harlan, and Stewart) dissented sharply: "I do not believe that any provision of the United States Constitution forbids any one of the 50 states of the Union, including Louisiana, to make it unlawful to stage 'sit-ins' or 'stand-ups' in their public libraries for the purpose of advertising objections to the State's public policies."[46] Black found no issue of racial discrimination in the case—the defendants were "granted every consideration to which they were entitled" in the library. Moreover, he denied the contention in the majority opinion that racial discrimination was practiced in the library.[47]

Finally, he challenged the basic notion in the majority opinion that the activity engaged in was protected:

It is high time to challenge the assumption in which too many people have too long acquiesced, that groups that think they have been mistreated or that have actually been mistreated have a constitutional right to use the public's streets, buildings, and property to protest whatever, wherever, and whenever they want, without regard to whom it may disturb.[48]

Thus, Black challenged both the finding of the majority that the conduct did not violate the statute and Fortas's position that the conduct was protected by the Constitution. Alluding to his own long struggle to extend the protection of the First Amendment, Black observed:

The First Amendment, I think, protects speech, writings, and expression of views in any manner in which they can be legitimately and validly communicated. But I have never believed that it gives

[46]383 U.S. 151-152.

[47]The majority and dissenting opinions both acknowledged discrimination in access to bookmobiles, but could not agree whether there was conclusive evidence of discrimination at the library building.

[48]383 U.S. 162.

any person or group of persons the constitutional right to go wherever they want, whenever they please, without regard to the rights of private or public property or to state law. . . . Though the First Amendment guarantees the right of assembly and the right of petition along with the rights of speech, press, and religion, it does not guarantee to any person the right to use someone else's property, even that owned by the government and dedicated to other purposes, as a stage to express dissident ideas. . . . It is an unhappy circumstance in my judgment that the group, which more than any other has needed a government of equal laws and equal justice, is now encouraged to believe that the best way for it to advance its cause, which is a worthy one, is by taking the law into its own hands from place to place and from time to time.[49]

Finally, Black alluded to the political context of the times, revealing what was going on in his mind and probably in the minds of many in the society at large:

But I say once more that the crowd moved by noble ideals today can become the mob ruled by hate and passion and greed and violence tomorrow. If we ever doubted that, we know it now. The peaceful songs of love can become as stirring and provocative as the Marseillaise did in the days when a noble revolution gave way to rule by successive mobs until chaos set in.[50]

After examining briefly a few more demonstration cases, I want to return to this point, for it is crucial to understanding the gradual growth in division in the Court over civil rights demonstrations, and the reversal in majority that took place.

Brown was a high water mark, for the next two important civil rights demonstration cases were the first major cases decided against the demonstrators. The cases discussed so far are but a sampling of a great number that had been decided

---

[49]383 U.S. 166, 167-168.
[50]383 U.S. 168.

in their favor.[51] In addition to public demonstrations involving picketing and mass gatherings, there was a long line of cases involving sit-ins in public accommodations. These cases will be treated in detail in the chapter dealing with equality. Suffice it to say here that the bulk of these cases up to 1966 had been decided in favor of the demonstrators. Most were decided not on First Amendment grounds, but upon a finding of state action in favor of racial discrimination (and hence a violation of the Equal Protection Clause of the Fourteenth Amendment); however, they too indicated the sympathy of the Court to civil rights activities.

The *Adderley* case

In 1966 and 1967, the Court upheld the convictions of civil rights demonstrators in two cases, *Adderley* v. *Florida*[52] and *Walker* v. *Birmingham.*[53] The five-four *Brown* majority dissipated with the defection of Justice White.[54] Thus, the dissenting minority of four in *Brown* in 1966 became the majority of 1967.

[51]According to Grossman, 57 of the 61 demonstration cases decided by the Supreme Court during the 1957-1967 period were in favor of the demonstrators. See Joel B. Grossman, "A Model for Judical Policy Analysis: The Supreme Court and the Sit-In Cases," in J. Grossman and J. Tanenhaus, *op. cit.,* pp. 405-460, 438.

[52]385 U.S. 39 (1966).

[53]388 U.S. 307 (1967). In *Walker,* a five-justice majority upheld conviction of Martin Luther King and four others for violation of an injunction forbidding marches during the 1963 demonstrations in Birmingham. The majority framed the question very narrowly: Did the demonstrators have the right to violate an injunction without first exhausting legal remedies that might have held it unconstitutional. The dissenters argued that given the history of activities by officials in Alabama, it was clear that such remedies would not have been of any avail and that the ordinance under which the injunction was issued was unconstitutional. Two years later, in *Shuttlesworth* v. *Birmingham,* 394 U.S. 147 (1969), a conviction arising out of the same Good Friday march was overturned and the ordinance was held unconstitutional as a prior restraint in violation of the First Amendment.

[54]Justice White had concurred in the *Brown* decision on the narrow ground of lack of evidence that the behavior of the defendants constituted a violation of the breach of peace statute.

In *Adderley*, a group of demonstrators had been convicted for "trespassing with a malicious and mischievous intent," after a demonstration on the grounds of a jail to protest the previous arrest of other demonstrators. The majority opinion, upholding the conviction, was written by Justice Black. He denied the petitioner's contention that this case was controlled by *Edwards* and *Cox*. This case was different from *Edwards*, he argued, because the latter involved the state capitol grounds (which are traditionally open to the public) while *Adderley* involved the jail (which, built for security purposes, was not generally open). Moreover, the *Edwards* and *Cox* convictions had been overturned because the statutes were vague and could be used to attack protected activities. This, Black argued, was not true of the Florida statute, which was reasonably precise and afforded due warning. Though the statute did involve the concept of "malicious" and "mischievous intent," this did not so broaden the offense of trespass as to make it unconstitutionally vague.

Not only was the statute sufficiently clear, but, unlike previous cases, Black argued, here there was clear evidence of violation. There was assembly on jail grounds, some blockage of vehicular traffic, and notice to the defendants that they were in jeopardy of arrest if they refused to move. Therefore, Black concluded, the conviction must stand:

Nothing in the Constitution of the United States prevents Florida from even-handed enforcement of its general trespass statute against those refusing to obey the sheriff's order to remove themselves from what amounted to the curtilage of the jailhouse. The State, no less than a private owner of property, has power to preserve the property under its control for use to which it is lawfully dedicated. . . . Such an argument [made by the petitioners] has as its major unarticulated premise the assumption that people who want to propagandize protests or views have a constitutional right to do so whenever and however they please.[55]

[55]385 U.S. 47, 48.

Thus, echoing the words of his *Brown* dissent but this time speaking for a majority, Black's opinion upheld the conviction.

Justice Douglas, joined by Justices Warren, Brennan, and Fortas, dissented. Their dissent emphasized the peaceful nature of the protest, the absence of violence, and the relative lack of interference with the operation of the jail facility. Douglas's opinion stressed black people's general lack of access to the political system and the media and hence their reliance upon public demonstrations to express their grievances. "Their methods should not be condemned as tactics of obstruction and harassment as long as the assembly and petitioner are peaceable, as these were."[56]

There may be some public places which are so clearly committed to other purposes that their use for the airing of grievances is anomalous. There may be some instances in which assemblies and petitions for redress of grievances are not consistent with other necessary purposes of public property. . . . But this is quite different than saying that all public places are off limits to people with grievances. . . . And it is farther yet from saying that the 'custodian' of the public property in his discretion can decide when public places shall be used for the communication of ideas, especially the constitutional right to assemble and petition for redress of grievances. . . . Such power is out of step with all our decisions prior to today where we have insisted that before a First Amendment right may be curtailed under the guise of a criminal law, any evil that may be collateral to the exercise of the right, must be isolated and defined in a narrowly drawn statute. . . . Today a trespass law is used to penalize people for exercising a constitutional right. Tomorrow a disorderly conduct statute, a breach-of-the-peace statute, a vagrancy statute will be put to the same end. It is said that the sheriff did not make the arrests because of the views which petitioners espoused. That excuse is usually given, as we know from the many cases involving arrests of minority groups.[57]

[56] 385 U.S. 51.
[57] 385 U.S. 54, 55, 56.

Thus, the dissent dwelt upon the lack of any disorder—a clear and present danger notion—and argued that therefore the activities were expression protected by the First Amendment.

Looking at *Edwards*, *Cox*, *Brown*, and *Adderley* together leaves one somewhat confused. All involved public demonstrations against racial discrimination; all involved public property (with the possible exception of *Cox*, which was in the vicinity of a courthouse though not directly on its premises); all involved peaceful activity; all involved statutes generally recognized as valid, but which were somewhat vague; all involved, therefore, exercise of discretion by the authorities in deciding that the statutes should be enforced. All involved deep division within the Court over the proper grounds upon which to decide the cases. Elements of the clear and present danger rule were used; the character of the statute, especially its vagueness, was sometimes fixed upon; the issue of whether the activity itself was protected was debated. What this all amounts to is the suggestion that it is difficult to find doctrinal issues making it clear why *Adderley* came out differently from the preceding cases. The institutional opinion in *Brown* could have been easily tailored to decide *Adderley* in favor of the demonstrators; by the same token, the *Adderley* majority opinion was quite apposite as grounds for deciding *Brown* (and perhaps *Cox*) the other way (in fact Black's *Adderley* majority opinion, as suggested above, was his *Brown* dissent, but this time with four instead of three colleagues willing to join it). Thus, to understand changes in the Court's treatment of these issues, one must go beyond the doctrine.

Trends in support for civil rights demonstrators

Support for the civil rights movement began to wane in the second half of the 1960s. The movement of the early 1960s, bringing together a coalition of northern whites, labor unions, leading political figures like Presidents Kennedy and

Johnson, a receptive Supreme Court, and the civil rights organizations had, at the doctrinal level at least, produced a revolution in the treatment of blacks in America. The 1964 Civil Rights Act forbade discrimination in public accommodations and provided a mechanism—the cut-off of federal funds to recalcitrant school districts—that seemed a possibly potent device to speed the pace of school desegregation in the South. The Voting Rights Act of 1965 provided, again potentially at least, the means by which blacks could begin to exercise effective power in the arena of electoral politics. However, by the middle of the decade things began to change. A split began to develop between the more militant civil rights organizations (e.g., CORE and SNCC) and those with more a traditional bent like the NAACP and the Urban League. The rhetoric of "black power" became increasingly representative of the civil rights movement. Perhaps more importantly, the struggle over equal rights began to move north and to become less nonviolent. The years 1964 and 1965 saw riots in Harlem and Watts. The movement of the civil rights struggle is suggested in Figure 1.

Thus, the civil rights movement changed in character, becoming more violent both in its rhetoric and activity, and moving out of the South. Northern whites grew concerned, for they could see equal rights for blacks in the South as a fairly simple moral issue. Equal rights in the North provided some troublesome practical issues, for black equality might well involve economic competition for jobs, proximity in living patterns, school bussing and the like. Thus, in the elections of 1966, the concept of white backlash entered America's political rhetoric, and many candidates exploited the frightening connotations of black power.

The falling off in white support for civil rights activity cannot be simply explained by pointing out the threatening character of the movement of the civil rights issue north, fear of competition, and backlash. It probably has something to do with a kind of growing national weariness with the civil

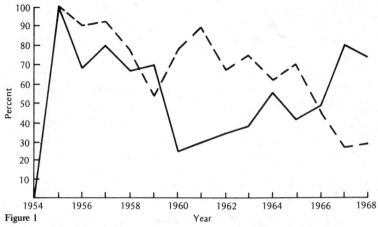

Figure 1

Year

The dashed line indicates the percentage of all reported civil rights demonstrations that took place in the eleven southern states. The solid line indicates the percentage of all reported incidents that involved violence.
Source: *The New York Times Index.*

rights issue. The Viet Nam War began to dominate the political horizon. There was a natural tendency of people to react to continuing cries for equality by pointing out the passage of legislation designed to ameliorate racial inequality. For blacks, it was reality and the relative absence of change that counted. For many whites, the symbolic satisfactions of having passed laws probably led to some diminution of interest in and support for civil rights activity.[58] In any event, the coalition in favor of civil rights appeared to begin to crumble. The 1966 civil rights legislation, with open housing provisions, failed of passage. Only in the aftermath of the assassination of Martin Luther King did the federal open housing legislation pass.

[58]For an imaginative discussion of the relationship between the passage of legislation and subsequent abatement of movement for reform—even in the absence of substantive behavioral change—see Murray Edelman, *The Symbolic Uses of Politics* (Urbana: University of Illinois Press, 1964), especially Chapter 2.

These developments in the civil rights movement were also reflected in the doctrine developed by the Court in decisions like *Adderley* and *Walker*. No simple mechanical explanation is offered—for example, that the Court, seeing the falling off of support for civil rights, simply followed suit. Decisions in favor of civil rights did not cease in 1967. Moreover, the decisions of individual justices and of the Court as a whole involved complex men and interactions. A crucial figure in the Court's turn was Justice Black; he was a man of too consistent principle to suggest that the pressure of the times led to a sudden switch in his view. Yet recall his words in *Brown* in 1966.

> But I say once more that the crowd moved by noble ideals today can become the mob ruled by hate and passion and greed and violence tomorrow. *If we ever doubted that, we know it now.* The peaceful songs of love can become as stirring and provocative as the Marseillaise did in the days when a noble revolution gave way to rule by successive mobs until chaos set in.[59]

One can't help thinking that what he urged "we know" now has something to do with his view of the developments undergone by the civil rights movement. Given what we have seen of the difficulty in reconciling the decisions of the Court simply on grounds of doctrine or principle, it is fair to at least advance the argument that the political and social developments alluded to above have a good deal to do with understanding the outcomes that occurred in the Supreme Court.

Before turning to the last section of this chapter, dealing with developments in freedom of expression outside the realm of loyalty-security and civil rights, a brief summary seems in order.

I have argued that the political and social climate surrounding the loyalty-security effort in this country is crucial to understanding the decisions made by the Court. These decisions were part of a continuing dialogue between the Court and the political system in which it operates. The

[59]383 U.S. 168. (Emphasis added.)

early civil rights cases involved some departure from the doctrine developed in dealing with alleged subversives. Though the issues raised were somewhat different—the organizations were more public and competed openly in the political arenas, the cause espoused differed—what differentiated the Court's treatment of governmental activity designed to suppress the freedom of expression of the two groups of participants was not just the nature of the issue, but the nature of their place in the political system. What was permissible in dealing with "subversives" was not permissible in dealing with civil rights workers. The attitudes in our society toward the two groups and the activities of other governmental institutions and interest groups were crucial to understanding the Court's treatment of the two groups. Finally, within the context of civil rights cases alone, we again have seen the interplay between doctrine and outcome produced by the Court and developments in the broader political system.

Now we turn to a brief discussion of some more recent issues of freedom of expression, and to some speculations about the future course that may be taken in the struggle over freedom of expression.

OTHER RECENT DEVELOPMENTS IN FREEDOM OF EXPRESSION

Several developments touching upon freedom of expression but not tied directly to the loyalty-security or civil rights movements have occurred in recent years. Some of them will be briefly discussed here, to give some more perspective upon both the breadth of governmental activities that involve freedom of expression and the nature of the Court's attempts to deal with them.[60]

[60]One major area of litigation dealing with freedom of expression not discussed here deals with attempts by the government to restrict the dissemination of allegedly pornographic or obscene material. Since 1957, the Court has wrestled quite unsuccessfully with this issue. The majority has consistently held that obscene material does not enjoy the

Libel of public officials

The Court has attempted to fashion and modify the law dealing with libel and slander to reduce the potential restriction upon political expression that sanctions for libel might produce. The landmark case, decided in 1964, involved a suit for libel against *The New York Times*.[61] The paper had published an advertisement in which civil rights advocates had accused the police in Montgomery, Alabama of abusing demonstrators. Some of the statements in the ad turned out to be false. An Alabama jury awarded damages to the local police commissioner in a libel suit. The Supreme Court reversed the judgment. The Court pointed out that the democratic process, especially electoral politics, required a good deal of latitude in making statements about public officials, for such discourse was at the heart of the process by which officials can be chosen. Fear of libel suits might, the Court argued, produce self-censorship by critics, perhaps unsure of themselves, who feared the sanction of a libel action. Thus, statements about officials that an individual might believe to be true, but which turned out to be false, might, under traditional rules of libel, be subject to sanction. And moreover, even those statements that were true might be suppressed, for fear that they could not be demonstrated to

---

protection of the First Amendment. The Court has thus been forced to deal with the issue of what constitutes obscenity and has attempted to develop definitions dealing with the characteristics of materials that make them obscene (or not obscene and hence enjoying the protection of the First Amendment). See, for example, *Roth* v. *United States*, 354 U.S. 476 (1957); *Manual Enterprises* v. *Day*, 370 U.S. 478 (1962); *A Book Named "John Cleland's Memoirs of a Woman of Pleasure"* v. *Massachusetts*, 383 U.S. 413 (1966); *Ginzburg* v *United States*, 383 U.S. 463 (1966); *Mishkin* v. *New York*, 383 U.S. 502 (1966). This area of litigation is omitted because of space limitations and because of the emphasis here upon the exercise of civil liberties in overtly political contexts. Though the obscenity cases caused a great deal of controversy, the issue itself seems less intimately tied to the operation of the political process than most of those discussed here.

[61]*New York Times* v. *Sullivan*, 376 U.S. 254 (1964).

be true. Thus, the Court reasoned, the First Amendment's "profound national commitment to the principle that debate on public issues should be uninhibited, robust, and wide-open"[62] required that the usual rules for libel—under which, in most states, truth and demonstration of good motives were the only sure defense against such an action—must be modified. The rule enunciated by the Court suggested that in order for a statement to lose the protection of the First Amendment, it must be demonstrated that it was made with "actual malice—that is, with knowledge that it was false or with reckless disregard of whether it was false or not."

In the same year, in *Garrison* v. *Louisiana*,[63] the Court further explicated the rule. In a case involving criminal libel, the Court held that truth itself was an absolute defense for libelous statements about public officials, regardless of the motive which informed the statements, and that even false statements about officials were protected, provided that they were not made with the "actual malice" discussed in the *New York Times* case. In 1966, *Rosenblatt* v. *Baer*,[64] the Court liberally construed the concept of a public official—for whom the *New York Times* rule applied—by suggesting that a public official included government employees "who have or appear to have, substantial responsibility for or control over the conduct of governmental affairs."[65] In this case, such a public official was held to include the head of a local government-owned ski resort. In 1968, the Court further amplified the concept of what constitutes malice.[66] The Court held that "reckless" conduct in expressing an untrue statement about a public official is:

[62]376 U.S. 270.
[63]379 U.S. 64 (1964).
[64]383 U.S. 75 (1966).
[65]383 U.S. 85.
[66]*St. Amant* v. *Thompson*, 390 U.S. 727 (1968).

... not measured by whether a reasonably prudent man would have published, or would have investigated before publishing. There must be sufficient evidence to permit the conclusion that the defendant in fact entertained serious doubts as to the truth of his publication.[67]

Thus, as the majority opinion admitted, to some extent the Court's ruling "puts a premium on ignorance." But the value of promoting free discussion was said to outweigh the possible danger of the expression of untruthful statements about public officeholders.

It is difficult to assess the impact of this line of cases. There has been little or no systematic research dealing with the incidence of libel actions by public officials for statements made about them. Moreover, as the reasoning of the Court suggests, the most important impact of the use of libel laws probably lies not in their application but in the fear of their use. Thus, the primary effect lies in the process of anticipated reactions—the stifling of potential expression for fear that it might lead to a libel action. Assessing the degree of "nonexpression" that might have been produced had the Court not weakened the law on libel of public officials is difficult, if not impossible. Thus, about all one can say about the decisions is that they potentially increased the amount of political discourse in the society. By placing the activities of public officials in a special category—and removing or decreasing one of the potential sanctions exercised against critics of public officials—the Court attempted to broaden the spectrum of political expression.

The emerging right to privacy

Another recent doctrinal development, the shaping of a "right to privacy" protected by the Constitution, has a potentially very important impact upon the protection of freedom of expression. However, the nascent state of this doctrine makes both the road the Court will take and the

[67]390 U.S. 731.

impact of its approach hard to gauge. Most of the litigation involving the notion of a right to privacy has occurred in contexts not directly dealing with freedom of expression— particularly the areas of searches and seizures and electronic surveillance in pursuit of criminal activity. Yet the relationship between privacy and expression is clear. The ability to express views, to associate with others in organizations designed to support points of view without fear of a "Big Brother" government keeping track of what one is saying or with whom one is associating, would seem crucial to the maintenance of a society in which people are free to hold and express divergent views and associate with others of a like mind. The notion of associational privacy was implicit in some of the cases already discussed: the loyalty-security investigations dealing with associations and the attempts to make public membership in civil rights organizations. The right to privacy and its relationship to the right of association and expression was in a sense the basis for the civil rights association decisions.

The *Griswold* case

The crucial decision suggesting most explicitly the right of privacy involved a Connecticut statute outlawing the use or counseling of the use of birth control devices.[68] The majority opinion in *Griswold* v. *Connecticut*, written by Justice Douglas, held that there was a right to privacy, though it was not specifically mentioned in the Bill of Rights. Examining the Court's rulings dealing with the rights of association and expression protected by the First Amendment, the Third Amendment prohibition on the quartering of soldiers in private houses in time of peace, the Fourth Amendment's protection against unreasonable searches and seizures, and the Fifth Amendment's protection against self-incrimination, the Douglas opinion argued:

[68]*Griswold* v. *Connecticut*, 381 U.S. 479 (1965).

... specific guarantees in the Bill of Rights have penumbras, formed by emanations from those guarantees that help give them life and substance.... The present case, then, concerns a relationship lying within the zone of privacy created by several constitutional guarantees.[69]

The statute, involving private marital relations, was held to unconstitutionally infringe this right of privacy.

Justice Goldberg (joined by Justices Warren and Brennan) concurred in the decision, but on somewhat broader grounds. His opinion stressed the long-forgotten Ninth Amendment to the Constitution, which provides "The enumeration in the Constitution, of certain rights, shall not be construed to deny or disparage others retained by the people." The Ninth Amendment had never been actively used by the Court as a restriction upon governmental activities; rather it had been taken, in conjunction with the Tenth Amendment,[70] mainly as a rhetorical injunction pointing out the limited power of the *federal* government vis-a-vis the states. Goldberg's opinion suggested, however, that the Ninth Amendment should be used as a tool to protect basic liberties not specifically enumerated in the Bill of Rights:

Nor do I mean to state the Ninth Amendment constitutes an independent source of rights protected from infringement by either the States or the Federal Government. Rather, the Ninth Amendment shows a belief of the Constitution's authors that fundamental rights exist that are not expressly enumerated in the first eight amendments and an intent that the list of rights there not be deemed exhaustive.[71]

[69]391 U.S. 484-485.

[70]"The powers not delegated to the United States by the Constitution, nor prohibited by it to the states, are reserved to the states respectively, or to the people."

[71]381 U.S. 492.

Thus, in this view, the Bill of Rights provides a floor of rights below which the federal government may not penetrate, but not a ceiling.

Justice Black (joined by Justice Stewart) dissented. He stressed that the Bill of Rights meant what it said, and that without any specific reference to a right of privacy, the Court could not on its own create such a general right.

> I like my privacy as well as the next one, but I am nevertheless compelled to admit that government has a right to invade it unless prohibited by some specific constitutional provision.[72]

Black's opinion stressed the lack of any standards controlling the Court in determining what rights fell within the bounds of the Ninth Amendment, and that the Court could not assume such a power:

> My point is that there is no provision of the Constitution which either expressly or impliedly vests power in this Court to sit as a supervisory agency over acts of duly constituted legislative bodies and set aside their laws because of the Court's belief that the legislative policies adopted are unreasonable, unwise, arbitrary, capricious or irrational.[73]

Citing the use in the past of the Due Process Clause to invalidate economic regulation during the early twentieth century, he asserted that the Ninth Amendment approach likewise invested the Court with an indiscriminate power that it simply did not possess. Ironically enough, Justice Black, a *bête noire* of the conservatives, is the author of one of the most eloquent defenses of the "strict construction" that conservatives so greatly cherish. In fact, his whole judicial career, with its emphasis upon a rather literal interpretation of the words of the Constitution, is a paradigm of "strict

[72]381 U.S. 510.
[73]381 U.S. 520-521.

construction." This term—usually used to denote a judge who does not tamper with the activities of other branches of government—is thus susceptible of a variety of meanings.

Problems of the right to privacy

The notion of a right to privacy has been mentioned in later cases, especially those involving electronic surveillance, which are discussed in Chapter Five. The potential importance of developments in this area are great. Technological advances in record-keeping and surveillance make feasible the gathering and storage of tremendous quantities of information about individuals in our society.[74] Such activities are not only the province of government but also of private organizations like credit agencies, employment services, private investigators, and the like. In the governmental realm, the increased use of police informers and undercover agents, the compilation by the Army and Secret Service of lists of individuals participating in political organizations and rallies, the assertion by the attorney general that the government possesses power, without judicial scrutiny, to engage in electronic surveillance of the activities of domestic groups thought to threaten the safety of the nation are but a few examples of the invasions of privacy that are becoming routine activities of the government. Since much of this surveillance and information gathering involves the activities of those opposed to government policy, the relationship between such activity and expression—and the potential chilling effect of such activity upon expression—is manifest.

Clearly, though, it is no answer simply to assert that these activities must cease because they violate the privacy of the individual. Other values compete with privacy, including those of public order, suppressing criminal conduct, and the like. The point I want to suggest, however, is that some invasions of privacy are intimately tied to the exercise of

---

[74]For an excellent discussion of the privacy issue, see Allen Westin, *Privacy and Freedom* (New York: Atheneum, 1967).

expression. And the Court will gradually have to arrive at some position on this matter. Just as freedom of expression competed with order and the preservation of the government in the loyalty-security area, so now the right of privacy—whatever it means, whatever it contains—is coming into conflict with similar values.

The libel of public officials suggests one of these conflicts—between free expression and the operation of the political process and the privacy of those holding public office. In another important case, *Time* v. *Hill*,[75] the Court dealt with a clash between freedom of the press and the privacy of the individual. The case arose from a *Life* magazine article which asserted that a play was in fact based directly upon the experience of a family that had been held captive by some escaped convicts. The family sued under a New York right-to-privacy statute. The award to the family was overturned by the Supreme Court. The majority held that the risk of occasionally having one's private life exposed to public scrutiny "is an essential incident of life in a society which places primary value on freedom of speech and of press."[76] The Court applied the same type of test to "newsworthy" private citizens as was applied to comment upon public officials and public affairs. Untrue statements about such newsworthy persons "if innocent or merely negligent, . . . must be protected if the freedoms of expression are to have the 'breathing space' they need to survive."[77]

Thus, in dealing with the clash between freedom of speech and press and the right to privacy, the Court has generally come down in favor of protecting the rights of expression, at least in dealing with those who occupy—by virtue of their political position or activities of public importance—prominent places in the society.

This is one area in which the conflict between the right to

[75] 385 U.S. 374 (1967).
[76] 383 U.S. 388.
[77] *Ibid.*

privacy and other freedoms or values had already been the subject of extensive litigation. Where the Court will come out in other areas of such conflict is in doubt. But the development of a doctrine of privacy both recognizes the growing threat to privacy in our society and possibly provides the Court with a tool to deal with restrictions upon expression by means of surveillance, name-gathering, and the like.

Freedom of expression and dissent from the Viet Nam War

One final area of freedom of expression litigation is worthy of attention, though, like the privacy cases, it is still in a nascent state. A few cases have come to the Court involving expression in opposition to the draft and the Viet Nam War. One of the most important, *U.S.* v. *O'Brien*,[78] attempted to raise squarely the question of whether there exists something called "symbolic speech"—action that is a form of expression and hence protected by the First Amendment. O'Brien burned his draft card as a symbol of his opposition to the draft and the Viet Nam War. After the practice of draft-card burning had begun, Congress added a provision to the Selective Service Law (which already made criminal nonpossession of draft cards) making it an offense to knowingly destroy or mutilate a draft card. Under this law, O'Brien was convicted.

O'Brien argued, among other things, that his act was protected under the First Amendment because it constituted "symbolic speech" or the "communication of ideas by conduct."[79] The Court, in an opinion by Chief Justice Warren, rejected this argument:

> We cannot accept the view that an apparently limitless variety of conduct can be labeled 'speech' whenever the person engaging in the conduct intends thereby to express an idea. However, even on the

[78]*United States* v. *O'Brien*, 391 U.S. 367 (1968).
[79] 391 U.S. 376.

assumption that the alleged communicative element in O'Brien's conduct is sufficient to bring into play the First Amendment, it does not necessarily follow that the destruction of a registration certificate is constitutionally protected activity. This Court has held that when 'speech' and 'nonspeech' elements are combined in the same course of conduct, a sufficiently important governmental interest in regulating the nonspeech element can justify incidental limitations on First Amendment freedoms.[80]

Thus, the majority opinion took it both ways. First, it cast doubt that the conduct was in fact speech; second, even if it were speech, it held that the government's interest in having registrants not destroy their cards was sufficient justification for the statute.

Justice Douglas dissented, arguing that the Court should have ordered reargument and considered whether the draft itself was constitutionally permissible in the absence of a declaration of war by Congress.

Though upholding the draft-card burning statute, the Court did move to restrict the practice of using the delinquency provisions of the Selective Service Law as a means of speeding up the induction of registrants who turned in their cards. Thus, the draft process itself could not be used to penalize those engaging in anti-war activities, though the Congress did have the power to punish criminal conduct such as draft-card burning or turn-ins.[81]

Other prosecutions of dissidents raised important free expression issues as the decade of the 1960s came to a close, but most did not or have not as of this writing reached the Supreme Court. The prosecution of Dr. Spock and his codefendants for conspiring to unlawfully "counsel, aid and abet diverse Selective Service registrants to unlawfully, knowingly, and willfully neglect, fail, refuse and evade service

[80]*Ibid.*

[81]E.g., *Gutknecht* v. *United States*, 396 U.S. 295 (1970); *Breen* v. *Selective Service Board Number 16*, 496 U.S. 460 (1970).

in the armed forces of the United States . . ." and other offenses dealing with possession of draft notices resulted in convictions of some of the defendants at the trial stage that were reversed on nonconstitutional grounds by the First Circuit Court of Appeals, and the cases were dropped by the government.[82]

The Chicago Eight

The celebrated trial of the Chicago Eight raised even more serious free expression issues. They were accused and five were convicted of violating a provision of the 1968 Civil Rights Act which made it a crime to travel in interstate commerce "with the intent to incite, organize, promote, encourage, participate in, and carry on a riot" and of conspiring to violate this section of the law. The vagueness of the law, the rather liberal definition of what constitutes a "riot," the selection of particular defendants out of an apparently large pool of candidates, the flimsy nature of the evidence against them—all suggest that the law has very grave implications for the protection of freedom of expression. Though at this point we don't know whether convictions will be upheld, whether the law itself will be held constitutional, the implications of this and other cases like Spock-Coffin seem ominous. The use of the conspiracy weapon, which permits dragging in numbers of defendants whose relation to the "crime" is tenuous, the selection of certain defendants rather than others, the general attack upon dissent by the Administration—all are troublesome developments. Has the Smith Act been resurrected in the antiriot statute? Is the country heading for a new period of repression in which the rights not of Communists but of white radicals and black militants are to be sacrificed in the name of law and order and national security? At this point there is no way of making any firm prediction. And there is no way of knowing what posture the Court will take towards such developments.

[82]*United States* v. *Spock,* 416 F. 2d 165 (1st Cir, 1969).

The appointment by 1971 of four new justices, including a new chief justice, makes prediction hazardous. Statements by President Nixon and other Administration officials have indicated strong dissatisfaction with the expression and activities of many who have disagreed with government policy. In addition, the President has made it clear that he hopes his appointees to the Supreme Court will mirror his views of the Constitution. Thus, the new justices may bring with them to the Court a somewhat more restricted view of the extent to which the Constitution should be used to protect the freedom of expression of those who intensely disagree with the activities being pursued by the government.

CONCLUSION

The two chapters dealing with freedom of expression have covered a lot of ground—a long period of time, a great number of cases, many different periods in American politics—but have a common theme. Understanding what freedom of expression means—what is protected, what is not; who can speak freely, who cannot—in the context of American politics requires much more than concentrating upon the decisions enunciated by the Court. Not only are these decisions—the doctrine dealing with freedom of expression—often ambiguous, but they are in a state of constant change and flux. And in part this change and flux is intimately related to the broader political context in which the cases arose and were decided.

Consider for a moment the doctrinal positions we have been discussing here; more specifically, the so-called "tests" that have been used to determine what expression is protected and what is not. Clearly, these tests have changed over time. In the 1920s the bad-tendency rule was combined with deference to legislature to produce few restrictions upon its power to punish speech thought inimical to the national interest. The clear and present danger test developed in the dissents of Holmes and Brandeis in the 1920s came, in the

1930s, to dominate a Court much more protective of the rights of expression. The Cold War period saw a retreat to the gravity of the evil and balancing tests. These tests were coupled with strong sentiment in favor of judicial modesty, which validated the often oppressive measures of the era of loyalty-security. The growth of the civil rights movement produced new doctrine, relying heavily upon the flavor if not the letter of clear and present danger. While it is by no means clear that the protective doctrine of the 1960s extended to Communists or alleged subversives, a general spirit of freedom and tolerance dominated the doctrine of the Court. As the 1960s ended, tensions once more appeared to be rising, social polarization was growing, and a somewhat identifiable set of dissidents—the New Left and black militants—appeared in danger of restrictions upon their freedom of expression.

Assuming that the above characterization of the approaches taken by the Court toward issues of freedom of expression is generally true, if admittedly rather simplified, what are we, as students of the Court, to make of it? Clearly, the words of the First Amendment have not changed during the past 50 years. Thus, to look at "the law" or "the Constitution" as a source of the changing approaches is not sufficient. A cogent argument can be made that some of the changes suggested above can be in part attributed to changes in the nature of the issues facing the Court. The threat to national security posed in the 1920s and the 1950s by supposedly close-minded idealogues dedicated to the destruction of our system of life was, perhaps, different from the relatively open organization of workers into labor unions or the fight by blacks for rights to which they were constitutionally entitled. This argument suggests, then, that it was the nature of the issues involved in the periods, and of the goals being pursued by those attempting to exercise their freedom of expression, as well as the strength of competing goals, that differentiates the more libertarian doctrine and tests from the less libertarian.

Yet this is not enough. To understand why the Court acted as it did requires us to look at the broader political context in which the Court was operating—the attitudinal structures of the population at large and of political influentials; and the behavior occurring in the society supportive of or in opposition to the protection of the right of free expression. The allusions to indicators of such attitudes and behavior made in this chapter suggest that they may be useful in understanding the shifts in doctrine that have occurred.

What are the mechanisms by which these other dimensions affect doctrine? One is the appointment process, for it is through appointments that a new and more or less tolerant majority coalition can make its preferences felt on the Court.[83] Another operates more directly—through the passage of legislation or attempts at constitutional amendment—aimed at reversing doctrine currently thought by other political participants and the public at large to be wrongheaded. Even when such direct attempts fail of passage, they provide pointed cues to the Court. Though appointed for life, justices are citizens and also members of the political stratum in our society.[84] Thus, it is not unnatural for their preferences, which are reflected to some extent in their decisions, to be informed by the changes in attitude that affect the broader political spectrum of the society. In a sense, to affirm that attitudes and behavior dealing with civil liberties are often reflected in doctrinal change is simply to affirm the obvious: Freedom of expression is a *political* issue in our society and the choices made by the Court about the issue

[83]See Robert A. Dahl, "Decision-Making in a Democracy: The Supreme Court as a National Policy-Maker," *Journal of Public Law*, 6 (1958), pp. 279-285, esp. pp. 284-286.

[84]For an overview of the general background characteristics of justices of the Supreme Court, see John Schmidhauser, "The Justices of the Supreme Court: A Collective Portrait," *Midwest Journal of Political Science*, 3 (1959), pp. 1-57. For a discussion of the utility of the use of background characteristics in explaining judicial decision-making, see Joel B. Grossman, "Social Backgrounds and Judicial Decision-Making," *Harvard Law Review*, 79 (1966), pp. 1551-1564.

are influenced by and at the same time part of the collective choices made by our society.

This argument appears to be, and to a large extent is, a complicated way of expressing Mr. Dooley's famous dictum that the Court "follows the election returns." Two comments are in order, however. First, the process is much more complex than this—for the Court can and does lead, can and does make mistakes in judging what the "returns" are (this is what I have tried to argue about the 1956-1957 loyalty-security decisions), and the process of interaction between the Court and its doctrine and the attitudes and behavior in the society is so complex that we by no means completely understand it. The second point is equally crucial. Mr. Dooley's dictum and the view it expresses is often taken to suggest that there is something "wrong" in the interaction between Court decisions and the broader political system; it is usually associated with a kind of cynicism that implies that the Court *ought* to be doing something different, ought to be adhering to a firmer foundation than is provided by the exigencies of the political process. This firmer foundation is supposed by many to be something called "the law," or "the Constitution." I hope that the examination of the cases discussed here makes it clear that such things simply do not exist: "The law," whether it be statute or precedent, is rarely clear, and is subject to many often equally plausible yet contradictory interpretations. Though logic or analogy may seem to point in one direction, often they point in several. Thus, the firmer foundation one supposes the Court ought to rely on often turns out to be made of sand.

Moreover, even if "the law" or the Constitution did provide unambiguous guidance to the Court, it would be unreasonable to believe that the Court would apply them consistently. For to look at the issues before the Court in this fashion is to misunderstand them. Such a view implies that there is something peculiarly legal about the issues, that they are simply disputes to be resolved on the basis of some standards removed from the criteria—prejudices, preferences, views of what is good public policy—that are used to decide questions that are political rather than legal. As I have tried to suggest, the very nature of the issues involved in the freedom of expression cases places them quite clearly outside of the realm of anything peculiarly legal. The issues touch deeply felt preferences and prejudices in the society; they are often highly allocative, affecting who gets what, when, and how—for the question of who can express himself and join with others to espouse a common cause and who cannot may affect the process of collective decision and its outcome. Thus, the interaction of doctrine dealing with freedom of expression and other aspects of the political system—attitudes and behavior—is not "right" or "wrong"; it is a defining character of American politics.

What, then, of the future? Predictions are hazardous in 1971, for it appears that we are in a period of transition. I think it not an exaggeration to say that in terms of doctrine and behavior dealing with freedom of expression we are today probably better off than we have ever been in the past. This is not to say we are as well off as we ought to be, for groups—especially the black, the poor, the politically dissident—still do not enjoy the freedom of expression open to the affluent, the white, the conventional in political belief. But we as a society have come a long way from the 1920s and the 1950s in developing both doctrine favoring the protection of freedom of expression and activity by political figures and interest groups in favor of the protection of such freedom.

But if the past experience traced here suggests anything, it is that we had better not take our gains for granted, especially today. Statements deploring dissent by high government officials; a disdain for freedom of expression on the part of segments of the radical left in our society; a spate of prosecutions using the conspiracy weapon under laws aimed not at action but at speech; a growing polarization of the society in which a minority believed to represent dangerous and alien ideas faces a majority unsure of itself and its own ideas—these are ominous developments, and they are all too familiar.

What will happen is, then, unclear. The survey data dealing with public attitudes toward civil liberties cited several times suggest that the seeds of repression are ever-present in our society. They sprout and bear fruit regularly. The Court is not able, by itself, to combat such repression, even if it wishes to. Besides the Court, the protection of freedom of expression depends upon other political institutions and leaders, organized interest groups committed to the protection of such freedom, and the public at large. Thus, the protection of this right—so essential to the maintenance of a democratic and open society—ever hangs in a delicate balance. The balance can and has been tipped against this liberty. The role of the Court is but one aspect of the complex political process in which civil liberties are inextricably enmeshed.

FOUR
EQUALITY

EQUALITY is another value that has been the subject of controversy in our society, and about which much litigation has centered. Like freedom of expression, the concept of equality—nondiscrimination against individuals regardless of such characteristics as sex, race, religion, etc.—has both intrinsic and instrumental value.

EQUALITY AS A VALUE: PRELIMINARY CONSIDERATIONS

Intrinsically, equality of treatment is valued because discrimination tends to devalue a man, to violate his integrity as an individual. To attach infirmities to a man because of characteristics like race, religion, etc.—those very characteristics which make him up as an individual—is to attack his humanness. Instrumentally, equality may be viewed as an integral part of a democratic political system. If democracy is defined, at least in part, as a system in which the preferences of the majority of citizens determine the collective decisions of a polity, then restrictions upon the ability of some citizens to participate in the system—which give more weight to the preferences of others—

reduce the degree of democracy of a system.[1]

Thus, most definitions of democracy treat equality as a value that ought to be pursued. Obviously, though, the matter does not end there, for a question immediately arises as to what kinds of discrimination ought to be reduced or eliminated? Presumably not all, for some kinds of inequality simply can't be erased. People differ in such characteristics as appearance, intelligence, education, wealth, sex, race, religion, status, preferences, and the like. Some of these differences can be diminished (e.g., wealth, education), but some cannot. Some we might wish to eliminate, others we might not (e.g., differences in preferences, religious beliefs, etc.). Moreover, since we deal here with public law, we are basically concerned not with discrimination by private persons—for example, associating with those whose appearance, views, characteristics one finds pleasing and avoiding those with characteristics one doesn't like—but with various forms of discrimination that involve the activities of public institutions. However, as we shall see, there has been a trend in our society toward widening the scope of discrimination that is under the aegis of government and hence subject to its remedial action, especially the legal system.

Some notions of equality

What kind of equality do we desire in our society? Two rather distinct formulations can be suggested. One is the notion of equality of opportunity. This formulation suggests that our society ought to strive to provide every individual with the opportunity to gain the benefits of life that his talents or abilities permit him to attain—that we should not place infirmities upon the ability of the individual to compete in the marketplace of life (economic, social, political, etc.) and reap the rewards that he can achieve. This is an appealing formulation and one that dominates much of

---

[1]For a discussion of the theory stressing this view, see Dahl, *A Preface to Democratic Theory, op. cit.,* especially ch. 2.

those not sharing equally in the values—that it is these issues our rhetoric about equality. However, this view has its own quite inegalitarian strain.[2] For people do not have similar degrees of talent, intelligence, creativity, drive, and the like. Thus, equality of opportunity is a form of social Darwinism—a social system in which the fittest (the most talented) will receive more of the material and cultural benefits of life than those less talented. In a sense, then, the notion of equality of opportunity may be conservative, for it tends to produce a kind of meritocracy.

Another conception of equality stresses not the equality to compete—a "process" equality in which individuals are not handicapped before they enter the race—but an equality of outcome. Under this view, equality means that members of society should enjoy equally the benefits—material, cultural, spiritual, intellectual, or whatever—that the society has to offer. Taken seriously, this view of equality probably involves rather extensive discrimination among individuals, for given the inequalities in talent and motivation, insuring inequality in outcome probably requires some discrimination in favor of the less talented. Thus, what might be called "substantive" equality reflects not so much the Darwinian notion of a competition as the Marxian notion of "From each according to his ability, to each according to his need."

Most of the legal controversy over equality in this country has involved equality of opportunity rather than substantive equality. Reasons for the dominance of this concept are not completely clear. As some of the survey data I will discuss shortly suggest, perhaps it is because Americans simply do not believe in substantive equality. Or, perhaps it is because our society has so long been dominated by quite conscious discrimination at the level of opportunity—discrimination that prevents people from competing equally for the values the society has to offer, much less discriminating in favor of

[2]John R. Schaar, "Equality of Opportunity and Beyond," in J. Roland Pennock and John W. Chapman, eds., *Equality* (New York: Atherton Press, 1967), pp. 228-249.

which have been faced first. Perhaps before we can begin to think seriously about substantive equality, we must overcome the inequality of opportunity that has so long characterized our society. In any event, these two conceptions of equality are quite different. In discussing the trends in our society toward the elimination of inequality of opportunity, we should keep in mind that this is not the only version of equality which might be valued; thus, a system which achieved complete equality of opportunity would not necessarily be a society viewed by everyone as maximizing the value of equality.

Beyond the somewhat abstract distinction in the concept of equality suggested above, another practical distinction arises in considering the relationship between the government and the individual (or relationships between individuals which are in some sense under the control of government). That is the question of how much equality ought we to pursue (or require)? Should the government in its relations with citizens, *never* discriminate among them, giving some more or less than others? Presumably this is not the policy we wish to pursue. For example, driver's licenses are not available to the blind; the rich are supposed to pay more taxes than the poor; some occupations are open only to those with certain training and skills. In all of these cases, and innumerable others, complete equality of treatment does not exist, for the government distinguishes between its citizens, gives things to some, denies them to others. The point, and it is an obvious one, is that equality, like freedom, competes with other values the society may wish to pursue—public safety, order, or private property for example—and is often sacrificed for another value.

TESTS FOR DISCRIMINATION

Some of the legal issues dealing with the principle of equality discussed in this chapter suggest the kinds of inequality that our society has practiced: discrimination on the basis of such characteristics as race, religion, economic status, place of residence, etc. Such discrimination has taken place in the context of education, voting, housing, public accomodations, employment, the criminal justice process. Are these justified because such discrimination is the result of the predominance of other, competing values, or are they not? This is the question that has faced our society and its public institutions. Are there "tests" that can be applied to decide such issues? Or is it simply a matter of personal balancing, with no principled approach possible? In evaluating what the Court has done in the area of equality, the reader will decide for himself whether such principled tests have informed its view.

Some tests do seem at least possible. Perhaps the most simple one is based upon the notion of equality of opportunity. This view would suggest, at a minimum, that equality requires no minority suffer infirmities preventing its participation in the political system. The notion of preferred position discussed in Chapter Two suggests this view: no insular minorities ought to be excluded from participation in the political system, and the Court ought to take upon itself the special role of intervening in behalf of such groups. Thus, this notion of equality suggests, at the very least, that the government must not prevent individuals or groups from participating in the political process—from speaking, voting, joining organizations, and the like.

But what of substantive equality? Again, speaking only of the government's relations with its citizens, one might suggest the simple principle that when the government provides goods or services or imposes burdens upon its citizens, it must treat all equally—give to all and take from all in the same measure. Obviously, this will not do. Licensing, taxation, welfare programs are all examples in which the government treats people differently, and in ways that most of us would hold proper. What, then, ought the principle to be? What comes to mind has something to do with the notion that discrimination ought not to be based upon characteristics that are in some sense "irrelevant" to the provision of the service or imposition of the burden; thus, governmental discrimination on the basis of race or religion is discrimination on the basis of a characteristic that is "irrelevant" and hence impermissible.

Another way of saying the same thing is to apply the concept that government discrimination in its treatment of citizens ought not be "arbitrary," or "invidious" or "without rational basis." These are all phrases that have been used by the Court in dealing with equality issues. Unfortunately, these phrases do not decide concrete questions, for their meaning, and hence application, is often ambiguous at best. Why, for example, is it more "reasonable" or less "arbitrary" to impose higher tax rates upon the rich than it would be to tax blacks or Catholics more heavily than others? Presumably the answer to this question—which most of us would find manifest though perhaps hard to express—lies in the goal that is to be pursued by the discrimination or its effect. In the former case, the goal can be characterized either in terms of equalization of income or in terms of insuring that those who have the most difficulty keeping their heads above water economically are not put in more jeopardy than we should like; in the latter, the goal is not so clear, though it might be to discourage people from adopting a particular religion or to prevent blacks from earning as much income as whites. Most would agree that the former goal is proper or morally correct, while the latter is not. But it is difficult to express coherently the differentiation. In fact, for a long period, the former goal—equalizing income, reducing the incidence of taxation upon the poor—was one which was not found by the Court to be constitutionally acceptable.

Another approach to this problem is to suggest that certain characteristics simply cannot be the basis for discrimination, regardless of the character of the goal or the effect of such discrimination. Thus, we could argue that race, sex, religion can never be the basis for governmental discrimination in the treatment of its citizens. However, this also seems unsatisfactory. First, we might disagree about what characteristics should appear on the proscribed list. Second, many would argue that certain characteristics—today, two that immediately occur are race and economic status—should never be permissible subjects for the *imposition of penalities or burdens by the government*, but are permissible classifications to use in *discrimination in favor* of the groups. Thus, it might be argued, blacks and the poor ought to receive differential—preferential—treatment by the government. The consequence of this position, of course, is that the general characteristics—race and economic status—*are* permissible characteristics for the imposition of burdens, for presumably aiding blacks and the poor involves to some extent placing burdens on whites and the more affluent.

The answer to this issue may be that it simply is not feasible to talk about equality in the abstract; rather we should talk about the distribution of costs and benefits in the society. This suggests that equality like freedom, is at its core a political issue, one which is fought over as other values are. Further, like freedom of expression, the conflict over equality involves the legal system not in dessicated arguments about principle, but about highly allocative, and hence political, issues.

To sum up, one might well argue that the principle of equality does have some abstract meaning when dealing with the question of access to the political system. We might begin with the abstract proposition that the government must protect and preserve complete equality of opportunity for all groups and individuals to participate freely in the political process: speaking, joining groups, voting, and similar activities. Beyond this, though, the search for abstract principles becomes much more difficult. And since the legal system inevitably becomes involved in equality issues beyond this point, one may well expect that it is functioning as part of the broader political system, making allocative choices, subject to many of the uncertainties of preference and prejudice that characterize all political choices.

Attitudes toward equality

Do Americans believe in equality? As the preceding discussion suggests, such a question is full of ambiguities: Equality is a term with different connotations and the concept of "belief" in such a principle or value is ambiguous (e.g., do people adhere to it in the abstract? in applications of the principle?). Different subgroups of the population may have different degrees of attachment to such principles. Given these constraints, some survey research will permit us a few generalizations at this point; as we discuss various issues in equality (e.g., racial and economic discrimination), some more detailed data are available.

Studies of the belief systems of Americans have found that those active in politics and (a related characteristic) those with more education, and higher socioeconomic status have somewhat different beliefs about equality than other citizens. It appears that when thinking about the issue of *political equality* (e.g., principles about participation in the political process, the ability of people to make intelligent choices about candidates and issues, the principle of majority rule in the society) the political stratum is more attached to the notion of equality than other citizens. As McCloskey says, "Support for equalitarian features of 'popular' democracy is greater among the elite than among the masses."[3]

On the other hand, attachment to the value of *economic equality*—something more akin to what I have called substantive equality (e.g., that labor does not get its fair share of what is produced, that everyone ought to have the right to a decent job and house)—is higher among the bulk of citizens than among members of the political stratum. For some of these items, even the mass is not close to consensus, but their attachment to principles of substantive equality is greater. At

---

[3] Herbert McClosky, "Consensus and Ideology in American Politics," *American Political Science Review*, LVIII (1964) 361-82, p. 367. A similar conclusion is reached in James W. Prothro and Charles M. Grigg, "Fundamental Principles of Democracy: Bases of Agreement and Disagreement," *Journal of Politics*, 22 (1960), pp. 276-294.

the same time, most people in both groups seem attached to the principle of *equality of opportunity*—the notion that individuals ought to compete for the benefits of the society, with the more talented receiving a disproportionate share: "Thus, approval is widespread for public policies (such as social security) that are designed to overcome gross inequalities, but is equally strong for certain features of economic life that promote inequality, such as private enterprise, economic competition, and unlimited pursuit of profit."[4]

On values of social and ethnic equality, both the mass and the political stratum are somewhat split, though when we talk shortly about race, we shall see that there has been a distinct trend toward belief in equality.

In short, Americans are ambivalent about equality, reflecting the various meetings and implications of the concept, differences in attachment to the value itself, and perceptions about what the application of equality would mean to the life and life-style of individuals. And, as in the case of freedom of expression, survey research seems to suggest that it is the politically sophisticated and active who are more attached to the concept of political equality than are the average citizens. As Robert Lane says:

> Whatever the reason, however, it is not to "The People," not to the business class, not to the working class, that we must look for consistent and relatively unqualified defense of freedom and equality. The professional class, at least in the American culture, serves as the staunchest defender of democracy's greatest ideals.[5]

Thus, a general ambivalence and disagreement about the basic notion of equality provides a crucial context for understanding the development of doctrine dealing with this

[4]McCloskey, *Ibid.*

[5]Lane, *Political Ideology, op. cit.*, p. 81. Chapter 4 in Lane's book, entitled "The Fear of Equality," provides an imaginative discussion of some of the reasons for Americans' ambivalence about equality.

issue. It is in great part because people are ambivalent, and because their attitudes can and do change, that we have seen and are seeing important shifts in the law (doctrine) dealing with the application of the principle of equality. Moreover, because the application of the principle of equality is potentially so distributive, directly touching the material life of the members of our society, the development of doctrine in this area presents fertile ground for political dispute. Equality as a principle, like freedom, is not simply the province for learned discussion and dispute by judges, lawyers, and members of the legal community. Disputes that take the form of lawsuits and result in court decisions are themselves integral elements of a broader political struggle.

RACIAL EQUALITY

The struggle against the repression of blacks in most aspects of social, political, and economic life has long been dominated by litigation and Supreme Court decisions. The Court's decision in the Dred Scott case, voiding the Missouri Compromise, was one factor precipitating the Civil War. The emasculation by the Court, after the Civil War, of legislation aimed at promoting racial equality was important in the growth of Jim Crow in the South. The Court's sanctioning of the doctrine of separate but equal lent further legitimacy to Jim Crow laws and systematic oppression of blacks in the South. By the same token, the Court in the twentieth century—particularly in the last thirty years—has been at the forefront of the movement toward the destruction of legal impediments to racial equality. Of course, the Court was by itself no more responsible for past racism in this country than for recent attempts at rooting out some of the most obvious legal manifestations of this racism. The interplay of the Court's decisions with developments in the broader political system are as crucial in the area of racial equality as they are in the area of freedom of expression. But the Court has been the most salient public institution in race relations in recent years. In part this is a function of the fact that the Court has served as a point of access to the political system for blacks who have been systematically denied access in other areas.

Early developments

The close of the Civil War saw the passage of the Thirteenth, Fourteenth, and Fifteenth Amendments to the Constitution, all apparently aimed at alleviating legal discrimination against blacks. The Thirteenth forbade slavery, the Fourteenth forbade states to "deprive any person of life, liberty, or property, without due process of law" or to "deny to any person within its jurisdiction the equal protection of the laws"; the Fifteenth provided that "The right of citizens of the United States to vote shall not be denied or abridged by the United States or by any State on account of race, color, or previous condition of servitude."

These Amendments have been the basis for most of the litigation and Court decisions dealing with racial equality, and two general comments may be useful in understanding this litigation. First, the meaning of the Amendments—particularly the Due Process Clause of the Fourteenth—has been the subject of a great deal of dispute. Especially important in the context of civil liberties and civil rights has been the relationship between the "due process" protected by the Fourteenth Amendment against state infringement and the provisions of the Bill of Rights (the first ten amendments to the Constitution). In 1833,[6] the Court had held that the provisions of the Bill of Rights applied only to the federal government and did not restrict the activities of state governments. The Due Process Clause of the Fourteenth Amendment obviously does provide some restrictions upon state activities. A controversy has long raged over whether the Fourteenth Amendment "incorporated" all, some, or none of the provisions of the Bill of Rights. In Chapter Two, we saw that the Court held that the speech, press and

[6]*Barron* v. *Baltimore*, 7 Pet. 243 (1833).

association guarantees of the First Amendment are incorporated into the Fourteenth Amendment and hence applicable to state action. In the next chapter, we shall see that most of the provisions dealing with procedural rights of those accused of crime have also been held to be incorporated. In any event, the controversy over the meaning of the Due Process Clause suggests the ambiguity of many of the important phrases of the Constitution and their relative malleability.

The second feature of the Civil War amendments—and one especially crucial in dealing with racial discrimination—was the use of the phrase in both the Fourteenth and the Fifteenth forbidding "States" from engaging in various forms of discrimination. One of the first important cases to come before the Supreme Court dealing with racial discrimination, the *Civil Rights Cases*,[7] raised the issue of the constitutionality of the Federal Civil Rights Act of March 1, 1875 which forbade racial discrimination in public accommodations like hotels, public transportation, and theaters. The Supreme Court declared the law unconstitutional. In its opinion, the Court held that the Fourteenth Amendment's Equal Protection and Due Process Clauses applied only to acts of state governments, not individuals or private businesses, and denied that private discrimination was a form of servitude or slavery. The Court held, in reference to the Fourteenth Amendment, that "It is State action of a particular character that is prohibited. Individual invasion of individual rights is not the subject-matter of the amendment."[8] The decision was important for two reasons. First, it appeared to deny Congress the power to pass legislation dealing with private racial discrimination. Second, it seemed to validate the constitutionality of private segregation, making the prohibitions of the Fourteenth Amendment applicable only to the activities of institutions of state

[7]109 U.S. 3 (1883).
[8]109 U.S. 11.

government. As we shall see in discussing the sit-in cases of the 1960s, the search for the hand of the state in various forms of racial discrimination became a crucial issue in racial discrimination litigation.

Plessy and the doctrine of separate-but-equal

The Court's lack of sympathy in the nineteenth century with racial equality was further manifested in the *Plessy* decision in 1896[9] in which the Court coined the famous "separate but equal" doctrine. At issue was a Louisiana law requiring segregation in railroad cars which was attacked as a violation of the Thirteenth and Fourteenth amendments. The Supreme Court upheld the constitutionality of the state segregation law.

The *Plessy* decision will be discussed in some detail, first because it was the most authoritative Court statement on racial discrimination for more than 50 years and validated state-imposed segregation; second, because the decision overturning *Plessy*, *Brown* v. *Board of Education*, has been severely criticized for its reliance on so-called "sociological" evidence. Examination of the *Plessy* decision reveals that it too relied heavily upon "sociological" assumptions, if not evidence. The implication of this fact is not that both were "bad" decisions but that the very notion of equality is one which changes over time, depends upon individual and social perspectives, and hence is always a "sociological" concept.

The majority opinion in *Plessy*, by Justice Brown, first dismissed a Thirteenth Amendment argument, stating that:

A statute which implies merely a legal distinction between the white and colored races—a distinction which is founded in the color of the two races, and which must always exist so long as white men are distinguished from the other race by color—has no tendency to destroy the legal equality of the two races, or reestablish a state of involuntary servitude.[10]

[9]*Plessy* v. *Ferguson*, 163 U.S. 537 (1896).
[10]163 U.S. 543.

The opinion then turned to the issue of whether such laws violated the Equal Protection Clause of the Fourteenth Amendment, and rejected this argument as well:

> The object of the [Fourteenth] amendment was undoubtedly to enforce the absolute equality of the races before the law, *but in the nature of things* it could not have been intended to abolish distinctions based upon color, or to enforce social, as distinguished from political equality, or a commingling of the two races upon terms unsatisfactory to either. Laws permitting, and even requiring, their separation in places where they are liable to be brought into contact do not necessarily imply the inferiority of either race to the other, and have been generally, if not universally, recognized as within the competency of the state legislatures in the exercise of their police power.[11]

The Court opinion went on to cite discrimination in schools in the North and laws against intermarriage as indications of the generally recognized power of states to enforce racial segregation. In rejecting the hypothetical argument that this view of the Fourteenth Amendment could also validate discrimination on the basis of hair color, laws dealing with the color of houses and the like, the majority opinion observed that "every exercise of the police power must be reasonable, and extend only to such laws as are enacted in good faith for the promotion for the public good, and not for the annoyance or oppression of a particular class."[12]

With respect to the reasonableness of the Louisiana segregation law, the Court observed:

> In determining the question of reasonableness [the state] is at liberty to act with reference to the established usages, customs and traditions of the people, and with a view to the promotion of their comfort, and the preservation of the public peace and good order.

[11]163 U.S. 544. (Emphasis added.)
[12]163 U.S. 550.

Gauged by this standard, we cannot say that a law which authorizes or even requires the separation of the two races in public conveyances is unreasonable. . . .*We consider the underlying fallacy of the plaintiff's argument to consist in the assumption that the enforced separation of the two races stamps the colored race with a badge of inferiority. If this be so, it is not by reason of anything found in the act, but solely because the colored race chooses to put that construction upon it.* The argument necessarily assumes that if, as has been more than once the case, and is not so unlikely to be so again, the colored race should become the dominant power in the state legislature, and should enact a law in precisely similar terms, it would thereby relegate the white race to an inferior position. We imagine that the white race, at least, would not acquiesce in this assumption. *The argument also assumes that social prejudices may be overcome by legislation, and that equal rights cannot be secured to the negro except by an enforced commingling of the two races. We cannot accept this proposition. If the two races are to meet upon terms of social equality, it must be the result of natural affinities, a mutual appreciation of each other's merits and a voluntary consent of individuals. . . . If one race be inferior to the other socially, the Constitution of the United States cannot put them upon the same plane.* [13]

There are three crucial assumptions implicit in this reasoning. The first deals with the character and impact of racial discrimination: The Court asserted that a majority passing a law segregating itself from a minority was not practicing invidious discrimination, was not thereby placing a "badge of inferiority" upon the minority; more particularly, that, in the context of black-white relations in the South, this was neither the intention nor the effect of enforced segregation. This was an assumption (argument) that depended heavily upon hypotheses about the effects of discrimination upon those discriminated against. Second, the Court argued—in a fashion similar to Sumner's later work on

[13] 163 U.S. 550, 551, 552. (Emphasis added.)

folkways—that it was not possible to change attitudes by legislation. It denied the proposition that "social prejudices may be overcome by legislation."[14] Regardless of one's evaluation of the validity of this proposition (and there is substantial research to suggest that it is simply incorrect), it is clearly that: an empirical proposition about the nature of prejudice. Finally, there was an assumption, or argument, that in fact blacks were inferior to whites. This emerges implicitly in the Court's statement that "in the nature of things" the Fourteenth Amendment could not have been intended to enforce "social" equality, and in the statement, in conjunctive form, "If one race be inferior to the other socially. . . ." Again, a few may argue, even today, about whether blacks are in fact "inferior" to whites in any respect, but the fact remains that such statements—upon which the *Plessy* opinion relies—are empirical propositions, not neutral principles or logical propositions.

Thus, the *Plessy* opinion was itself a series of "sociological" arguments. Neither citing nor based upon "sociological" *evidence*, but still quite clearly a set of empirical propositions presented under the guise of obvious truth or the common wisdom.

However, as with the *Brown* decision of 1954, it was not the rhetoric or reasoning, but the outcome of *Plessy* that was crucial: It validated state legislation discriminating against blacks. Though *Plessy* dealt with discrimination in public transportation, later decisions applied the doctrine to public

[14]William Graham Sumner, *Folkways* (Boston: Ginn, 1907). On the concept of prejudice, see Gordon W. Allport, *The Nature of Prejudice* (Cambridge, Mass.: Addison-Wesley, 1954). Studies suggesting that attitudes can be modified by legislation or court decision include: Morton Deutsch and Mary Evans Collins, "Interracial Housing," in William Petersen, ed., *American Social Patterns* (Garden City, N.Y.: Doubleday, 1956), pp. 7-57; William K. Muir, Jr., *Prayer in the Public Schools* (Chicago: University of Chicago Press, 1967); Richard M. Johnson, *The Dynamics of Compliance* (Evanston, Ill.: Northwestern University Press, 1967).

schools.[15] The Court's posture, until the late 1930s, was that the provision of separate facilities for blacks was constitutionally permissible. Moreover, the Court did not take it upon itself to inquire very deeply into whether such separate facilities were equal. In point of fact they were consistently and manifestly—especially in the case of schools—unequal, for the resources put into and the quality of education provided to blacks were typically inferior to that provided to whites.

In the area of housing, the Court overturned in 1917 a city zoning ordinance which set aside certain areas for whites and others for blacks.[16] The Court's opinion was based not on the Equal Protection Clause, but upon the Due Process Clause, and held that such zoning ordinances violated an individual's right to dispose of his property as he wished.

The elimination of racial zoning led to the development of private agreements—called restrictive covenants—by which groups of owners would agree (and make part of their leases to property) not to sell property to blacks or other minority group members. The Court held that this system of "private" agreements—contracts among private individuals—did not violate the Due Process Clause of the Fifth Amendment (the case arose in the District of Columbia).[17] The absence of state action in the agreement made it immune to the prohibitions of the Constitution. Such contracts, though, were enforceable in court, and hence the power of the state could be invoked to insure that they were not broken.

During the late 1930s and the 1940s the Court began to examine racial discrimination much more critically, eroding the *Plessy* doctrine by striking down state-imposed discrimination in voting, housing, and schools. A brief look at some

[15]*Cummings* v. *Board of Education*, 175 U.S. 528 (1899) and, especially, *Berea College* v. *Kentucky*, 211 U.S. 45 (1908).

[16]*Buchannan* v. *Warley*, 245 U.S. 60 (1917).

[17]*Corrigan* v. *Buckley*, 271 U.S. 323 (1926).

of these cases will provide the backdrop for the revolution of the 1950s.

Movement toward equality

The major issue in the suffrage cases involved the systematic exclusion of blacks from voting in the South. The Court had, in 1915, struck down one highly overt form of discrimination, the so-called grandfather clause.[18] The grandfather clause scheme involved both rigorous educational requirements for voting—which most blacks could not meet—and an exception to these requirements permitting voting by descendants of voters in the period before 1866 (thus enfranchising most whites). After *Guinn*, the main thrust of black exclusion then turned from elections themselves to the primaries. Since the Democratic Party dominated in southern states, the important choices were those made in the primary, not the general election, which usually was a formality validating the choice made by the Democrats. The first major primary cases to come to the Court involved the passage by Texas, first, of a law forbidding blacks to vote in primary elections, and, later, a statute authorizing the state party central committees to determine who was eligible to vote. Both these schemes were struck down: the first[19] on the grounds that the statute was state action in violation of the Fourteenth Amendment; the second[20] because the discrimination was sanctioned by statute. The state took no further action, but the Democratic convention in Texas then passed a resolution making all whites eligible for membership in the party and hence eligible to vote in the primary. This scheme was upheld by the Court[21] on the ground that discrimination was the product of the activities of a private group, and hence not in violation of the Fourteenth Amendment.

[18]*Guinn* v. *United States*, 238 U.S. 347 (1915).

[19]*Nixon* v. *Herndon*, 273 U.S. 536 (1927).

[20]*Nixon* v. *Condon*, 286 U.S. 73 (1932).

[21]*Grovey* v. *Townsend*, 295 U.S. 45 (1935).

In 1944, the Court overruled the *Grovey* doctrine, holding that the white primary was not a permissible means of discriminating against black voting:

> The United States is a constitutional democracy. Its organic law grants to all citizens a right to participate in the choice of elected officials without restriction by any state because of race. This grant to the people of the opportunity for choice is not to be nullified by a state through casting its electoral process in a form which permits a private organization to practice racial discrimination in the election. . . . The privilege of membership in a party may be, as this Court said in *Grovey* v. *Townsend*, no concern of a state. But when, as here, that privilege is also the essential qualification for voting in a primary to select nominees for a general election, the state makes the action of the party the action of the state.[22]

Thus, the fact that the state law provided for the mechanism of primary elections provided state action requisite for application of the Fifteenth Amendment. *Smith* did not end the voting litigation. The white South had by no means exhaused its ingenuity in attempting to exclude blacks. But *Smith* marked an important step in the gradual movement of the Court towards protection of the rights of blacks against discrimination and its increasing willingness to find the state action requisite for application of the safeguards of the Fourteeenth and Fifteenth amendments.

In the area of housing, the Court also moved forward in the 1940s, dealing a blow to private discrimination via the use of restrictive covenants. Recall that these private agreements to discriminate had been validated in 1926 as lacking the requisite state action required to make applicable the provisions of the Fourteenth Amendment. In 1948, in *Shelly* V. *Kraemer*[23] the Court took a different stance toward

[22]*Smith* v. *Allwright*, 321 U.S. 649 (1944) at 664-665.

[23]334 U.S. 1 (1948). For a fascinating account of the restrictive covenant litigation, see Clement Vose, *Caucasians Only* (Berkeley: University of California Press, 1959). Vose's study traces the role of the

restrictive covenants and declared them unenforceable by courts. In arriving at this conclusion, the Court used a somewhat novel and potentially far-reaching doctrinal approach. The opinion agreed that restrictive covenants themselves were not in violation of the Fourteenth Amendment, for they were simply agreements among private individuals. But, the majority of the Court argued, it was the intervention of an arm of the state—the courts—that gave the agreements force and life:

> It is clear that but for the active intervention of the state courts, supported by the full panoply of state power, petitioners would have been free to occupy the properties in question without restraint. These are not cases, as have been suggested, in which the States have merely abstained from action, leaving private individuals free to impose such discriminations as they see fit. Rather, these are cases in which the States have made available to such individuals the full coercive power of government to deny to petitioners, on the grounds of race or color, the enjoyment of property rights in premises in which petitioners are willing and financially able to acquire and which the grantors are willing to sell. The difference between judicial enforcement and nonenforcement of the restrictive covenants is the difference to petitioners between being denied rights of property available to other members of the community and being accorded full enjoyment of those rights on an equal footing.[24]

The doctrine of *Shelley* was somewhat novel because the state was pursuing a general policy—the enforcement of contracts entered into by private individuals—which was itself granted to be legitimate. *Shelley* had great potential significance, for it appeared to suggest that the state's power could not be used to enforce the wishes of private individuals to

---

NAACP in litigation attacking restrictive covenants over a forty-year period, and provides perhaps the best study of the activities and importance of interest groups in the legal system.

[24]334 U.S. 19.

discriminate, an issue that was to arise later in cases involving the enforcement of trespass laws by private establishments desiring to discriminate. In addition to its doctrinal novelty, *Shelley* was important because it suggested the willingness of the Court to strike out in new directions in attacking racial discrimination.

The Court and school segregation

In the area of school segregation, perhaps the most potent and invidious form of southern racism, the Court began in the late 1930s to move toward a reevaluation of the separate-but-equal doctrine. The movement by the Court took the form of a much more critical attitude toward what constituted "equality" in separate educational facilities provided by the state. In 1938, *Missouri ex rel Gaines* v. *Canada*,[25] the Court was faced with a suit by a black who had been denied admission to the University of Missouri law school. The state did not have a separate law school for blacks, but offered to pay Gaines' tuition at various law schools in nearby states if he could succeed in gaining admission. The Supreme Court held that this program violated the Equal Protection Clause of the Fourteenth Amendment. The question, the Court said, was not whether the law schools in other states were equal, but whether Missouri itself was providing equal facilities for blacks and whites; and, they held, by providing a law school for whites but not for blacks, the state denied the equal facilities to which blacks were entitled.

In *McLaurin* v. *Oklahoma*[26] the Court held that the enforced segregation in classrooms, libraries, and lunchrooms of a black graduate student at the University of Oklahoma violated the requirement of the Equal Protection Clause that black students be accorded the same treatment as other students.

[25]305 U.S. 337 (1938).

[26]*McLaurin* v. *Oklahoma State Regents*, 339 U.S. 637 (1950).

In another milestone case in 1950, *Sweat* v. *Painter*[27] the Court dealt with the exclusion of a student from the University of Texas law school. In this case, the state did provide a law school for blacks, but it had a smaller faculty, fewer books in its library, and fewer courses. Following the separate-but- equal approach, the Court argued that the white law school was "superior" in terms of its facilities. Moveover, it "possesses to a far greater degree those qualities which are incapable of objective measurement but which make for greatness in a law school. Such qualities, to name a few, include reputation of the faculty, experience of the administration, position and influence of the alumni, standing in the community, traditions and prestige."[28] Thus, Sweatt followed the traditional separate-but-equal approach, but growing attention to the "equality" of separate facilities was significant. Thus, the law school cases suggested the possibility of a successful attack upon racial discrimination in the public schools. What remained an open question was whether the Court would deal with such an attack under the framework of the traditional separate-but-equal approach or through a rejection of the formula itself.

This question was answered in the 1954 *Brown* v. *Board of Education* decision, which rejected the separate-but-equal formula.[29] This decision was the beginning of a revolution in doctrine dealing with racial discrimination, and in a sense the birth of the activist civil rights movement that came to fruition in the 1960s. Before turning to the later litigation, something should be said about changes in attitudes and

[27]339 U.S. 629 (1950).

[28]339 U.S. 634.

[29]*Brown* v. *Board of Education of Topeka*, 347 U.S. 483 (1954); *Bolling* v. *Sharpe*, 347 U.S. 497 (1954). The school segregation issue came to the Court in four suits originating in Kansas, South Carolina, Virginia and Delaware (decided together by the Court in the *Brown* opinion) and a suit coming from the District of Columbia (decided in the *Bolling* opinion).

behavior that provided a context for the doctrinal movement toward racial equality.

Changing attitudes toward racial discrimination

As the twentieth century approached its midpoint, the doctrine dealing with racial discrimination was undergoing some modification, with a movement toward more racial equality. As the theme of this book suggests, such a trend should not be viewed in isolation: The doctrine of the Court and the outcomes of cases before it are intimately related to attitudinal structures and behavioral patterns in the broader political system. Thus, the reduction in the Supreme Court's willingness to embrace white supremacy was related to shifts in public attitudes toward racism and to activities in the political system.

Table 6 examines some survey data dealing with public attitudes toward racial integration and blacks. The table suggests that within a twenty-year period there was a revolution in attitudes toward racial discrimination in this country. From minorities (sometimes quite small) favoring

Table 6   Attitudes toward racial integration and blacks

	Percent approving				
Issue	1942	1944	1948	1956	1963
Approve school integration	30			49	63
Approve residential integration	35			51	64
Approve public transportation integration	44			60	78
Approve passage of federal legislation prohibiting discrimination in voting			43		86
Believe blacks as intelligent as whites		44		78	80

Sources: Roper Public Opinion Research Center, Williamstown, Mass. and Paul B. Sheatsley, 'White Attitudes Toward the Negro," *Daedalus*, 95 (1966), 217-238.

integration, our society moved to approval by overwhelming majorities. In 1940, for example, fewer than a third of our citizens approved of racial integration in the schools; this grew to about half in 1956 and to almost two thirds in 1963. Perhaps the decisions of the Supreme Court were in part responsible for the dramatic shift between 1956 and 1963. More probably, the dynamics discussed here between the Court and the people are responsible for the changes both in doctrine and in attitudes.

The 1940s also saw events in the political arena that are important in understanding the movement of the Court. The activities of black soldiers in World War II and the subsequent integration of the Armed Forces indicated movement toward acceptance of the principle of racial equality. The Report of President Truman's Committee on Civil Rights in 1947[30] indicated Presidential concern and demonstrated that even in the eyes of a relatively moderate group of prestigious citizens the plight of the black man was the subject of growing concern. The report highlighted both violence and brutality towards blacks by white police and vigilante groups and the systematic exclusion of blacks from political activity as well as from decent living and working conditions. The Dixiecrat revolt in 1948 indicated a nascent split, as the South gradually became isolated from national political institutions. The increased activities of groups like the NAACP in promoting litigation and legislation in favor of civil rights were another indication of the growing strength of the civil rights movement.

Thus, the stage was in a sense set by the 1950s for the historic Supreme Court decisions dealing with racial discrimination. These decisions were partly the product of the shift in attitudes and activity in the political system and were themselves contributors to further attitudinal and behavioral change.

[30] *To Secure These Rights*, U.S. Government Printing Office, 1947.

Brown and its progeny

Brown v. *Board of Education*, the landmark case in racial discrimination, came in 1954. The Court had five cases before it, all challenging racial discrimination in public schools; in all the physical facilities and curriculum were about equal, so the Court was faced directly with the question of the separate-but-equal doctrine. The suits were argued twice before the Court. After the first argument, the Court ordered reargument, asking for detailed discussion of the intention of the framers of the Fourteenth Amendment with regard to racial segregation and for suggestions about the nature of the decree that the Court ought to issue should it find that racial discrimination was in violation of the Equal Protection Clause. The Court, led by its new chief justice, Earl Warren, announced its decision on May 17, 1954, unanimously holding that legally imposed segregation in public schools violated the Equal Protection Clause of the Fourteenth Amendment. The opinion of the Court, by Chief Justice Warren, first discussed the evidence dealing with the intention of the framers of the Fourteenth Amendment, and concluded that such evidence was equivocal. Not only were proponents of the Amendment apparently divided about its intended impact, but the fact that there was almost no public education in the post-Civil War South suggested that some of the framers may simply have had no intention at all regarding an institution that was not particularly salient. Turning then directly to the question of the separate-but-equal doctrine, Warren observed:

> In approaching this problem, we cannot turn the clock back to 1868 when the Amendment was adopted, or even to 1896 when *Plessy* v. *Ferguson* was written. We must consider public education in the light of its full development and its present place in American life throughout the nation. Only in this way can it be determined if segregation in public schools deprives these plaintiffs of the equal protection of the laws.[31]

[31]347 U.S. 492-493.

The opinion then emphasized the importance of public education in inculcating civic and cultural values and in providing the basic skills that determine the life-chances of individuals. The opinion concluded that separation of the races violated the Constitution: "To separate [blacks] from others of similar age and qualifications solely because of their race generates a feeling of inferiority as to their status in the community that may affect their hearts and minds in a way unlikely ever to be undone."[32] Quoting a lower court opinion suggesting that segregation would retard learning, the Court agreed with this conclusion. In what became a cause-celebre, the opinion then stated:

> Whatever may have been the extent of psychological knowledge at the time of *Plessy* v. *Ferguson*, this finding [that segregation has deleterious effects upon black children] is amply supported by modern authority.[33]

The opinion at this point referred in a footnote to the work of psychologists and sociologists, including Kenneth B. Clark and Gunnar Myrdal, that supported the Court's conclusion about the invidious effects of racial discrimination upon black students. The opinion concluded this argument by saying:

> We conclude that in the field of public education the doctrine of "separate but equal" has no place. Separate educational facilities are inherently unequal. Therefore, we hold that the plaintiffs . . . [have been] deprived of the equal protection of the laws guaranteed by the Fourteenth amendment.[34]

The opinion concluded by ordering reargument on the question of the nature of the decree the Court ought to issue to implement its decision.

[32]347 U.S. 494.
[33]*Ibid.*
[34]347 U.S. 495.

A great deal of criticism was levelled at the Court for its apparent reliance upon "sociological" evidence, specifically for the citation of the work of social scientists. It is worthy of noting that in fact there are very strong parallels between the *Brown* and *Plessy* opinions. Recall the argument of the *Plessy* opinion that there was no badge of inequality implied by segregation, and, by inference, that no one was therefore disadvantaged by it. The opinion offered no justification for this proposition. The *Brown* opinion ran along the same ground, but arrived at a contrary conclusion, and offered some reasonably persuasive evidence to support its view. Such evidence was not unknown to Supreme Court opinions; the use of empirical evidence dealing, for example, with the effects of working conditions upon employees had characterized the so-called "Brandeis brief" used in economic regulation cases.[35]

Two major objections might be offered to the Court's use of such evidence. First, that the state of the social sciences was such that crucial social, legal and political decisions should not rest upon the results of what are only pseudo-sciences.[36] Second, that the Court opened itself up to unnecessary criticism by citing such evidence because the effects of racial discrimination upon black children were already well known and recounting it was thus in a sense gratuitous. Both of these criticisms suggest that, strategically, the Court might have been wiser to follow the *Plessy* approach: simply to state as absolute truth what was in fact

[35]See Clement E. Vose, "The National Consumers' League and the Brandeis Brief," *Midwest Journal of Political Science*, 1 (1957), pp. 267-290

[36]As Edmund Cahn argued: "I would not have the constitutional rights of Negroes—or of other Americans—rest on any such flimsy foundation as some of the scientific demonstrations in these records. . . . Since the behavioral sciences are so very young, imprecise, and changeful, their findings have an uncertain expectancy of life. Today's sanguine asseveration may be cancelled by tomorrow's new revelation—or new technical fad." "Jurisprudence," *New York University Law Review*, 30 (1955), pp. 150-169, 157-158, 167.

empirical proposition, without bothering to adduce any evidence. Thus, the Court could well have simply eliminated the footnote and stated the proposition alone.

At this point, we have no way of knowing why the Warren opinion chose to cite the empirical research. Perhaps, as some have argued, the citation, which was indeed in a footnote, was simply thrown in as a kind of fillip and the members of the Court misjudged the reaction that it would generate.

Another explanation is possible, though it too remains in the realm of speculation. Many of those critical of the reliance on "sociological" evidence[37] also urged that the Court should not have referred at all to the effect of segregation upon the education of students. Rather, the Court should have simply laid down the abstract principle that the use of a race as a criterion in classifying citizens was itself simply impermissible by virtue of the Fourteenth Amendment. This, some have argued, would have been a more "principled" decision, one more befitting a court of law.

There are two possible objections to this last approach, and perhaps some members of the Court had them in mind. First, since the government cannot be prevented from classifying citizens on all criteria, justifications must be offered for saying that some criteria are impermissible bases for classification. If race is to fall within this class, then a reason must be given for this choice. In fact, evidence about

---

[37]Such critics included both those sympathetic to the outcome of the *Brown* decision—elimination of racial discrimination—and those who disliked both the outcome and the reasoning. Among critics of the reasoning of the opinion who were sympathetic toward integration, see Cahn, *ibid.*; Herbert Wechsler, "Towards Neutral Principles of Constitutional Law," *Harvard Law Review*, 73 (1959), pp. 1-35, especially 26-34. For defenses of the Supreme Court, see Louis H. Pollak, "Racial Discrimination and Judicial Integrity: A Reply to Professor Wechsler," *Pennsylvania Law Review*, 108 (1959), pp. 1-34; and Charles L. Black, "The Lawfulness of the Segregation Decisions," *Yale Law Journal*, 69 (1960), pp. 421-430. For a criticism both of the reasoning of the Brown opinion and of the outcome, see Carleton Putnam, *Race and Reality* Washington, D.C.: Public Affairs Press, 1967).

deleterious effects of racial classification would seem a quite reasonable way to justify its elimination. The alternative to offering such evidence—simply stating that using the criterion of race is impermissible—is perhaps appealing, but possibly somewhat less "principled" than citing some justification.

A second justification might be suggested for the somewhat narrow holding of *Brown*. Some members of the Court might have predicted (as indeed has occurred) that the elimination of racial discrimination might require various compensatory steps (e.g., benevolent quotas in education, housing, or employment) that involved the use of race as a classification. To state as a principle that race simply could not be used at all would have made such compensatory programs more difficult. By focussing upon the deleterious effects of the invidious use certain racial classifications rather than upon all use of race, the Court left open the option of using race as a classification in governmental activities designed to alleviate the effects of previous discrimination. Thus, *Brown* might be read as standing for the proposition that race cannot be used as a classification in placing burdens upon black citizens, though it may, in some circumstances, be used as a classification in distributing benefits through compensatory programs designed to alleviate previous discrimination.

The *Brown* opinion provoked criticism from those sympathetic to the result it reached and provided quasi-respectable grounds for criticism by those who opposed the outcome. The *Brown* opinion seems to suggest something also discussed in connection with *Plessy*: The very concept of "equality" is not an unchanging and principled value, but is something that changes over time as the values and perceptions of the populace change. What is "equal" treatment in one era may be the rankest inequality and insult in another. The *Brown* opinion was honest in its recognition and treatment of this fact. However, in law as in politics, honesty may not always be the best policy if one wishes his decisions to be met with acquiescence.

The pace of school integration

The *Brown* decision was probably the most important made by the Court during the twentieth century. In terms of the growth of the civil rights movement, it was crucial; in terms of the integration of southern schools, the second *Brown* decision was almost equally important. In *Brown* I, the Court ordered reargument on the question of the nature of the decree that ought to be issued—what instructions it should offer lower federal and state courts in handling further suits dealing with racial discrimination. At least three choices were available to the Court. The first would be the traditional response to a finding that a practice violated the constitutional rights of citizens: an order to stop immediately the offending practice in the instant case and, by implication, in future similar cases. This, for example, was to be the pattern followed in the later reapportionment and school prayer cases. A second alternative might have been to set a future time limit (e.g., five years from the current time) and indicate to lower courts that they should not accept plans that would produce anything less than full integration by that date. Such an alternative would have the advantage of recognizing the complexity of school reorganization and the intensity of feeling that implementation would involve. It would perhaps have had the disadvantage of insuring that recalcitrant districts would make no move to integrate until the time limit was about to expire. The third alternative was to turn the pace of integration over to the lower courts, ordering neither immediate compliance nor compliance by a specified date, but leaving in the hands of lower courts the pace that integration was to take in different areas.

The Court chose the last alternative. The *Brown* II[38] opinion recognized the complexity of the process of integration and the fact that school districts differed in their characteristics and ability to comply quickly with integration orders:

[38]*Brown* v. *Board of Education of Topeka*, 349 U.S. 294 (1955).

... the [lower] courts may consider problems related to administration, arising from the physical condition of the school plant, the school transportation system, personnel, revision of school districts and attendance areas into compact units to achieve a system of determining admission to the public schools on a nonracial basis.[39]

The Court ended its opinion, remanding the original five desegration cases decided in *Brown* I to the lower courts, with the injunction to "enter such orders and decrees consistent with this opinion as are necessary and proper to admit to public schools on a racially nondiscriminatory basis with all deliberate speed the parties to these cases."[40]

Thus, the Court turned desegregation over to lower courts. Its abdication was underscored by the fact that the Court rarely spoke out on school segregation cases in subsequent years. It did issue an opinion in the 1958 Little Rock Case,[41] denying a request for further delay and indicating that opposition in the community was not sufficient justification for failing to implement an integration plan. Beginning in 1963, the Court began to speak more often on the need for a speed-up in the pace of integration, and eventually, in 1969,[42] the Court abandoned the doctrine of all deliberate speed and stated that all dual school systems must be eliminated immediately. But, the Court's general hands-off policy resulted in a proliferation of evasive schemes—pupil placement schemes, transfer plans, school-closings, etc.— which succeeded in delaying integration substantially. For example, in 1964, ten years after the *Brown* I opinion, 2.14 percent of black children in the eleven southern states were in schools with whites.[43]

[39] 349 U.S. 300-301.

[40] 349 U.S. 301.

[41] *Cooper* v. *Aaron*, 358 U.S. 1 (1958).

[42] *Alexander* v. *Holmes County Board of Education*, 396 U.S. 19 (1969).

[43] See *A Statistical Summary, State by State, of School Segration and Desegration* (Nashville: Southern Education Reporting Service, 1964), p. 2.

What had happened? The Supreme Court—the highest court in the land—had held that school segregation violated the Constitution, but the practice continued almost completely unabated. In part, as suggested above, the reason could be traced to the Court itself, for it hadn't exerted itself very greatly to insure that its policy was followed. But the experience shows also the importance of the context in which doctrine is implemented. Decisions of the Court are not self-executing: If they are to be followed they depend upon compliant activities of others. For a policy like integration of the public schools, the number of individuals who must comply was enormous and included lower court judges, school officials, community leaders, state government officials, parents. In addition, effective compliance would have been greatly aided by supportive behavior on the part of other federal government institutions, including the President and the Congress.

Those whose behavior was most directly affected—parents, local officials, and the like—didn't want to integrate. In 1956, for example, a sample of white southerners revealed that only 14 percent approved of school integration; by 1963, this had risen to about 33 percent.[44] Thus, people whose behavior was most directly affected were not initially inclined to obey. Equally important were the lower court judges, for the Supreme Court had placed the burden upon them. Not only did they have the authority to issue orders in desegregation suits arising out of the localities in which they served (which is always true in such a situation), but they had been given a great deal of discretion by the Court. For those judges not sympathetic to integration—and there were many federal judges in this category—the discretion gave them freedom to thwart the intent of the *Brown* I decision. For those who were sympathetic to integration, or to the notion of following the dictates of the Supreme Court, the discretion made them vulnerable to the often intense pressures of the

[44]Sheatsley, *op. cit.*, p. 219.

communities in their jurisdiction. These judges were, after all, members of their communities, subject to the social pressures that all of us are, desiring to be liked and respected as we all are. Life tenure eliminated the immediate sanction of removal from office if they made unpopular decisions; it did not insulate them from the social and political forces that could make life unpleasant if integration was forced. These pressures were often effective, for various forms of evasive schemes were accepted by lower federal courts. In a fascinating account of the activities of the lower federal court judges in school integration cases, Jack Peltason observed in 1961:

What the district judges need—and what most of them want—is not the responsibility for making choices, but rigid mandates that compel them to act. . . . It was, and is, politically unrealistic to think that a southern judge could, or would, cut through the Supreme Court's vague instructions to initiate action hostile to segregation. . . . What is needed is a hierarchy of scapegoats. . . . The Supreme Court is in a better position than the district judge to "take the heat." It has a national constituency; it can withstand locally generated pressures. . . . All policy-makers in a free society are the focus of contending pressures. Judges are no exception. The judiciary is subject to competing claims in a somewhat different fashion from, say, the legislature; nevertheless the difference is one of degree and not of kind. And just as the laws enacted by the legislature reflect the dominance of certain values in the community, so do the decisions of judges. It is so today; it has always been so.[45]

Peltason's argument suggests that the *Brown* II opinion was a mistake, that a more forceful attitude toward desegregation—a stronger order, more frequent opinions—would have produced a much quicker pace. Some support for this argument can be found in the fact that some communities moved toward compliance in the interim between *Brown* I

[45]Jack Peltason, *Fifty-Eight Lonely Men* (New York: Harcourt Brace Jovanovich, 1961), pp. 245-247.

and *Brown* II, slowing or stopping after the Court made it clear that it was not going to demand speedy compliance. Perhaps the majority of the Court[46] simply didn't think a fast pace was wise, but felt instead that the social implications of integration were so great that it should proceed slowly; perhaps the Court misjudged the degree of opposition the decision would entail; perhaps they felt they were not in a position to dictate the means by which integration was to take place, as the task was complicated and various means might be used in different districts, and hence consciously wished to turn it over to the lower court judges and local school officials closer to the reality of the individual communities. Perhaps it was all of these.

Moreover, we should recall that the 1957-1960 period was not a happy one for the Court; its freedom of expression decisions had produced an onslaught of attacks upon the Court. Peltason observes:

> As long as it is merely taking on the defenders of segregation, the Court has ample power to withstand the onslaught. But if it takes on too many enemies at the same time, the Court could find its own power curbed. One major battle at a time is good strategy in politics as well as in war.[47]

Thus, whatever the motivation for the 1955 *Brown* II decision, perhaps the Court found shortly that more affirmative and aggressive action in favor of integration was politically infeasible or unwise.

The pace of integration proceeded slowly to say the least,

---

[46]As in the discussion of the possible reasons for the *Brown I* opinion, there is a difficulty here in anthropomorphizing the Court—and treating it as though it is an individual with intentions. It is rather an institution—made up of nine individuals—and bargaining among them and compromise are crucial aspects of their decision-making process. Hence, to speak as though the Court or a majority of the Court had a single intention is to simplify, and perhaps oversimplify.

[47]Peltason, *op. cit.*, 246.

illustrating once more that there is more to civil rights and liberties than court doctrine, that the political context in which the doctrine exists is crucial to understanding which rights and liberties our citizens enjoy and which they do not.

Other forms of racial discrimination

We shall return to school integration shortly. Suffice it to say that for the first ten years after *Brown* I the Court was not particularly active in the area of school desegregation, and that the pace of such integration lagged badly. The Court showed much less reticence in dealing with segregation in other public places. A brief laundry list of the types of segregation found unconstitutional suggests the breadth of the Court's work. Segregation was outlawed in public golf courses,[48] interstate busses,[49] airports,[50] public parks,[51] and courtrooms.[52] In none of these areas did the Court utilize the all-deliberate-speed formula; rather, it simply held such discrimination in violation of the Constitution and told lower courts to offer immediate relief.

As discussed previously in some detail, the late 1950s and early 1960s saw a great deal of litigation before the Court dealing with the direct-action tactics of the civil rights movement and with attacks upon interest groups working for racial equality. One of the major tactics used by civil rights advocates was the sit-in, the occupation of private accommodations that refused to serve blacks. The first publicized sit-in took place at a lunch-counter in Greensboro, North Carolina on February 1, 1960. The movement spread quickly, and by the end of 1961, it has been estimated that 70,000

---

[48]*Holmes* v. *Atlanta*, 350 U.S. 879 (1955).

[49]*Boynton* v. *Virginia*, 364 U.S. 454 (1960).

[50]*Turner* v. *Memphis*, 369 U.S. 762 (1962).

[51]*Watson* v. *Memphis*, 373 U.S. 526 (1963).

[52]*Johnson* v. *Virginia*, 373 U.S. 61 (1963).

individuals engaged in sit-ins and that about 3600 were arrested.[53]

The arrests in the sit-ins cases typically involved charges of trespass, breach of peace, loitering, failing to obey an officer, etc. These cases led to a great deal of litigation, some of which reached the Supreme Court. The goals of the sit-in demonstrators were mixed and covered the range of testing the constitutionality of segregation laws; placing direct economic and moral pressure upon those practicing segregation; and drawing national attention to the practice of racial discrimination, thereby rousing the conscience of the nation in opposition to such discrimination.

The sit-in cases raised a variety of constitutional issues, some of which involved rather traditional concepts, some of which were highly innovative. Three types of doctrinal arguments could typically be used to overturn a sit-in conviction. First, if state action in favor of discrimination (e.g., a statute requiring segregation) existed, then the traditional application of the Equal Protection Clause could be used to overturn the conviction. A somewhat broader argument suggested that generally unexceptionable and valid state laws—like those against trespass upon private property—could not be constitutionally applied to enforce private racial discrimination. This was an extension of the doctrine set forth in *Shelley* v. *Kraemer*, the restrictive covenant case. Finally, some lawyers urged the unconstitutionality of segregated public accommodations in the absence of overt state action. Under this view, either the somewhat tenuous connection of the state in the form of licensing of public establishments, or the very fact that public accommodations held themselves out as open to the public, rendered them subject to the application of the Equal Protection Clause.

In addition to these constitutional arguments, the typical sit-in case involved technical issues as well—for example the

[53]Report of the Southern Regional Council, "The Student Protest Movement: A Recapitulation," No. 21, 1961.

question of the sufficiency of evidence to establish an offense like breach of peace, the possibility of vagueness in such statutes, and the like.

The Supreme Court proved highly favorable to the sit-in demonstrators, but tended to decide their cases on rather narrow grounds. This approach was supported by the Solicitor General, who often submitted *amicus curiae* briefs urging reversal on narrow grounds. Most of the cases were decided on the basis that state action supported discrimination, but the Court often had to reach rather far to find evidence of this. For example, they found the requisite state action necessary to overturn convictions in statements by local officials apparently urging establishments to practice discrimination[54]; the existence of state toilet regulations requiring separate washrooms for white and black employees[55]; the fact that a special policeman making an arrest in an amusement park was also a deputy sheriff.[56] After the passage of the public accommodations section of the Civil Rights Act of 1964, the Court held that all prosecutions of demonstrations not completed and appealed were abated by the passage of the act.[57]

Thus, the major thrust of the sit-in movement, the integration of public accommodations, met with eventual doctrinal success in the legislative rather than the legal arena. Its proponents had been pursuing a mixed strategy—lobbying the courts, the legislature, the national conscience—and eventually they did win at the doctrinal level. Their failure to win in the legal arena is probably partly attributable to the Court's unwillingness to act on an issue that was before the

[54]*Lombard* v. *Louisiana*, 373 U.S. 267 (1963).

[55]*Robinson* v. *Florida*, 378 U.S. 153 (1964).

[56]*Griffin* v. *Maryland*, 378 U.S. 130 (1964).

[57]*Hamm* v. *Rock Hill*, 379 U.S. 306 (1964). For a review of the Court's handling of the sit-in cases, see Monrad G. Paulson, "The Sit-in Cases of 1964: 'But Answer There Came None!' " Philip B. Kurland, ed., *Supreme Court Review* (Chicago: University of Chicago Press, 1964), pp. 137-170.

legislature as well. The Supreme Court had been asked to promulgate, as a matter of constitutional right, the policy that was established by statute in the Civil Rights Act of 1964. They refused to do so, with the support of the Solicitor General and the Administration, and though they reversed convictions, they did so on relatively narrow and well-established doctrinal grounds. The sit-in cases thus illustrate the interplay between the development of doctrine through litigation and legislation, for they suggest that change can come from either arena, and that activity in one is related to what happens in the other. Had the public accommodations law failed of passage, perhaps the Court would have stepped in. In *Bell* v. *Maryland*[58] at least three justices appeared willing to hold that discrimination in the absence of overt state action was violative of the Equal Protection Clause. The constitutionality of the public accommodations law was considered and upheld with unusual dispatch by the Court on the basis of Congress's power to regulate interstate commerce.[59]

The attack on voting discrimination also proceeded in both the legal and legislative arenas. The Civil Rights Act of 1965 established the power of the federal government (through the Attorney General) to file suit in behalf of black voters in the South, to suspend literacy tests, to send in federal registrars when the state was demonstrated to be unwilling to register black voters. The Court upheld the validity of these measures[60] and registration of blacks in the South rose dramatically (see Table 7).

Also contributing to the growth of black voting registration was the adoption in 1964 of the Twenty-fourth Amendment forbidding poll taxes in federal elections and a

[58]378 U.S. 226 (1964).

[59]*Heart of Atlanta Motel* v. *United States,* 379 U.S. 241 (1964); *Katzenbach* v. *McClung,* 379 U.S. 294 (1964).

[60]*United States* v. *Mississippi,* 380 U.S. 128 (1965) and *South Carolina* v. *Katzenbach,* 383 U.S. 301 (1966).

Table 7   Registration of voting-age blacks, 1940-1967

Year	Estimated number of voting-age blacks registered	Estimated percentage of voting-age blacks registered*
1940	250,000	5
1947	595,000	12
1952	1,008,614	20
1956	1,238,038	25
1958	1,266,488	25
1960	1,414,052	28
1964	1,907,279	38
1966	2,306,434	46
1967	2,810,763	57

*In eleven Southern states

Source: Donald Matthews and James Prothro, *Negroes and the New Southern Politics* (New York: Harcourt Brace Jovanovich, 1966) and United States Commission on Civil Rights, *Political Participation* (Washington, D.C.: GPO, 1968).

1966 Supreme Court decision[61] which held that the use of poll taxes as a condition for voting in state elections violated the Equal Protection Clause.

School integration, 1963-1970

In addition to dealing with the sit-in movement and the issue of discrimination in public accommodations and voting, the Court began in the mid-1960s to speak once more to the question of segregation in the schools. As suggested before, between *Brown* II in 1955 and 1963, the Court had generally left the pace of school desegregation up to the lower courts; and it had been slow indeed. In 1963, the Court began to speak out again on the issue of desegregation. In *Goss* v. *Board of Education*[62] the Court struck down a transfer plan permitting students to move out of schools to which they had been assigned under a Memphis desegregation plan if their new school had previously served a majority of the

[61]*Harper* v. *Virginia Board of Education*, 383 U.S. 663 (1966).

[62]373 U.S. 683 (1963).

opposite race—essentially a scheme whereby whites assigned to black schools could avoid attendance at such schools. The following year, the Court held that the closing of public schools in Prince Edward County, Virginia was an unconstitutional method of evading desegregation and indicated its impatience with the pace of desegregation.[63] In *Bradley* v. *School Board*[64] the Court observed that "delays in desegregating school systems are no longer tolerable."[65]

Thus, the Court began to indicate that it was concerned about the pace of integration and that it would begin to measure various proposed integration schemes in terms of how effectively they produced tangible degrees of integration.

Legislation aimed at promoting desegregation was also passed during the mid-1960s. The 1964 Civil Rights Act, in addition to its public accommodations section, included a provision authorizing the federal government to issue guidelines insuring that federal funds would not be utilized in discriminatory programs. Agencies were authorized to cut off funds to state and local institutions continuing to discriminate. HEW issued school integration guidelines in 1965 which stipulated that localities must either submit a form indicating compliance, be under a final court order requiring the elimination of the dual school system, or submit a plan indicating a program for voluntary desegregation. The last category was the most significant, for it permitted the so-called "freedom of choice" plans. Under this scheme, each student was given the opportunity to choose which school he wished to attend. The difficulty with such plans, from the standpoint of producing substantial integration, was that they required affirmative action on the part of blacks. They could choose to transfer to integrated schools, but in the

[63]*Griffin* v. *School Board of Prince Edward County*, 377 U.S. 218 (1964).

[64]382 U.S. 103 (1965).

[65]382 U.S. 105 (1965).

absence of such action, blacks would remain in their old segregated schools.

The Supreme Court considered the freedom-of-choice concept in 1968. In this case, a Virginia school district had instituted a freedom-of-choice plan to comply with the HEW guidelines, but it had produced almost no actual integration. The Court measured the plan against its result, and indicated to the lower courts that they should do likewise:

> The obligation of the district courts, as it always has been, is to assess the effectiveness of a proposed plan in achieving desegregation. We do not hold that 'freedom of choice' can have no place in [an integration] plan. We do not hold that a 'freedom of choice' plan might of itself be unconstitutional, although that argument has been urged upon us. Rather, all we decide today is that in desegregating a dual system a plan utilizing 'freedom of choice' is not an end in itself. . . . The New Kent School Board's 'freedom of choice' plan cannot be accepted as a sufficient step to 'effectuate a transition' to a unitary system. . . . Rather than further the dismantling of the dual system, the plan has operated simply to burden children and their parents with a responsibility which Brown II placed squarely on the School Board.[66]

Thus, the Court again indicated its impatience and concern not only with the removal of racial classifications in the abstract but with the actual results that integration plans would produce.

The Court finally formally announced the demise of the all-deliberate-speed doctrine in 1969. In a brief, unanimous *per curiam* opinion, the Court ordered the Fifth Circuit Court to require the immediate abolishment of dual school systems in 33 Mississippi school districts. The federal government had argued, with the school districts, that more time was needed, but the Supreme Court refused to agree:

[66]*Green* v. *School Board of New Kent County*, 391 U.S. 430 (1968) at 441-442.

... The Court of Appeals should have denied all motions for additional time because continued operation of segregated schools under a standard of allowing 'all deliberate speed' is no longer constitutionally permissible. Under explicit holdings of this Court the obligation of every school district is to terminate dual school systems at once and to operate now and hereafter only unitary school systems.[67]

Fourteen years after its promulgation, all deliberate speed was no longer a viable constitutional doctrine. Its life and gradual demise had permitted extensive noncompliance with the *Brown* I holding that school segregation was not permissible under the Constitution.

Thus, as the decade of the 1960s came to a close, *de jure* desegregation of Southern schools was moving toward a reality. A combination of court action and legislation produced doctrine that provided a somewhat effective mechanism for achieving compliance. And there was some evidence that compliance produced increased attitudinal change. One observer has suggested:

... a solid majority of Southern whites (58 percent), in those few places where there has been (as of 1963) considerable integration of schools, declared that they approved of school integration. In Southern communities which had accepted only some token desegregation, 38 percent approved; while in the hard-core segregationist communities, only 28 percent were in favor of integration. Though the sample sizes are small, particularly in the desegregated areas, the correlation is clear: Where integration exists in the South, more whites support it.

It is dangerous to try to unravel cause and effect from mere statistical correlation, yet a close analysis of the data indicates that official action to desegregate Southern schools did not wait for

[67]*Alexander* v. *Holmes County Board of Education*, 396 U.S. 19 (1969) at 20.

majority opinion to demand it, but rather preceded a change in community attitudes.[68]

This argument, though admittedly somewhat tentative, suggests a more hopeful future. The use of somewhat coercive measures to induce Southern schools to desegregate may produce a climate in which integration will gradually encounter less intense or widespread opposition. As of this writing (June 1971), the equivocal attitude of the Nixon Administration toward further vigorous enforcement of integration makes the future somewhat hard to predict. However, the experience in the South suggests that the sociological argument of *Plessy*, which denied that "social prejudices may be overcome by legislation," was probably false.

De facto segregation

If Southern *de jure* segregation was on the way to extinction as a result of Court decisions and legislation by the end of the 1960s, the question of *de facto* segregation in the North was very much up in the air. Even at the doctrinal level, much less the behavioral, the question of whether localities had an obligation to alleviate racial segregation resulting from residential patterns was not clear. The Supreme Court had simply refused to hear cases on the question. Conflicting decisions had emerged from the lower courts, but the Supreme Court refused to review them. Does the Constitution forbid, require, or say nothing about action by school boards to insure integration in localities where a neighborhood school system produces segregated schools? The thrust of some of the Southern school cases seemed to suggest an affirmative duty on the part of school districts to insure that integration occurs.[69] On the other hand, *Brown* I might be

---

[68]Sheatsley, *op. cit.*, 221.

[69]E.g., *United States* v. *Jefferson County Board of Education*, 385 F. 2d. 380 (5th Cir., 1967).

read to indicate that racial classifications are impermissible, whether to promote segregation or integration.

In dealing with Northern *de facto* segregation, lower courts have taken contradictory positions. Some have held that *de facto* segregation is not in violation of the Equal Protection Clause[70]; some have suggested a positive duty to alleviate *de facto* segregation[71]; other decisions have, without indicating a positive duty to alleviate *de facto* segregation, validated schemes that involve racial classifications as a means of producing integration.[72] The Supreme Court has ducked the issue, refusing to review these conflicting statements by lower courts.[73]

As suggested in the previous decision of the *Brown* I opinion, the argument advanced in the original desegregation opinion would appear to leave the door open to the position that alleviation of *de facto* segregation is a constitutional requirement. If *Brown* I was based on the invidious effects of segregated education upon learning, then the difference between *de facto* and *de jure* discrimination may disappear. As one proponent of this view has suggested:

> As for education, the necessary import of *Brown* and its predecessors is that whatever the cause of the separation, Negroes in a dominant white culture cannot obtain equal educational opportunities within the mandate of the Constitution in an educational environment separate and apart from white students. . . . The teaching of *Brown* and its predecessors is that the central issue is whether

[70]*Bell* v. *School Board of the City of Gary*, 324 F. 2d 209 (7th Cir., 1963).

[71]E.g., *Blocker* v. *Board of Education*, 226 F. Supp. 208 (1964).

[72]E.g., *Balaban* v. *Rubin*, 14 N.Y. 2d 193 (1964).

[73]In a recent decision, the Court held that busing was a permissible and perhaps in certain circumstances a constitutionally required remedy in eliminating segration in school systems that previously practiced *de jure* segregation. The implication of this opinion for *de facto* segregation is as yet unclear. See *Swann* v. *Charlotte-Mecklenburg Board of Education*, 402 U.S. 1 (1971).

the Constitution's warrant of equal education opportunity has been met, and the critical constitutional fact is that segregated education, however it occurs, denies Negroes what the Constitution is said to secure .... it is singularly immaterial whether a denial of equal educational opportunities is characterized as 'de jure' or as 'de facto.' Still remaining is the fact of segregation with all of its resulting harm and inequality.[74]

The alternative argument, that *Brown* I stands simply for the proposition that the state may not constitutionally require segregation but has no duty to act when it results accidentally from housing patterns, has also been advanced, and, as suggested above, accepted by some courts.

Why has the Supreme Court failed to speak? One of the situations in which the Court nominally is supposed to exercise its control over its docket and accept cases for review[75] is a conflict in lower court opinions. The issue of *de facto* segregation is a prime example of this situation, yet the Court has simply refused to act. One can only speculate, but the political climate seems a fertile field to look for an explanation. Busing, pairing, and similar schemes for insuring racial balance have not been popular in the North. The Congress, in passing the Civil Rights Act of 1964, made clear that it opposed attempts to alleviate *de facto* segregation by inserting the following provision at the beginning:

'Desegregation' means the assignment of students to public schools and within such schools without regard to their race, color, religion,

---

[74]Robert L. Carter, "Equal Educational Opportunity for Negroes— Abstraction or Reality," in John H. McCord, ed., *With All Deliberate Speed* (Urbana: University of Illinois Press, 1969), pp. 56-84 at 62, 65, 67.

[75]The Supreme Court has extensive discretion over the docket of cases it chooses to decide. Its Rule 19 specifies that one circumstance in which the Court is likely to agree to hear a case includes: "When a court of appeals has rendered a decision in conflict with the decision of another court of appeals on the same matter." 398 U.S. 1030 (1970).

or national origin, but 'desegregation' shall not mean the assignment of students to public schools in order to overcome racial imbalance.[76]

In addition to a general hostility on the part of Congress and many leading white northern political figures, the position of black community leaders has been somewhat ambivalent. The growth of the call for quality education rather than integration—for a greater share of resources in the ghetto schools rather than busing of children into and out of the often delapidated facilities—and the growing call for community control of schools via decentralization indicates that many of the most vocal blacks in the North are not so much interested in integration as they are in improving and changing the facilities within their own communities.

The preceding discussion suggests one reason for the Court's failure to speak on the issue of *de facto* segregation: the attitudinal and behavioral dimensions. In addition, there are doctrinal difficulties. If the Court is to hold that *de facto* segregation violates the Equal Protection Clause, what test can it develop to determine how much segregation is "too much"? In addition, the simple fact that the jurisdictions for school districts in many cities are fixed by the states makes remedial action difficult. In many large cities, school jurisdictions fall along the same lines as units of government. Many such units contain large numbers of blacks. Real integration is often simply not possible without changing the boundaries of the school district. Finding a doctrinal tool that will require either changing district boundary lines (e.g., placing a suburban and urban area in same district) or busing across local governmental units is problematical. Hence, even at the doctrinal level, there are problems in developing approaches to the aleviation of *de facto* segregation.

Thus, perhaps one reason the Court has not spoken out on this issue is that there is no clear indication of what the

[76]Public Law 88-352, Title IV, section 401.

"best" policy is (in terms of doctrine or the preferences of affected individuals). This issue is highly divisive; the Court has, during the 1960s, been fighting battles on many fronts—Southern school segregation, criminal justice, obscenity, school prayer—and adding a new front was perhaps viewed as bad tactics. Moreover, as indicated above, the position of those allegedly being injured by *de facto* desegregation—the blacks—has been somewhat unclear, since many of the most vocal voices of the black community appear indifferent if not hostile to programs for integration. Thus, the Court has remained mute, perhaps waiting for a more clear concensus to emerge as to what is a viable approach to the problem of *de facto* segregation.

Summary

In a vast area of relations between individuals, public and private, the Court moved to eliminate discrimination on the basis of race, in an attempt to insure that blacks were treated the same as whites. The path was not a smooth one; Court decisions are not self-executing, and both the changes in doctrine itself and their implementation depended greatly upon the political context in which the decisions were made. The product of this litigation and the decisions of the Court has not, of course, been the elimination of discrimination or racism in our society. Such an accomplishment is beyond the reach of the Court; but the interaction of the Court and its doctrine with changes in the values and perceptions of people in the system has removed some of the most overt forms of institutional discrimination. Perhaps the elimination of such formal barriers will assist in further attitudinal changes among the people in the society. Though one cannot say that the Court has eliminated racial discrimination, its participation has been crucial in diminishing it.

DISCRIMINATION ON THE BASIS OF ECONOMIC STATUS

The thrust of the racial discrimination cases was the opportunity to participate in social and political life, to share equally in the benefits offered by government activity and not be denied them on the basis of race. Another area in which inequality has long characterized our society is inequality of wealth, or material resources. Some are richer than others. Can the government discriminate against citizens on the basis of their economic status? As in the case of compensatory programs to overcome past discrimination against blacks, this question raises the conflict between the two notions of equality discussed at the outset of this chapter—equality of opportunity to some extent presumes a resulting substantive inequality. That is, if people have differing motivations and talents, one would expect that some would capture a greater share of the resources in the society than others. Thus, the notion of equality of opportunity implies that the government should not discriminate on the basis of economic status and everyone should have an equal chance to gain benefits in the society; however, this approach may result in substantial economic inequality.

On the other hand, a notion of substantive equality implies a good deal of government intervention. Substantive equality suggests, for example, that the government should take from the rich in order to give to the poor. Thus, under an income redistribution model of substantive equality, economic status is an essential ground for classifying citizens and distributing the benefits of government. To some extent, we recognize this model and have incorporated it into our doctrine: The progressive income tax, the concept of welfare benefits and unemployment compensation programs are examples of the use by government of economic status as a criterion for distributing benefits.

What of the other side of the coin, though? Granted that we are committed in a limited way to the propriety of the use of economic status as a criterion for distributing benefits, what of the use of economic status as a criterion for distributing burdens? Can the poor be made to bear heavier burdens than the rich? The implication of the above discussion is that they cannot, for if we are committed to producing some degree of substantive equality by redistribution of income, then it would not make much sense to practice discrimination against the poor at the same time.

But such discrimination has been consistently practiced in our society, perhaps reflecting a general confusion over the concept of equality. As Herbert McClosky has observed:

> In short, both the public and its leaders are uncertain and ambivalent about equality. The reason, I suspect, lies partly in the fact that the egalitarian aspects of democratic theory have been less adequately thought through than other aspects, and partly in the complications connected with the concept itself. . . . Another complication lies in the diffuse and variegated nature of the concept, a result of its application to at least four separate domains: political (e.g., universal suffrage), legal (e.g., equality before the law), economic (e.g., equal distribution of property or opportunity), and moral (e.g., every man's right to be treated as an end and not as a means).[77]

Such complications and confusions have been reflected in the doctrine developed surrounding the concept of equality. Thus, though we tax the rich (at least in theory) more heavily than the poor and provide services to the poor (e.g., welfare) not available to the rich, we have accepted practices in the administration of justice (e.g., bail, the right to counsel), in the administration of certain governmental programs (e.g., the welfare system itself), and in the right to vote that themselves disadvantage the poor in relation to the affluent.

Recent years have seen doctrinal movement toward reducing some of these inequalities and contradictions, and this section discusses some of these developments.

Criminal justice

When a man becomes enmeshed in the machinery of the criminal justice system, should his chance to emerge successfully—to exonerate himself, to receive the minimum sen-

---

[77]McCloskey, *op. cit.*, p. 368.

tence, etc.—depend in part upon his wealth? In the abstract, of course, none of us would reply that the answer ought to be yes. Yet there can be little doubt that this is in fact the reality of the American criminal justice system. Recent developments have attempted to remove some of the infirmities attached to being poor, though they have not yet resulted in removing them completely.

The right to counsel

The Sixth Amendment to the Constitution provides, among other things, that persons accused of crime have the right to be represented by counsel. Since our criminal justice system putatively operates under the adversary model, and the state is generally represented by an attorney, this right to representation possessed by the defendant seems eminently fair. But suppose the defendant is poor and cannot afford a lawyer? Does the state have the obligation to provide him with a lawyer? Again, logic would suggest that equality—in this case, not placing the poor man at a disadvantage relative to the rich man who can retain his own attorney—would suggest that the answer is yes. The crucial question facing the Court during this century has been that of whether this right to counsel extends to state criminal proceedings.[78]

The first question was whether the Due Process Clause of the Fourteenth Amendment applied the right to counsel to state proceedings. The Court first spoke on this issue in the celebrated Scottsboro case of 1932.[79] In this case, a group of young blacks had been accused of raping two white women, and were tried in an atmosphere of great public outrage and hostility without effective representation of counsel. The

[78] For useful discussions of the right to counsel, see David Fellman, *The Defendant's Rights* (New York: Holt, Rinehart & Winston, 1958), ch. 7; William Beaney, *The Right to Counsel in American Courts* (Ann Arbor: University of Michigan Press, 1955); Lee Silverstein, *Defense of the Poor in Criminal Cases in American State Courts* (Chicago: American Bar Foundation, 1965).

[79] *Powell* v. *Alabama*, 287 U.S. 45 (1932).

Supreme Court held that under certain circumstances the Due Process Clause did require the state to provide counsel. The crucial circumstances in *Powell* v. *Alabama* were the youth, illiteracy and inexperience of the defendants and the fact that they were charged with a capital crime.

However, in the next landmark case the Court made it clear that the Due Process Clause did not require the provision of counsel to all indigent defendants. In *Betts* v. *Brady*,[80] the defendant was a more mature individual, not charged with a capital crime, who was able to understand the charge and apparently able to conduct his own defense in a fairly effective manner. The Court concluded that the Due Process Clause did not require appointment to Betts. The issue in such cases, the Court reasoned, involved "an appraisal of the totality of facts in a given case."[81] This gave rise to the so-called "special circumstances" rule in right-to-counsel cases: The state was not required to provide free counsel to an indigent defendant in noncapital cases unless there were special circumstances—e.g., youth, immaturity, lack of education or intelligence, inexperience, etc.—that made it inherently unfair for him to be tried without counsel. The general reasoning at this point dwelt not upon the notion of equality, the difference between the rich and the poor, but rather upon an examination of the "fairness" of the proceedings. Justice Black dissented from the *Betts* decision, and his view was eventually to be vindicated.

During the 1950s, the Court began to indicate increasing concern for the indigent defendant. Though still deciding the cases in rhetoric that stressed attention to the degree of prejudicial error that lack of counsel produced, the Court appeared to be paying less attention to weighing the importance of the error in determining whether due process was denied.[82]

[80]316 U.S. 455 (1942).

[81]316 U.S. 462.

[82]For example, *Cash* v. *Culver*, 350 U.S. 633 (1959); *Hudson* v. *North Carolina*, 363 U.S. 697 (1960).

Finally, in 1963, the Court abandoned the special circumstances test and adopted a broad rule requiring the provision of counsel to all indigent defendants charged with serious crimes in state courts.[83] The majority opinion, written by Justice Black, who had dissented more than twenty years earlier in *Betts*, relied upon the Due Process Clause of the Fourteenth Amendment, but stressed also the inequalities imposed by the lack of attorneys for the poor:

> ... in our adversary system of criminal justice, any person hailed into court, who is too poor to hire a lawyer, cannot be assured a fair trial unless counsel is provided for him ... there are few defendants charged with crime, few indeed, who fail to hire the best lawyers they can get to prepare and present their defenses. That government hires lawyers to prosecute and defendants who have the money hire lawyers to defend are the strongest indications of the widespread belief that lawyers in criminal courts are necessities, not luxuries. ... This noble ideal [of fair trials before impartial tribunals] cannot be realized if the poor man charged with crime has to face his accusers without a lawyer to assist him.[84]

The Court has also moved to grant the right to counsel to indigent defendants at other stages of the proceeding, both before and after trial. The Court ruled that, under certain circumstances, counsel must be provided by the state to indigents before interrogation by police,[85] at the preliminary hearing,[86] at the first appeal from a criminal conviction,[87] and at a line-up.[88]

---

[83]*Gideon* v. *Wainwright,* 372 U.S. 335 (1963). For a fascinating account of this case, see Anthony Lewis, *Gideon's Trumpet* (New York: Random House, 1964).

[84]372 U.S. 344.

[85]*Miranda* v. *Arizona,* 384 U.S. 436 (1966).

[86]*White* v. *Maryland,* 373 U.S. 59 (1963).

[87]*Douglas* v. *California,* 372 U.S. 535 (1963).

[88]*United States* v. *Wade,* 388 U.S. 218 (1967).

The provision of counsel to indigent defendants raises severe practical problems. For example, attempts to provide counsel at the police interrogation stage have proved somewhat difficult to implement.[89] In addition, devising programs to provide effective counsel at formal proceedings is not simple: If systems of assigned counsel[90] are used, then adequate compensation must be paid if competent attorneys can be induced to take cases. The danger of low fees is that attorneys will not pay much attention to cases for which they are not adequately compensated, or that lower income attorneys will tend to take on a large number of such cases and turn them over quickly (e.g., by pleading guilty, not raising all possible defenses) in order to generate sufficient fees to live on. Many localities have chosen to develop public or quasi-public agencies (e.g., public defender offices) to handle the defense of indigents, but again the problem of case overload tends to plague such programs. Moreover, simply to provide a defendant with counsel is not to give him an adequate defense, or to make him equal to the richer defendant. Effective defense against a criminal prosecution often requires such services as independent investigation and the use of expert witnesses. Unless the state provides them to the indigent defendant, he is not truly in a position of equality with the richer defendant who can afford to pay for such activities out of his own pocket. The question of whether our society is willing or able to provide the resources for such assistance is moot. At this point, though, one can suggest that the movement toward requiring the provision of

[89]For a discussion of difficulties encountered in devising schemes to provide counsel to suspects at the custodial interrogation stage, see Richard J. Medalie, et al., "Custodial Police Interrogation in Our Nation's Capital: The Attempt to Implement Miranda," *Michigan Law Review*, 66, (1968), pp. 1347-1421, especially 1379-1394.

[90]Under assigned counsel systems, attorneys in private practice are assigned by the trial court to defend individual indigents accused of criminal offenses. The major alternative is the establishment of a public or quasi-public agency (e.g., Public Defender office) which supplies counsel to all indigents.

counsel to indigent defendants is a step toward reducing inequality in the treatment of individuals in the criminal justice process.

Bail

Another, even more obvious form of economic discrimination is the system of money bail. The very concept of money bail means that the rich will be more likely to be free during the period between arraignment and trial than the poor. This period can be crucial and it can be long. During this period a defendant can assist in developing evidence in his defense, and, more importantly, is in a position to continue to work and support his family.

There have been few Supreme Court decisions dealing with bail. In 1951, the Court indicated that the only constitutionally permissible function of bail was insuring that a defendant would appear at trial, and indicated that bail set at a "higher figure than an amount reasonably calculated to fulfill this purpose is 'excessive' under the Eighth Amendment."[91] But what constituted such an amount has never been discussed in detail, and it seems probable that other factors—for example, the nature of the offense, the judge's calculation about the dangerousness of the defendant—are also considered by judges in setting a bail amount. The major changes in the bail system have emerged from Congress and from the activities of private organizations, particularly the Vera Institute of Justice.[92] The Vera system involves a relatively speedy fact-finding procedure designed to gather data about characteristics of the defendant that are relevant to the probability of his appearing at trial—e.g., employment history, stability of family life, relatives in the city, extent of

[91]*Stack* v. *Boyle*, 342 U.S. 1 (1951) at 5.

[92]For a discussion of the Vera Foundation project, see Charles E. Ares, et al., "The Manhattan Bail Project—An Interim Report on the Use of Pre-Trial Parole," *New York University Law Review*, 38 (1963), pp. 67-95.

his roots in the community. If the defendant appears to have roots in the community, and hence is judged unlikely to flee, he is released on his own recognizance without requiring money bail (with the exception of certain violent crimes like homicide and some drug offenses). Such systems, which have been adopted in many communities in over half the states are designed to reduce the reliance upon the discriminatory practice of money bail. A similar system was adopted for the federal courts in the Bail Reform Act of 1968.

Appeals costs and fines

Two other forms of economic discrimination practiced in the criminal justice system are worthy of mention. One involves the cost of preparing appeals after conviction. As indicated before, the Court has decided that states are obliged to provide an attorney to indigent defendants at the first appeal stage, which is in most states a matter of right. In 1956, the Court held that an indigent defendant must be provided a copy by the state of the transcript of his trial if such transcript is an essential element in filing an appeal.[93]

In dealing with another issue of discrimination in the administration of criminal justice, the Court has recently begun to restrict the practice of providing defendants the option of paying fines instead of receiving a term in jail.[94]

The upshot of recent litigation and legislation is that some of the most blatant forms of discrimination between rich and poor within the system of criminal justice are being ameliorated. One cannot say that the quality of justice offered the poor is equal that offered the rich. The trend of doctrine is in the direction of this goal, though its realization may by necessity await more radical forms of income redistribution in our society that reduce economic disparities themselves.

[93]*Griffin* v. *Illinois*, 351 U.S. 12 (1956).

[94]*Williams* v. *Illinois*, 399 U.S. 235 (1970); *Tate* v. *Short*, 401 U.S. 395 (1971).

Welfare

The Court also moved against discrimination within the welfare system itself. In cases dealing with the administration of welfare programs, the Court dealt with the so-called "man in the house rule" of many state welfare programs, which reduced or denied benefits to mothers of children eligible for welfare payments if a man lived with the family. In *King* v. *Smith*[95] the Court held that Alabama's "substitute father" provision was invalid, because it was in conflict with HEW regulations. Man-in-the-house rules were often justified on the basis of discouraging promiscuity in sexual relations by withdrawing benefits for which a woman and her children were generally entitled if she lived with a man to whom she was not married. Thus, such rules involved a clear discrimination against the poor, for they penalized conduct for which the rich suffered no similar penalty.

The Court also moved to strike down residency requirements common to welfare programs in the states.[96] Under such regulations, a potential recipient of welfare benefits had to establish a certain period of residence before becoming eligible for benefits. The justifications offered for waiting periods involved both administrative convenience and the need to discourage indigents from leaving states with lower welfare benefits and travelling to those · offering higher benefits. The Court rejected the latter justification, stressing that such an objective was in conflict with the constitutionally protected right of citizens to move about from one state to another, and discriminated against indigents in particular:

> . . . a State may no more try to fence out those indigents who seek higher welfare benefits than it may try to fence out indigents generally. In sum, neither deterrence of indigents from migrating to

[95]392 U.S. 309 (1968). This ruling was reaffirmed in *Lewis* v. *Martin*, 397 U.S. 552 (1970).

[96]Shapiro v. *Thompson*, 394 U.S. 618 (1969).

the State nor limitation of welfare benefits to those regarded as contributing to the State is a constitutionally permissible state objective.[97]

What do the welfare decisions amount to in terms of the concept of equality? First, the very programs themselves are based upon economic discrimination, for they are open only to individuals below certain income standards. They are designed to advance the goal of substantive equality and they utilize economic status as a criterion in distributing governmental benefits. The Supreme Court decisions on welfare programs stand, to some extent, for the proposition that once the government decides to offer a benefit, it cannot condition the enjoyment of such a benefit upon a classification of citizens for which it can demonstrate no compelling interest. Thus, in the man-in-the-house cases, the state was held not to have a sufficiently compelling interest in discouraging sexual promiscuity (and the nexus between this goal and the means chosen to achieve it was somewhat tenuous) to permit it to deny benefits to mothers living with men not their husbands. In the residency case, it was asserted that such benefits could not be denied if such a denial inhibited exercise of a constitutionally protected right. Thus, two tests inform the welfare cases: first, the traditional balancing test seen in the free association cases (e.g., *Barenblatt, Shelton* v. *Tucker*), which asserts that a classification of citizens must be nonarbitrary and related to a valid state objective; second, that if a classification touches directly a constitutionally protected freedom, the state's interest must be compelling:

> Thus, even under traditional equal protection tests a classification of welfare applicants according to whether they have lived in the State for one year would seem irrational and unconstitutional. But, of course, the traditional criteria do not apply in these cases. Since the

[97]394 U.S. 631, 633.

classification here touches on the fundamental right of interstate movement, its constitutionality must be judged by the stricter standard of whether it promotes a *compelling* state interest.[98]

Another welfare case, *Dandridge* v. *Williams*,[99] reinforces this argument, though its import is somewhat unclear. Maryland's administration of the Aid to Families with Dependent Children placed a maximum on the grants available to families. Thus, the size of the grant was computed on the basis of the number of children, but families above a certain size could receive no more than the maximum grant allowable. This was challenged as a violation of the Equal Protection Clause in that it discriminated against citizens merely on the basis of the size of their family. Maryland responded that the discrimination was constitutionally permissible because it was designed to encourage citizens to obtain employment, maintained some kind of balance between those on welfare and those who worked, and encouraged family planning. In a five-to-four decision, the Court held that the program did not violate the Equal Protection Clause. Justice Black wrote the institutional opinion for the Court, and asserted a kind of "reverse preferred position" argument:

> If this were a case involving government action claimed to violate the First Amendment guarantee of free speech, a finding of "overreaching" would be significant and might be crucial. For when otherwise valid governmental sweeps so broadly as to impinge upon activity protected by the First Amendment, its very overbreadth may make it unconstitutional. But . . . here we deal with state regulation in the social and economic field, not affecting freedoms guaranteed by the Bill of Rights. . . . In the area of economics and social welfare, a State does not violate the Equal Protection Clause merely because the classifications made by its laws are imperfect. If the classification

[98] 394 U.S. 638.
[99] 397 U.S. 471 (1970).

has some "reasonable basis," it does not offend the Constitution simply because the classification "is not made with mathematical nicety or because in practice it results in some inequality."[100]

Thus, the *Dandridge* case seems to stand for the proposition that if the state, in distributing benefits such as welfare, administers these programs in such a way as to affect a right protected by the Bill of Rights, it must produce a *compelling* reason for such activity. If the administration of the program does not touch such a right, the state must merely exhibit a *reasonable* relation between the classification and the goal to be achieved. A somewhat open question, though, is what constitutes a constitutionally protected right and, especially, how doctrinal developments dealing with the developing right to privacy may affect the administration of welfare programs.[101]

Summary

These, then are some of the areas of discrimination on the basis of economic status that have been the subject of litigation in recent years. Can we draw from the cases a consistent theme? The basic principle underlying them would appear to be some commitment to the notion that a lack of economic resources should not result in disadvantage in one's dealings with the government. Those lacking resources should not be placed at a disadvantage when enmeshed in the criminal justice process, and those receiving benefits of economic and social aid should not be the subject of unreasonable infringements upon their liberty. Certainly, though, the litigation does not demonstrate a commitment to the principle of substantive equality: There is little in the doctrine thus far developed to suggest that every individual in

[100]397 U.S. 484-485.

[101]See, for example, *Wyman* v. *James*, 400 U.S. 309 (1971) which upheld the requirement of visits by a welfare worker to the homes of recipients of Aid to Families with Dependent Children as a condition for receipt of such aid.

this society has a right to a decent income, place to live, education, job, or other aspects of a pleasant life. In very limited areas, legislation has moved toward these goals. The Court has dealt kindly with such legislation, but it has not developed a great deal of new doctrine in using the Constitution, particularly the Equal Protection Clause, as a source of rights to substantive equality. The Court has demonstrated more initiative in the area of equality of opportunity. In large measure, the fact that the Court has not committed itself to the principle of substantive equality is probably attributable to a lack of commitment on the part of our society as a whole. Because of confusion about the meaning of the concept of equality—and the lack of consensual commitment to either substantive equality or equality of opportunity—it is not surprising that the Court has not attempted to turn the Equal Protection Clause into a warrant for substantial redistribution of resources in the society.

REAPPORTIONMENT

One of the most publicized areas in which the Supreme Court acted in the name of the value of equality was legislative reapportionment. The issue involved the inequality among voters in selecting members of legislatures. The inequality was based not upon race, economic status, religion or other demographic characteristics we commonly assoicate with discrimination but upon place of residence. Extensive changes in living patterns in our society over the past hundred years—from rural areas to cities to suburbs— combined with the retention of old apportionment schemes in federal and state legislative districts produced substantial inequalities in the sizes of such districts. Since most state legislatures were elected from single-member districts, such inequalities in district sizes meant that citizens in large districts were "underrepresented" in relation to citizens living in districts with smaller populations.

Of course, inequality in size of districts has a long history in this country. The Constitution itself condones such inequalities—all states, from the smallest to the largest, have two representatives in the Senate, and hence individuals living in the more populous states are "underrepresented" in the Senate. Seats in the House of Representatives are to be apportioned to the states on the basis of their populations, though the Constitution itself is silent about whether Congressional districts within states must be of equal population. Most state legislatures followed the federal pattern, with one house representing geographical districts (e.g., counties) of unequal population; and the other, districts of putatively equal size.

However, as indicated above, both in the United States House of Representatives and in most of the lower houses of state legislatures, changes in residence patterns, combined with retention of old apportionment schemes, produced substantial malapportionment (i.e., legislative districts of unequal size). Malapportionment tended to maintain itself because the power to reapportion state legislatures (either by statute or by constitutional amendment) lay in the hands of the legislatures themselves. Thus, controlling majorities in legislatures had much to lose and little to gain by reapportioning themselves. This type of stalemate—in which the "democratic" process was closed—was a paradigm of the type in which we might expect the Court to step in and vindicate the rights of those the subject of discrimination. This was, in its way, the model of the situation for which the preferred position test was designed, with the peculiar twist that the oppressed groups constituted not a minority but the majority.

The Court, however, was long reticent about intervening in the affairs of the House of Representatives or of state legislatures. In 1946, the Court was asked to enjoin an election for members of the U.S. House of Representatives from Illinois on the grounds that congressional districts were malapportioned. The state was operating upon an apportionment plan for Congressional districts established in 1901 and Illinois had since seen great population shifts from farm to city to suburb. The Supreme Court upheld a lower court's refusal to enjoin the election.[102] The seven justices who participated in the decision were divided into three blocs, with the decision resting on a four-man majority. Three justices, in an opinion by Frankfurter, held that the issue was not "justiceable"; that is, was not an issue that courts ought to attempt to resolve. Relying on the doctrine of political questions—the notion that there are certain kinds of disputes in which courts ought not to become involved—Frankfurter argued:

> Nothing is clearer than that this controversy concerns matters that bring courts into immediate and active relations with party contests. From the determination of such issues this Court has traditionally held aloof. It is hostile to a democratic system to involve the judiciary in the politics of the people.[103]

Frankfurter's opinion stressed the constitutional provisions that authorized Congress to determine whether its members had been elected properly and were fairly representative:

> To sustain this action would cut very deep into the very being of Congress. Courts ought not to enter this political thicket. The remedy for unfairness in districting is to secure State legislatures that will apportion properly, or to invoke the ample powers of Congress. The Constitution has many commands that are not enforceable by courts because they clearly fall outside the conditions and purposes that circumscribe judicial action.[104]

The Frankfurter view was part of the cloth of judicial modesty and deference to legislatures that informed his

[102]*Colegrove* v. *Green*, 328 U.S. 549 (1946).
[103] 328 U.S. 553-554.
[104] 328 U.S. 556.

judicial philosophy. The anomaly of his view was that the remedy he suggested—recourse to the legislature itself—was by definition difficult, if not impossible, to achieve.

In any event, the principle of the Frankfurter opinion appeared to suggest that the matter of legislative apportionment was one in which courts would not intervene. This principle was somewhat undercut by the fact that only three of the seven justices sitting in *Colegrove* adhered to it. The fourth member of the majority, Justice Rutledge, concurred in the result but on somewhat different grounds. Concluding that the issue was in fact justiceable, Rutledge agreed with the denial of the injunction on the ground that the shortness of time before the election and the possibility of an at-large election for the whole state if the apportionment system was declared unconstitutional made it doubtful that any equitable relief could be obtained in court at the time. Thus, he concurred in the view that the Supreme Court ought to rule on the substantive issue.

Despite this uncertainty about the constitutional import of *Colegrove*, it was followed by several cases in which the Court—relying on the *Colegrove* doctrine of the Frankfurter opinion—refused to interfere with elections and legislative apportionment.[105] One of the first intimations of a shift in the Court's approach came in 1960, in a case involving a racial gerrymandering of districts in Tuskegee, Alabama.[106] Though the decision did not rely upon the Equal Protection Clause of the Fourteenth Amendment but rather upon the right-to-vote guarantees of the Fifteenth Amendment, the Court did appear to weaken its blanket prohibition upon dealing with issues of legislative apportionment and voting. The case mixed together issues of malapportionment and racial discrimination, but was a straw in the wind and augured changes to come shortly.

[105]E.g., *McDougall* v. *Green*, 335 U.S. 281 (1948); *South* v. *Peters*, 339 U.S. 276 (1950).

[106]*Gomillion* v. *Lightfoot*, 364 U.S. 339 (1960).

The landmark case of *Baker* v. *Carr*[107] established the proposition that legislative apportionment was an issue with which the federal courts could and would deal. Holding that the issue was not one which fell under the rubric of "political questions" and hence nonjusticeable, the Court ruled that an attack upon legislative malapportionment (in this case, upon the apportionment of the Tennessee legislature) as a violation of the Equal Protection Clause was properly a matter for the federal courts. The major question that *Baker* left open, though, was what standards for apportionment the Fourteenth Amendment imposed upon the states. The Court shortly began to develop some standards.

In 1964, the Court dealt first with the problem of malapportionment in Congressional districts, and then with state legislatures. First, in a case dealing with the apportionment of Congressional districts,[108] the Court held that Article I, Section 2 of the Constitution requiring that Representatives be chosen "by the People of the Several States" meant that as nearly as possible one man's vote in a Congressional election should count for the same as another. In the same year, the Court decided six cases dealing with malapportionment in state legislatures.[109] In the words of the now famous "one man/one vote" opinion by Chief Justice Warren:

> We hold that, as a basic constitutional standard, the Equal Protection Clause requires that the seats in both houses of a bicameral state legislature must be apportioned on a population basis. Simply stated, an individual's right to vote for state legislators is unconstitutionally impaired when its weight is in a substantial

[107]369 U.S. 186 (1962).

[108]*Wesberry* v. *Sanders*, 376 U.S. 1 (1964).

[109]Alabama: *Reynolds* v. *Sims*, 377 U.S. 533 (1964); New York: *WMCA* v. *Lomenzo*, 377 U.S. 633 (1964); Colorado; *Lucas* v. *Colorado General Assembly*, 377 U.S. 713 (1964); Maryland: *Maryland Committee for Fair Representation* v. *Tawes*, 377 U.S. 656 (1964); Virginia: *Davis* v. *Mann*, 377 U.S. 678 (1964); Delaware: *Roman* v. *Sincock*, 377 U.S. 695 (1964).

fashion diluted when compared with the votes of citizens living in other parts of the State.[110]

Rejecting the so-called federal analogy, which suggested that if the Constitution permitted, in fact required, apportionment of one house of the federal legislature on a basis other than population, then it was somewhat anomalous to hold that it did not permit similar schemes in state legislatures, the Court held that both houses of state legislatures must be apportioned on the basis of equal population districts.[111] One week later, on June 22, 1964, the Court declared unconstitutional (either directly or by affirming lower court judgments) the legislative apportionments of nine other states. In a week, then, the Court had overturned apportionments of legislatures in nearly a third of the states. By 1968, congressional redistricting had taken place in 37 of the 50 states, and every state had taken at least some steps toward equalizing population in state legislative districts.[112]

In a later decision, *Avery* v. *Midland County*[113] the Court held that the one-man-one-vote principle applied also to the drawing of districts for units of local government having general governmental power over the unit's entire geographic area (in this case, a board of County Commissioners).

One major question left open by the 1964 decisions was that of precisely how much deviation from exact numerical equality was tolerable under the terms of the Equal Protection Clause. The Court's opinion eschewed mathematical

[110]377 U.S. 568.

[111]The majority opinion stressed the fact that states were recognized as governmental units by the provisions of the Constitution, while local governmental units and districts were themselves products of the state, subject to change at the will of the legislature, and hence somewhat less permanent than the states themselves.

[112]Robert McKay, "Reapportionment: Success Story of the Warren Court," in Richard H. Sayler, et al., eds. *The Warren Court* (New York: Chelsea House, 1969), pp. 32-45.

[113]390 U.S. 474 (1968).

exactness and implied that some deviations were constitutionally permissible. In a recent case, involving Congressional apportionment, the Court indicated that a deviation of only six percent was not permissible.[114] The Court has gradually narrowed the limits of deviation but has not settled upon a fixed mathematical standard.

Though to many the reapportionment decisions appeared simply inevitable—given the lack of other remedies to deal with malapportionment—they were hotly contested in the courts and the broader political arena.[115] Though the decisions, particularly the principle that both houses had to be apportioned on the basis of population, met with a great deal of criticism from political figures and an attempt was made to circumvent the decision by constitutional amendment, the reapportionment decisions did not arouse as much hostility among the public at large and indeed, compared with decisions in areas like civil rights, criminal justice, obscenity, or schoolhouse religion, were not particularly salient to the general public.[116]

The actual impact of the process of reapportionment is itself somewhat unclear. Chief Justice Warren has indicated that he considers the decisions dealing with reapportionment

---

[114]*Kirkpatrick* v. *Preisler*, 394 U.S. 526 (1969).

[115]For a discussion of the reapportionment litigation and response to the Supreme Court decisions, see Robert Dixon, *Democratic Representation* (New York: Oxford University Press, 1969), especially chs. 15 and 16; Arthur E. Bonfield, "The Dirksen Amendment and the Article V Convention Process," *Michigan Law Review*, 66 (1968), pp. 949-1000; Robert McKay, "Court, Congress, and Reapportionment," *ibid.*, 63 (1964), pp. 255-278.

[116]Survey research dealing with public perceptions and evaluations of Supreme Court decisions suggests that the reapportionment cases—as compared, for example, with those dealing with segregation, school prayer, and the rights of persons accused of crime—did not make a particularly great impression upon the public. See, for example, Walter F. Murphy and Joseph Tanenhaus, "Public Opinion and the United States Supreme Court," *Law and Society Review*, II (1968), pp. 357-384; and Kenneth M. Dolbeare, "The Public Views the Supreme Court," in Herbert Jacob, *Law, Politics and the Federal Courts* (Boston: Little, Brown, 1967), pp. 194-212.

to have been the most significant of his tenure.[117] The cases and their most publicized symbol, one man-one vote, have a fulfilling democratic ring to them, and exemplify the invocation of judicial review to protect the democratic process itself.

Moreover, the opposition that reapportionment met with in the legislatures, the furor that the decisions aroused among politicians, and the hopes of those urging reapportionment and supporting the suits that led to it were based in large measure upon the premise that reapportionment would affect party balances in legislatures and the kinds of public policies that emerged from legislatures. Ironically, much of the research that has inquired into the effects of reapportionment has raised doubts that reapportionment in fact does affect party balances or the public policies that are produced by legislatures.[118]

Regardless of the effects of the process of reapportionment upon outcomes in legislation, the cases represent what one scholar has called the "success story" of the Warren Court. They were successful in the sense that they appeared to vindicate an important manifestation of democratic equality and, moreover, the policy implicit in the Court decisions was obeyed. The Court did not resort to a policy of "all deliberate speed" in reapportioning legislatures, and most

[117]"I think the reapportionment, not only of state legislatures but of representative government in this country, is perhaps the most important issue we have had before the Supreme Court." *The New York Times*, June 27, 1969, p. 17. "I think *Baker* v. *Carr* was the most important case we decided in my time." *The New York Times Magazine*, October 19, 1969, p. 130.

[118]See, for example, Thomas R. Dye, "Malapportionment and Public Policy in the States," *Journal of Politics*, 27 (1965), pp. 586-601; Richard I. Hofferbert, "The Relation Between Public Policy and Some Structural and Environmental Variables in the American States," *American Political Science Review*, 60 (1966), pp. 73-82; for a somewhat contrasting view, using similar research techniques, see Allan G. Pulsipher and James L. Weatherby, Jr., "Malapportionment, Party Competition and the Functional Distribution of Governmental Expenditures," *ibid.*, 62 (1968), pp. 1207-1219.

legislatures were in fact reapportioned; though reapportionment plans are still the subject of debate and litigation, the general policy the Court tried to implement has resulted in action and movement in the direction intended. Two factors appear crucial to the success of the reapportionment decisions in producing behavioral compliance with the doctrine enunciated. First, unlike decisions dealing with civil rights or schoolhouse religion, the reapportionment decisions met with general public support, or, at worst, apathy. Unlike other, more controversial decisions, reapportionment did not touch directly the personal or social lives of citizens. The second factor crucial to compliance was the willingness of lower courts to supervise closely the activities of state legislatures and to step in and draw up their own plans when states were unwilling to do so. Thus, the attitudes and behavior of the population generally and of other political institutions interacted with the doctrinal change to produce a relatively high degree of compliance.

Political equality, at least in the form of nondiscrimination on the basis of place of residence, was one more area in which the principle of equality has seen doctrinal development in recent years. And, unlike some of the other areas of equality discussed here, especially racial equality, doctrinal developments produced substantial behavioral compliance.

CONCLUSION

These, then, are some of the areas in which doctrine has been developed to further the principle of equality. The use of such classifications as race, economic status, and place of residence has been restricted in areas of voting, education, public accommodations, the criminal justice process, housing, hiring, and the like. The doctrinal development has dealt mainly with equality of opportunity rather than substantive equality. Though developments such as the poverty program and the proposed minimum income program do indicate a concern with redistribution of resources in the direction of more substantive equality, even these programs have a distinct flavor of equality of opportunity about them. Compensatory programs to develop educational and occupational skills for the poor, to provide them with legal representation, to guarantee them an income floor below which they will not fall, are redistributive in a sense. But they are basically aimed at providing blacks and the poor with a base from which they can effectively compete in the political, social, and economic marketplaces of life.

Thus, both redistributive programs—which have come primarily from the executive and legislative branches—and the Court's attempt to remove infirmities attached to blacks and the poor in gaining effective access to and participation in the political and legal systems, are mainly aimed at increasing the value of equality of opportunity in our society, and at providing those who are disadvantaged with the skills and resources to compete with those more advantaged. In a sense, this stress upon equality of opportunity is, as John Schaar has argued, conservative:

> ... to be accurate, the equality of opportunity formula must be revised to read: equality of opportunity for all to develop those talents which are highly valued by a given people at a given time.
>
> When put in this way, it becomes clear that commitment to the formula implies prior acceptance of an already established social-moral order. Thus, the doctrine is, indirectly, very conservative. It enlists support for the established patterns of values. It also encourages change and growth, to be sure, but mainly along the lines of tendency already apparent and approved in a given society. The doctrine is "progressive" only in the special sense that it encourages and hastens progress within a going pattern of institutions, activities, and values. It does not advance alternatives to the existing patterns.[119]

Such "alternatives" might involve basic structural changes in the economic system and changes in the basic relations of

[119]Schaar, "Equality of Opportunity and Beyond," *op. cit.*, p. 230.

one human to another, with the development of a more intense sense of community. Whatever alternatives one might have in mind, I think Schaar's point is correct: Equality of opportunity is a Darwinian concept, implying a meritocracy of the talented and taking as given the value of the current system of distributing economic, social, and political values. And, as suggested above, it seems that most of the doctrinal development in the area of equality has been focused around the development and application of the principle of equality of opportunity, of permitting all groups in society to compete in the political, social, and economic marketplaces unencumbered by handicaps at the outset.

A few concluding obervations seem in order. First, though doctrinal and behavioral change have moved toward the ideal of equality of opportunity, we are by no means there yet. The poor, the black, the criminal, for example, are not by any means currently free to compete with the white and the affluent on an equal plane, even assuming that one accepts this model as desirable. Court, Congress and the President have moved us in this direction, but we are not yet there.

However, the doctrinal developments seen in the past fifteen years have been no mean feat. Given the ambivalence of Americans about the concept of equality—disagreement both about what the concept means and whether it is a value that ought to be pursued—the developments in the doctrine of equality, particularly of the black and the poor, have been an impressive achievement. Both of these groups have long been outside the mainstream of American social and political life, living in a state of partial citizenship. The decisions of the Court regarding their rights have not been self-executing, have not removed the blatant and invidious discrimination to which they have been subjected. But they have been important in placing the status of these groups on the agenda of our society and our political institutions, of making our society more self-conscious about the discrimination it has so long practiced. It is through the interplay of legal institutions and other political institutions that such issues have been raised, if not resolved.

The denouement of the drama is by no means clear. Equality of opportunity has not been provided to minority groups and one wonders if our society will ever be willing to do so. Moreover, many are suggesting that this goal itself, as yet unrealized, may be one that we should not pursue. In a sense, I think, the movement of many articulate and vocal black leaders from the goal and rhetoric of integration (which may be interpreted as the goal of making blacks and whites alike and equal to compete for the material goods of the society) toward separatism and stress upon community reflects in part a questioning of the goal of equality of opportunity; by the same token, many in the white radical community are questioning the basic social, political and economic structures of American society.

These developments suggest that perhaps the goal toward which so much of the energy and attention of the Court has been focused is coming under increasingly critical scrutiny. But, by the same token, much of this questioning owes its nascence to the willingness and ability of legal and political institutions to make us more self-conscious about the inequalities in our society and to begin the process of removing some of the most blatant forms of discrimination. Perhaps the answer is provided by the doctrine developed by the Court—equality of opportunity—will be modified or rejected by future generations. But the role played by the Court should not, I think, simply be dismissed as either misguided or unnecessary.

FIVE
CRIMINAL JUSTICE

THE third value in the American democratic trinity, in addition to freedom and equality, is due process or fair procedure. Not only does constitutional doctrine protect against governmental infringements on the freedom of citizens and discrimination against minority groups, it also provides that when government attempts to impose sanctions upon individuals, it must do so only under "due process" of law. What does "due process" mean? It is often referred to by the synonymous concept of "fair procedure," which isn't much more illuminating. Several elements are present in the notion of procedural fairness. One is an equalitarian value: that of treating equals equally or not discriminating invidiously on the basis of "irrelevant" characteristics like race, sex, or economic status. This was suggested in the preceding chapter. Another facet of procedural fairness involves the provision of certain rights to individuals caught up in government proceedings. When an individual is subjected to sanctions by the government, particularly by law-enforcement officials, he possesses certain rights that should be vouchsafed if he is to obtain due process. These include representation by the counsel of his choice, confrontation of his accusers, trial by an impartial jury of his peers, protection of his person and property from illegal searches and seizures, privilege against self-incrimination, etc.

These rights are at the heart of our system of justice, and are elements in the due process of law to which every individual in our society is supposed to be entitled. Though the government deals with people in myriad ways and imposes sanctions in such proceedings—administrative proceedings, contacts between government officials and citizens, legislative hearings, trials—the most salient area in which the concept of due process has been developed in recent years is within the context of the criminal justice system. The major disputes over the concept of due process in the past few decades have been over the protections to be afforded to individuals accused of crime.[1]

THE CONCEPT OF DUE PROCESS

The justifications for the protections inherent in the notions of due process or fair procedure flow from the need to protect the integrity and dignity of the individual and from a fear of governmental tyranny. The application of the criminal sanction is perhaps the most serious act against a citizen that the government can perform. The stigma and loss of freedom that the application of the criminal sanction can bring are highly destructive of the dignity of a citizen. This process should be guarded both from making mistakes and from capriciousness or malice on the part of government officials.

---

[1]This chapter discusses what has been called "procedural" due process—protections afforded to individuals in the process by which the government affects citizens (with special attention to criminal justice). During the period of 1880-1935, the Court used extensively the doctrine of "substantive" due process. This doctrine—used by the Court to strike down much economic regulation—invoked such "substantive" rights as freedom of an individual to offer his services to an employer without governmental restrictions upon the conditions of employment, and the inviolability of an individual's property from governmental regulation.

Thus, a series of procedural protections designed to limit the ability of the government to invoke the criminal sanction are generally deemed essential if a society is to remain free. As Herbert Packer has observed:

> ... there is the assumption that there are limits to the powers of government to investigate and apprehend persons suspected of committing crimes ... a degree of scrutiny and control must be exercised with respect to the activities of law enforcement officers, ... the security and privacy of the individual may not be invaded at will. [There is also] the notion that the alleged criminal is not merely an object to be acted upon, but an independent entity in the process who may, if he so desires, force the operators of the process to demonstrate to an independent authority (judges and jury) that he is guilty of the charges against him.[2]

The provision of procedural rights to defendants in criminal cases has involved both doctrinal and political controversy. That is, there has been acrimonious dispute within the legal community and among members of the Court about the substance of procedural rights available to defendants by virtue of the Constitution, and in the society as a whole about what rights ought to be available.

Dispute within the Court itself has centered around two questions: First, what is the substance of some of the protections afforded in the Constitution (e.g., what constitutes an "unreasonable" search and seizure? at what stage does the right to counsel become available? what is a "cruel and unusual" punishment?). The second question deals with the availability of such protections to defendants in state proceedings. By virtue of the early Court decision in *Barron* v. *Baltimore*, the provisions of the Bill of Rights were held to apply only to the activities of the federal government. Beginning with the *Gitlow* decision which dealt with the

---

[2]Herbert L. Packer, The Limits of the Criminal Sanction (Stanford, Calif.: Stanford University Press, 1968), pp. 156-157.

applicability of the First Amendment protections to state activities, the Court began to incorporate the protections of the Bill of Rights to proceedings of state governments. As indicated in the preceding chapter, the first of the procedural protections in criminal trials held applicable to states was that of the provision of counsel to indigent defendants under certain circumstances.[3]

After the *Powell* decision, the Court began to consider other procedural protections and their applicability to state proceedings. The Court moved, especially during the early 1960s, to incorporate almost all of the protections of the Bill of Rights into the Due Process Clause of the Fourteenth Amendment. The major doctrinal dispute within the Court on the issue of incorporation dealt with the question of "total" versus "selective" incorporation. One wing of the Court, led by Justice Black, argued that the Due Process Clause of the Fourteenth Amendment simply incorporated *all* of the provisions of the Bill of Rights and made them applicable to state proceedings. The other wing, led by Justice Frankfurter and, more recently, by Justice Harlan, argued that the Due Process Clause incorporated only those procedural protections which were essential to "fundamental fairness," or were "implicit in a concept of ordered liberty." Their approach, sometimes called selective incorporation, has dominated the Court during the twentieth century. Today, the two positions have essentially arrived at the same place, for, by the process of selective incorporation the Court has now incorporated all of the protections of the Bill of Rights (with the exception of the requirement that all defendants be indicted by grand juries).

One point on the general issue of incorporation is worthy

[3]*Powell* v. *Alabama.* 287 U.S. 45 (1932). See, for example, the various opinions in *Adamson* v. *California,* 331 U.S. 46 (1947). See also William Crosskey, "Charles Fairman, 'Legislative History' and the Constitutional Limitations on State Authority," *University of Chicago Law Review,* 22 (1954), 1-43; Charles Fairman, "A Reply to Professor Crosskey," *ibid.,* pp. 144-156.

of note. As suggested in the discussion in Chapter Three dealing with the right of privacy, what was once the position of maximum extension of liberty—Justice Black's total incorporation theory—became, at least as applied by him, somewhat less libertarian, for he recently used it to deny that protections not included within the provisions of the Bill of Rights exist at all. Thus, the lack of any specific mention of a right to privacy in the Bill of Rights led Black to argue that such a protection simply does not exist. In the same vein, Justice Black's position on wiretapping, which denied that such activities constitute a search and seizure under the terms of the Fourth Amendment, was somewhat less protective of liberty than the approaches taken by other justices, including many who adhere to the fundamental fairness approach.

These developments, which are discussed in more detail in this chapter, are suggestive of two elements in doctrinal developments in the area of due process and of the judicial decision-making generally. First, they indicate that "strict construction" is a concept susceptible of many meanings. In his own fashion, Justice Black was perhaps the "strictest constructionist" to have sat on the Court in this century. His literal interpretation of the provisions of the Bill of Rights— for example, of the First Amendment provisions dealing with freedom of speech or the Fourth Amendment provisions dealing with searches and seizures—was terribly strict, for it rigidly demarcated the limits of the other branches of government and of the Court in dealing with such activities. It was in fact the "looseness" of the selective incorporation position—its reliance upon concepts like fundamental fairness or ordered liberty—to which Black objected.

The second feature of constitutional development that Black's position vis-a-vis many of his colleagues suggests is that doctrinal change can lead to somewhat odd twists in position. During the period up to the mid-1960s, Black was a consistent dissenter in favor of liberty: His espousal of the doctrine of total incorporation in a sense put him "ahead" of many of his colleagues in extending procedural protections.

When the majority of the Court had finally incorporated nearly all of the provisions of the Bill of Rights and was grappling with the problems of further extensions of protections (e.g., the development of a notion of a right to privacy, the applicability of the search and seizure provisions to technologically advanced means of surveillance), Black frequently dissented from libertarian rulings. Reading his opinions, the suggestion is unmistakable that it was not Justice Black who has changed but the Court itself. What Black developed as a doctrine protective of liberty became, in recent years, one used to attack decisions protective of liberty.[4]

In addition to the doctrinal disputes that have characterized the Court's movement toward extending the procedural protections available to defendants in criminal cases, the decisions themselves have often met with opposition from political figures and the public at large. Again, as with decisions dealing with freedom and equality, this reception reflects in part some basic disagreements among the American people about the validity of the application of procedural protections. Though large majorities of our citizens agree that every man ought to be afforded the right to a fair trial, there is substantial disagreement about what constitutes such a proceeding. Thus, for example, though majorities favor the general thrust of the Fourth Amendment protection against unreasonable searches and seizures, substantial minorities do not.[5] Bare majorities agree with the

---

[4] See especially the opinions in *Adamson* v. *California*. Black argued that the Due Process Clause simply incorporated the provisions of the Bill of Rights. Justices Rutledge and Murphy agreed that the Bill of Rights was incorporated, but that other rights might also be protected against state infringement, though not explicitly mentioned in the Bill of Rights. The controversy over the "right to privacy" discussed in Chapter Three suggests the difference between Black's literal view and the more liberal view taken by some other justices.

[5] The CBS poll of 1970, *op. cit.*, found that 66 percent of those sampled believed that citizens should not be subjected to searches without warrants. A similar survey, almost 15 years earlier, produced similar

notion that an individual should not be compelled to testify against himself in court.[6] A majority of the American people apparently believe that the police should be permitted to hold a suspect in custody until they are able to obtain evidence against him.[7] A majority of citizens simply reject the notion that a man ought not to be tried twice for the same crime—the double jeopardy provision of the Fifth Amendment.[8] Thus, decisions of the Court extending rights to accused persons and amplifying the meanings of the provisions of the Bill of Rights are fertile ground for political dispute, for they embody policies that many people oppose.

Value conflicts in American criminal justice

Why is there disagreement about these procedural protections? As in the case of freedom and equality, ambivalence about due process values is a result of the conflict between them and other values that people also wish to pursue. Law enforcement and the control of criminal behavior appear, on the surface at least, to conflict directly with due process values. Herbert Packer suggests that there are, in America, two views of the criminal process: the Crime Control and the Due Process models.[9] That is, there are two ways of looking at the goals and procedures of the criminal process, two competing conceptions of how our criminal law ought to

---

results, with 81.8 percent of the respondents agreeing that law enforcement officials "should never be allowed to search a person or place without a warrant." Raymond W. Mack, "Do We Really Believe in the Bill of Rights?" *Social Problems*, 3 (1956), pp. 264-269, at 266-267.

[6] Fifty-four percent in the CBS poll; 56 percent in Mack's study.

[7] Fifty-eight percent of respondents in the CBS poll agreed that if a person is suspected of a serious crime, "the police should be allowed to hold him in jail until they can get enough evidence to officially charge him."

[8] Fifty-eight percent of respondents in the CBS poll and 72 percent of Mack's respondents agreed that retrials should be permitted for acquitted defendants if new evidence is discovered.

[9] Herbert L. Packer, *op. cit.*, ch. 8.

operate. He likens the Crime Control Model to an assembly line and the Due Process Model to an obstacle course:

> The value system that underlies the Crime Control Model is based on the proposition that the repression of criminal conduct is by far the most important function to be performed by the criminal process. . . . In order to achieve this high purpose, the Crime Control Model requires that primary attention be paid to the efficiency with which the criminal process operates to screen suspects, determine guilt, and secure appropriate dispositions of persons convicted of crime. . . . The image that comes to mind is an assembly-line conveyor belt down which moves an endless stream of cases, never stopping, carrying the cases to workers who stand at fixed stations and who perform on each case as it comes by the same small but essential operation that brings it closer to being a finished product, or, to exchange the metaphor for the reality, a closed file. . . . If the Crime Control Model resembles an assembly line, the Due Process Model looks very much like an obstacle course. Each of its successive stages is designed to present formidable impediments to carrying the accused any further along in the process. . . . The Due Process Model insists on the prevention and elimination of mistakes to the extent possible.[10]

Thus, one view of the criminal process stresses efficiency, speed, and the use of informal proceedings necessary to expeditious handling of criminal cases. The Due Process Model, on the other hand, stresses the gravity of applying criminal sanction, the grievous consequences of possible errors, and the reliance upon formalized, adversary proceedings in which the activities of law-enforcement officials are strictly controlled and the rights of the accused are jealously guarded.

These two models are designed to point up the tension in our view of the criminal justice process: between effective enforcement of the law and protection of the procedural

[10]*Ibid.*, pp. 158, 159, 163.

rights of the defendant. To some extent, the types of procedures that one would want to use if interested primarily in enforcement of the law (e.g., wide discretion for law enforcement officers in their dealings with suspicious individuals, in their ability to engage in searches for evidence of crime, in their questioning of suspects, in reliance upon informal proceedings to establish guilt or innocence) are the very types of practice that vigorous pursuit of due process protections would outlaw. In fact, as will be pointed out later, some empirical research upon the impact of various Court decisions dealing with due process protections (e.g., provision of counsel, informing suspects of their constitutional rights, etc.) tends to throw some doubt upon the extent to which emphasis on due process protections actually hampers law enforcement efforts. But law enforcement officials and the public generally tend to perceive a tension, if not contradiction, between the two sets of values.

As Packer points out, the two models, and our conceptions of the legal process, stress two different kinds of "guilt"— legal and factual.[11] Factual guilt is what usually comes to mind when we consider whether an individual is guilty of the crime with which he is charged: Did he do it? Legal guilt, on the other hand, deals not simply with the factual question of whether the accused committed the crime but with the question of whether the state can prove—under various procedural restraints dealing with the admissibility of evidence, the burden of proof, the requirement that guilt be proved beyond a reasonable doubt, etc.—that the individual did in fact commit the crime.

Thus, many of the procedures that are at the heart of what we call Due Process appear to make it more difficult to apprehend, convict, and punish the factually guilty. And, not unnaturally, given the ambivalence of people about the two values of law enforcement and due process, this fact causes

[11]A similar distinction is used by Skolnick in his excellent discussion of police behavior. See Jerome Skolnick, *Justice Without Trial* (New York: Wiley, 1966), ch. 9.

some people difficulty, makes them wonder about and often criticize Court decisions emphasizing due process values. This problem is exacerbated by the fact that many of the most publicized cases in which the Court has moved to protect due process values involve defendants who are in fact quite clearly factually guilty. In the area of search and seizure, for example, the crime involved is often possession of some contraband like narcotics or weapons. Thus, there would be no case if the allegedly illegal search had not produced evidence against the defendant. In such cases, when the Court chooses to hold that the search was unreasonable and hence the evidence obtained not admissible, it is quite clearly letting a "guilty" man go. Similarly, in many of the landmark cases involving the rights of defendants during interrogation by the police, apparently guilty men have been freed. Thus, in many of the significant and publicized criminal justice cases the Court, in protecting and extending due process values, has appeared to free men who apparently did commit the crimes with which they were charged.

The Court has moved in recent years to stress the Due Process Model, to judicialize the criminal justice process from the first encounter between police and suspect to the final appeal. This doctrinal movement has resulted in a good deal of opposition from political figures, law enforcement officials, and the public at large. "Law and order" has become a political catch-phrase, and implies an emphasis on the values stressed by the Crime Control Model and a denigration of the Due Process values being pursued by the Court.

In looking at the doctrinal developments in the area of criminal justice, we should keep in mind that such developments have occurred in a context of equivocal attitudinal support for such changes. And, since implementation of such doctrinal changes requires behavioral changes on the part of law enforcement officials often quite unsympathetic with the decisions themselves, we cannot assume that the doctrinal developments have been translated into the expected behavioral changes. Like its civil rights decisions, Supreme Court decisions dealing with criminal justice have not been self-executing but have met with resistance and sometimes evasion on the part of law-enforcement officials. Moreover, the nature of the criminal justice process, especially plea-bargaining (discussed later in the chapter), makes implementation quite difficult, for important legal issues are often suppressed in the normal operation of the criminal justice process. Examination of doctrinal developments in the area of due process values must be tempered by an awareness that, as with freedom or equality, changes in doctrine are the beginning, not the end, of understanding the rights available to persons accused of crime.

SEARCH AND SEIZURE

The Fourth Amendment to the Constitution provides that "The right of the people to be secure in their persons, houses, papers, and effects, against unreasonable searches and seizures shall not be violated, and no Warrants shall issue, but upon probable cause, supported by Oath or affirmation, and particularly describing the place to be searched, and the persons or things to be seized." The provision grew out of English common law that had dealt with the use of general warrants which were unspecific as to what was being searched for but granted broad powers to compel production of evidence and to permit officials to search persons and places. English case law had developed some restrictions upon the use of general warrants, but their use by customs officials in the colonies became a major grievance in the years before the American Revolution, and the provision of the Constitution restricting searches was an outgrowth of the distaste in America for the use of general warrants.

"Reasonable" searches

As with many provisions of the Constitution, the Fourth Amendment is, on its face, somewhat ambiguous. It does not prohibit all searches but only those that are unreasonable; it suggests that searches should not be conducted without warrants, yet it is not clear that all searches conducted without warrants are impermissible; it deals with searches and seizures, yet it is somewhat unclear what governmental activity falls within this category. This latter question has become especially relevant in recent years when technological advances have made it possible to obtain evidence without direct physical intrusions.

The *Boyd* case

Until the middle of the twentieth century, most of the important search and seizure cases arose in the context of the activities of federal law enforcement agencies, for the Fourth Amendment provision was not incorporated against state activities until 1949. One of the first milestone search and seizure cases, *Boyd* v. *United States*,[12] came to the Court in 1886. The Court dealt in *Boyd* with a federal act governing civil proceedings by which the government attempted to force the forfeiture of goods imported illegally. The law provided that in such proceedings the prosecution could ask and the court require the importer to produce invoices dealing with the material allegedly imported illegally, and that if the importer refused to produce the invoices the allegations of the government about the material would be regarded as admitted by the importer. The Supreme Court held the law unconstitutional, arguing that it violated the Fourth and Fifth Amendments because it authorized an unreasonable search and required the importer to provide testimony against himself. The Court's opinion was important because it treated the notion of a search and seizure more broadly than simple physical intrusion, and held that the Fourth Amendment protection applied to "all invasions on the part of the Government and its employees, of the sanctity of a man's home and the privacies of life."[13] Thus,

[12] 116 U.S. 616 (1886).
[13] 116 U.S. 630.

the Fourth Amendment protection was construed broadly, and its intimate relationship to the Fifth Amendment protection against self-incrimination was stressed.

The Court has since dealt extensively with the question of what constitutes a "reasonable" search and seizure. The general rule developed has been that searches are reasonable if they are based upon a warrant from a magistrate. Such a warrant may be issued only upon a demonstration that the law enforcement officials have probable cause to believe that some evidence of criminal activity will be uncovered by the search. The magistrate must determine whether probable cause exists and must rely upon more than a mere statement by the police that they believe some material will be found. Moreover, the warrant must describe in some detail the goods to be searched for and seized. Thus, in the case of searches with warrants, law enforcement officials must produce some evidence to an impartial magistrate to justify their request to be given permission to conduct a search.

The harder cases involve searches conducted in the absence of warrants. The major exception to the rule that law enforcement officials must obtain warrants deals with searches incident to a lawful arrest. The two crucial issues involved in such searches are: What is "incident to a lawful arrest?"; how much can be searched when the search is incident to a lawful arrest? The major justifications for searches (without warrants) incident to arrest involve the need for an officer to search a defendant to remove weapons (and thus protect the officer's safety) and to remove evidence that the defendant may destroy if the officer does not remove it. Neither of these justifications permits an officer simply to search anybody and then use evidence obtained as justification for the original arrest: In general, it is not permissible for an officer to use the fruits of a search as justification for the arrest; the grounds for arrest must exist before a search incident to the arrest is lawful.

These propositions sound authoritative in the abstract, but

in practice they are quite difficult to apply. First, consider the question of whether an officer ought to obtain a warrant to search rather than arresting and then searching incident to the arrest. In *Trupiano* v. *United States*,[14] the Court held that officers were required to obtain warrants before searching, if it was "reasonably practicable" to do so. Thus, when government agents had been observing an individual for a long period and had engaged in detailed planning of a raid on his property, they were required to obtain a warrant. The Court abandoned this rule only two years later in *United States* v. *Rabinowitz*.[15] Again, the officers had had time to obtain a warrant, but did not. The Court rejected the *Trupiano* rule, and relied upon the reasonableness of the search itself. Arguing that *Rabinowitz* involved a reasonable search since the arrest was valid and the search was restricted to a small area under the defendant's control, the Court held that the search was permissible. Thus, the crucial question was not the practicability of obtaining a warrant, but the reasonableness of the search itself.

This raises one of the crucial questions about warrantless searches: When is a search incident to a lawful arrest and hence permissible? This issue has most recently been raised in the context of the police practice of "stop and frisk," in which the police, observing an individual acting suspiciously, stop him and frisk him to see whether he possesses weapons or other contraband. In two important cases, the Court recently upheld some searches and seizures in the stop and frisk situation.[16] The state urged that stopping and frisking was not really searching and seizing; it was a tentative or preliminary action that might then give rise to evidence which could be the basis for a lawful arrest. The Court rejected this argument and held that a frisk was a search

[14]334 U.S. 699 (1948).
[15]339 U.S. 56 (1950).
[16]*Terry* v. *Ohio*, 392 U.S. 1 (1968); *Peters* v. *New York*, 392 U.S. 40 (1968).

under the terms of the Fourth Amendment. But, crucially, the Court did not reiterate the traditional doctrine that therefore the officer must have probable cause to make an arrest before he can frisk an individual.

Terry v. Ohio

The *Terry* case illustrates the complexity of the issue facing the Court. A police officer observed two men standing on the street. One left the other and walked down past a series of store windows, pausing to glance into a particular window, walked a few paces further and returned to his companion. His companion then repeated the trip, again stopping to look in the same window. A third man came up and talked with the two and then walked away. The original two had repeated their strolling a half dozen times, and then walked away together and met with the third man. The officer was convinced that the three were making preparations for an armed robbery. He approached the three men, stopped and frisked them, and found weapons on two of them. The trial court held that at this point the officer did not have probable cause for arrest, but that the searches were justifiable and reasonable, and the weapons could be introduced against the defendants. The Supreme Court agreed:

> When an officer is justified in believing that the individual whose suspicious behavior he is investigating at close range is armed and presently dangerous to the officer or to others, it would appear to be clearly unreasonable to deny the officer the power to take necessary measures to determine whether the person is in fact carrying a weapon and to neutralize the threat of physical harm. . . . there must be a narrowly drawn authority to permit a reasonable search for weapons for the protection of the police officer, where he has reason to believe that he is dealing with an armed and dangerous individual, regardless of whether he has probable cause to arrest the individual for a crime. The officer need not be absolutely certain that the individual is armed; the issue is whether a reasonably prudent man in

the circumstances would be warranted in the belief that his safety or that of others was in danger.[17]

In a case decided the same day,[18] the Court overturned a conviction for possession of narcotics in which the officer had observed a defendant for several hours talking with known addicts. The officer did not hear any of the conversation nor did he observe materials being exchanged between the defendant and the known addicts, but when he frisked the defendant he did find some heroin. On the facts, it appeared that although he did not have probable cause to arrest, he did have about as firmly grounded a suspicion of criminal activity as had the police officer in *Terry*. But the Court differentiated the cases, saying that the search for weapons was the crucial difference. That is, in a search not incident to lawful arrest, there must be some reasonable suspicion that the suspect is carrying weapons. Justice Douglas objected to the *Terry* decision, arguing that what it did was to grant the police powers that magistrates did not have. Since the majority opinion admitted the absence of probable cause for arrest, Douglas argued:

> Had a warrant been sought, a magistrate would, therefore, have been unauthorized to issue one, for he can act only if there is a showing of "probable cause." We hold today that the police have greater authority to make a "seizure" and conduct a "search" than a judge has to authorize such action.... To give the police greater power than a magistrate is to take a long step down the totalitarian path. Perhaps such a step is desirable to cope with more modern forms of lawlessness. But if it is taken, it should be the deliberate choice of the people through a constitutional amendment.[19]

---

[17]394 U.S. 24, 27.

[18]*Sibron* v. *New York*, 392 U.S. 40 (1968).

[19]392 U.S. 36, 38-39.

Thus, the general rule about warrantless searches appears to be that such searches must be incident to a lawful arrest, but that an exception is made in the case of encounters between police and citizens in which the officer has reasonable cause to believe that the individual is likely to be engaged in or contemplating illegal conduct and likely to be armed and dangerous.

Though the stop-and-frisk cases somewhat loosened restrictions upon police searches of the person or individuals suspected of criminal activity, another recent case dealing with searches has severely restricted the discretion of police officers. The cases discussed above dealt primarily with warrantless searches of the person; a related question deals with the issue of "how much" can the police search without a warrant? Only the person? The person and the room in which he is located? His whole house?

In 1947, the Court held that officers had fairly wide discretion in searching the premises of a validly arrested individual.[20] FBI agents arrested Harris with a valid arrest warrant and proceeded to conduct a very thorough search of all four rooms of his apartment for a period of about five hours, eventually finding some draft cards that he had no right to possess (which were, in fact, not the materials for which the agents were searching). A five-justice majority upheld the search on the grounds that the whole apartment was apparently under Harris's exclusive control and the documents that the agents were searching for (two cancelled checks) were quite small. Recall that in the *Rabinowitz* case discussed above, the Court validated as reasonable the search of the whole room in which the defendant was arrested. Thus, under the *Harris* and *Rabinowitz* doctrine, the police appeared to have rather wide latitude in searching premises under the control of validly arrested defendants.

[20]*Harris* v. *United States*, 331 U.S. 145 (1947).

The *Chimel* Case

The Court's decision in *Chimel* v. *California*[21] substantially tightened the requirements of the Fourth Amendment, and reversed the trend of *Harris* and *Rabinowitz*. Officers went to the defendant's house with an arrest warrant and were admitted by the defendant's wife. They waited about fifteen minutes until the defendant returned from work and arrested him. Over his objection, they proceeded to search the house for about an hour. No search warrant had been obtained. The state claimed that the search was valid, since it was incident to a lawful arrest and was restricted to premises (the house) under the control of the defendant. The Court, in an opinion by Justice Stewart, rejected this argument and overturned the conviction. The majority opinion stressed the reasoning used in *Terry* v. *Ohio*, the stop-and-frisk case discussed above, in which the legitimacy of a search turned upon the need to search for weapons or for evidence that might be destroyed. Using these two goals as the touchstone for a lawful search incident to arrest, the Court held that widespread searches of premises beyond the room in which the defendant was arrested were unreasonable:

> There is ample justification, therefore, for a search of the arrestee's person and the area "within his immediate control"—construing that phrase to mean the area from within which he might gain possession of a weapon or destructible evidence. There is no comparable justification, however, for routinely searching any room other than that in which an arrest occurs—or, for that matter, for searching through all the desk drawers or other closed or concealed areas in that room itself. Such searches, in the absence of well-recognized exceptions [e.g., of a car which might be moved out of the jurisdiction of the police if not searched immediately], may be made only under the authority of a search warrant.[22]

[21]*Chimel* v. *California*, 395 U.S. 752 (1969).
[22]395 U.S. 763.

Justices White and Black dissented, arguing that if the arrest were lawful and there was probable cause to believe that the defendant did possess incriminating evidence, searches of the whole premises ought to be allowed:

> Again assuming that there is probable cause to search premises at the spot where a suspect is arrested, it seems to me unreasonable to require the police to leave the scene in order to obtain a search warrant when they are already legally there to make a valid arrest, and when there must almost always be a strong possibility that confederates of the arrested man will in the meanwhile remove the items for which the police have probable cause to search.[23]

Thus, in the earlier search cases, the Court had dealt with the lawfulness of the arrest as the touchstone for determining whether a search was proper. So long as the arrest was lawful, the Court had developed rules quite tolerant of rather widespread searches. In a sense, cases like *Harris* and *Rabinowitz* had, by concentrating upon the question of the lawfulness of the arrest, lost sight of the original justification for the search-incident-to-lawful-arrest doctrine. The doctrine of permitting searches without warrants incident to arrest had been based upon the danger to the arresting officer that weapons on the defendant's person might cause or upon the possibility of the destruction of evidence if the defendant was not searched. Cases like *Harris* and *Rabinowitz*, stressing the reasonableness of the search *because* it was incident to a lawful arrest lost sight of these justifications. But when the Court was faced in *Terry* with a situation in which there was not a lawful arrest, but in which the Court felt there were grounds for a search, their attention returned to the *justification* for the search: protection of the officer and preservation of evidence. This perspective rendered the *Harris* doctrine anomalous, for searches of entire premises were not

[23]395 U.S. 774.

justified in terms of protection of the officer, and only hypothetically related to preservation of evidence.[24] Thus, a consequence of the stop-and-frisk cases—"victories" for law enforcement—was to further restrict law enforcement officials in another context.

The upshot of these cases—all of which deal with the question of what is a "reasonable" search under the terms of the Fourth Amendment—would appear to be that searches of the person of a defendant are always justified if incident to a lawful arrest. Searches of a defendant's person are sometimes justified even though not incident to a lawful arrest if the officer has good reason to believe that the defendant is armed. Searches of premises in which defendants are arrested must be restricted to areas from which the defendant might obtain a weapon or destroy evidence.

The somewhat tortured path followed by the Court in these cases illustrates the difficulty in fashioning broad rules to govern the conduct of police officers. The nature of their activities—their dependence upon instinct, observation, and intangible judgments about the activities of suspected criminals—makes the formulation of general rules quite difficult. Even proceeding in a case-by-case fashion to develop a concept like "reasonableness," the Court has moved in fits and starts, changing its mind frequently, and often groping for principles to guide behavior that is very difficult to control. [25]

---

[24] White's argument in *Chimel* stressed the possibility that a suspect's confederates or friends might come and destroy evidence. This possibility can presumably be circumvented either by stationing an officer at the premises until a search warrant can be obtained or, more simply, by obtaining a search warrant in advance.

[25] For useful discussions of police behavior, and the difficulties that both police superiors and outside agencies like courts encounter in attempting to establish rules governing police conduct, see Skolnick, *op. cit.*, and James Q. Wilson, *Varieties of Police Behavior* (Cambridge, Mass.: Harvard University Press, 1968).

Incorporation of the fourth amendment

A parallel line of cases dealing with searches and seizures occurred at the same time the Court was grappling with the question of what constitutes an unreasonable search and seizure. These cases dealt with the remedy available to a defendant who was the subject of an unreasonable search and seizure. The most obvious remedy would appear to be exclusion of evidence obtained illegally. This would insure that defendants would not be convicted on the basis of evidence obtained in violation of the Constitution, and would presumably offer a powerful deterrent to police misconduct, for the fruits of illegal searches would not be of use in convicting law violators.

In fact, this so-called exclusionary rule has been applied in the federal courts since 1914. In *Weeks* v. *United States*,[26] the Supreme Court ruled that evidence obtained illegally must be suppressed and excluded at the trial of defendants in federal couts.[27] Though the federal courts applied the exclusionary rule, most states did not, following an old common law rule that relevant evidence was admissible regardless of its source. In 1949, when the Court first faced squarely the question of applying of the exclusionary rule to state proceedings, thirty of the forty-eight states had refused to adopt the exclusionary rule. In *Wolf* v. *Colorado*,[28] the Court refused to apply the exclusionary rule to state proceedings. A six-justice majority held that the Due Process Clause of the Fourteenth Amendment did protect the privacy of individuals from arbitrary intrusion by state law enforcement officers. But the majority refused to hold that the remedy used in federal courts, the exclusionary rule, was also

[26] 232 U.S. 383 (1914).

[27] Later cases developing and refining the federal exclusionary rule include *Silverthorne Lumber Company* v. *United States*, 251 U.S. 385 (1920); *Rea* v. *United States*, 350 U.S. 214 (1956); *Elkins* v. *United States*, 364 U.S. 206 (1960).

[28] 338 U.S. 25 (1949).

applicable to state proceedings. The majority argued that the Due Process Clause guaranteed basic rights essential to a free society, but that exclusion of evidence was not necessarily one of these. The general Fourth Amendment protection was incorporated against state activities, but not the specific remedy used in federal courts. The majority opinion stressed that federalism argued for flexibility in permitting the states to experiment with various other remedies against unlawful activity by police (e.g., civil actions against offending officers). Thus, the majority incorporated the Fourth Amendment protection, while holding that the exclusionary rule did not have constitutional status but was simply a pragmatic remedy developed under the Court's power to supervise the federal judicial system. The dissenters in *Wolf* protested that the other remedies (e.g., civil suits against offending officers) had generally proved ineffective and that in the absence of the exclusionary rule, the incorporation of the Fourth Amendment protection was close to meaningless. Justice Black, pursuing his literal incorporation view, concurred with the majority in the case, holding that the Fourth was incorporated by the Fourteenth; yet since the Fourth Amendment made no reference to exclusion of evidence, he could not acquiesce in the view that the exclusionary rule was applicable to states.

In 1961, the Court abandoned the Wolf doctrine and held the exclusionary rule applicable to state proceedings.[29] Justice Clark, writing for the majority in *Mapp*, noted that the refusal of the Court in the *Wolf* case to apply the exclusionary rule relied heavily upon the fact that most states had not seen fit to adopt it and the assumption that means other than the exclusionary rule could be adopted by states to protect citizens against unreasonable searches. Clark then pointed out that these factual assumptions appeared to be incorrect. Though two-thirds of the states had, at the time of *Wolf*, not adopted the exclusionary rule, more than half of

[29]*Mapp* v. *Ohio*, 367 U.S. 643 (1961).

those which had passed on it since *Wolf* had adopted it. Moreover, he argued, experience in the states indicated reliance on other remedies (e.g., civil suits against officers engaging in illegal searches) "have been worthless and futile." Thus, Clark argued, the factual bases for *Wolf* had turned out to be incorrect.

Thus, the exclusionary rule was held applicable to states as essential to the incorporation of the Fourth Amendment privilege:

> Since the Fourth Amendment's right of privacy has been declared enforceable against the states through the Due Process Clause of the Fourteenth, it is enforceable against them by the same sanction of exclusion as is used against the Federal Government. . . . Without that rule the freedom from state invasions of privacy would be so ephemeral and so neatly severed from its conceptual nexus with the freedom from all brutish means of coercing evidence as not to merit this Court's high regard as a freedom "implicit in the concept of ordered liberty." . . . Having once recognized that the right to privacy embodied in the Fourth Amendment is enforceable against the States, and that the right to be secure against rude invasions of privacy by state officers, is, therefore, constitutional in origin, we can no longer permit that right to remain an empty promise.[30]

Justice Black concurred in the result, but still had some reservations about the proposition that the Fourth Amendment (and hence the Fourteenth, as a consequence of his total incorporation theory) included the exclusionary rule:

> For the Fourth Amendment does not itself contain any provision expressly precluding the use of such evidence, and I am extremely doubtful that such a provision could properly be inferred from nothing more than the basic command against unreasonable searches and seizures.[31]

[30]367 U.S. 655, 660.
[31]367 U.S. 661-662.

Black found justification for the exclusionary rule not simply in the Fourth but in the combination of the Fourth and Fifth Amendments—the point suggested in the *Boyd* case in the nineteenth century:

> When the Fourth Amendment's ban against unreasonable searches and seizures is considered together with the Fifth Amendment's ban against compelled self-incrimination, a constitutional basis emerges which not only justifies but actually requires the exclusionary rule.[32]

He proceeded to quote the portion of *Boyd* which argued that the Court was "unable to perceive that the seizure of a man's private books and papers to be used in evidence against him is substantially different from compelling him to be a witness against himself."[33] Black concluded in the *Mapp* case that "the Boyd doctrine, though perhaps not required by the express language of the Constitution strictly construed, is amply justified from an historical standpoint, soundly based in reason, and entirely consistent with what I regard to be the proper approach to interpretation of our Bill of Rights."[34]

A bloc of three justices, in an opinion by Justice Harlan, dissented from the *Mapp* decision. Arguing the selective incorporation position, and urging that what *Wolf* had applied to the states was not the provision of the Fourth Amendment but rather only the "principle of privacy 'which is at the core of the Fourth Amendment,' "[35] the Harlan opinion rejected the exclusionary rule. Harlan argued that the exclusionary rule was designed as a means of deterring police misconduct, but he did not "believe that this Court is empowered to impose this much-debated procedure on local courts, however efficacious we may consider the *Weeks* rule

[32]367 U.S. 662.
[33]116 U.S. 616.
[34]367 U.S. 662-663.
[35]367 U.S. 679.

to be as a means of securing Constitutional rights."[36] Federalism required, in his view, that the Court not impose upon states remedies for police misconduct simply "to suit [the Court's] notions of how things should be done."[37]

In any event, the remedy that the Court eventually arrived at to answer the question of what to do if police did engage in illegal searches and seizures was to exclude the evidence from court, either state or federal.

The Fourth Amendment and police practice

In the two lines of cases discussed thus far the Court has attempted to fashion rules defining an unreasonable search and seizure under the terms of the Fourth Amendment, and provided a mechanism for enforcement of the protection. As suggested in the discussion at the outset of this chapter, these cases epitomize the tension between the values of due process and crime control. Police officers would maintain, and probably correctly, that most people they search (or would like to search) are in fact guilty of some law violation. The rules for lawful searches place restrictions upon their ability to search (though the stop-and-frisk cases give them more latitude than they possessed before). Police officers tend to stress their special competence in recognizing criminal behavior, "that they are able craftsmen who can determine with high accuracy whether a suspect 'merits' a search."[38] The rules for probable cause, which stress tangible evidence of criminal activity rather than the policeman's instincts, tend to operate, in the police officers's view, to hamper his exercise of his special skills (though, again, *Terry* does place reliance upon these skills and permits some more leeway in their exercise). Moreover, the exclusionary rule comes into play directly *only* when some incriminating evidence is

[36]367 U.S. 683.
[37]367 U.S. 682.
[38]Skolnick, *op. cit.*, 214.

found. Though it is designed not only to protect the rights of offenders but also to discourage police misconduct in relations with the innocent, evidence is excluded only when it is found—for if nothing is found, there is nothing to exclude. Thus, the exclusionary rule appears to operate in a counterfactual fashion: It operates most clearly only to protect the guilty.

The developing rules on searches and seizures must be implemented by law enforcement officials who are quite hostile. As a result, Jerome Skolnick suggests, the exclusionary rule, and its intended impact upon police behavior, is in practice quite often modified, if not subverted:

> Consequently, all these reasons—the norm of police alertness; the requirement that police confiscate illegal substances; the tendency toward a presumption of the legality of the search once the illegal substance is found; the fact that in a "small pinch" the policeman is usually not interested in an arrest but in creating an informant; the sympathy of police superiors so long as policemen act in conformity with administrative norms of police organization; the difficulty of proving civil suits for false arrest; the denial of fact by the exclusionary rule ... —all militate against the effectiveness of the exclusionary rule. In short, the norms of the police are fundamentally pragmatic. ... To make these observations, however, is not to deny the possible effectiveness of sanctions on police behavior as a way of insuring compliance with procedural rules. *I do not wish to be understood as implying that the legal structure under which the police operate has no effect, but rather as stating the conditions under which its effects may be perceived.* The policeman is more likely to take seriously the more rigorous standard—"search incident to an arrest"—the better the anticipated pinch. Or, put another way, the exclusionary principle puts pressure on the police to work within the rules in those cases where prosecution is contemplated.[39]

Thus, the doctrinal developments that emerged from the Court interacted with the attitudes of enforcement officials

[39]*Ibid.*, 224.

whose behavior was the subject of the doctrine to produce changes in behavior. These changes, it appears, are not necessarily precisely those intended by the Court. The distribution of preferences, resources, and discretion within the legal system makes the translation of doctrine into behavior a complicated process; Supreme Court decisions, as I have suggested before, are by no means self-executing.

Wiretapping and bugging

A final line of cases involving the Fourth Amendment privilege against unreasonable searches and seizures is worthy of note, for it involves issues that are likely to become increasingly salient in American society. These cases involve the use of electronic devices for surveillance and information gathering. As such devices have become more sophisticated, evidence, particularly conversations of suspects, has become accessible without literal physical intrusion into the premises of suspects. The applicability of the Fourth Amendment to such activities has been a recurring problem with which the Court has grappled; technological advances have not only made the issue more prominent, but also more complex.

The Court's first major encounter with wiretapping came in 1928, *Olmstead* v. *United States.*[40] The Court held, in a five-to-four decision, that wiretapping did not violate the Fourth Amendment protection against unreasonable searches and seizures. The majority opinion by Chief Justice Taft argued that the protection of the Fourth Amendment reaches only material things (the Amendment speaks of "persons, houses, papers, and effects") and not conversations. "There was no searching. There was no seizure. The evidence was secured by the use of the sense of hearing and that only."[41] Moreover, there was no search because the activity of wiretapping did not involve a trespass upon the property of others. Thus, the *Olmstead* opinion appeared to exclude

[40]277 U.S. 438 (1928).
[41]277 U.S. 464.

wiretapping from the province of the Fourth Amendment. Justice Holmes dissented, calling wiretapping a "dirty business" and pointing out that the federal law enforcement officials in this case had violated a state law which forbade wiretapping and that the Court ought not to condone lawless activity by law enforcement officers. Justice Brandeis, also in dissent, warned of the possible extensive invasions of privacy that electronic eavesdropping might produce, and urged that such surveillance—like the searches undertaken under the old general search warrants—was completely unchecked, since everything was heard, not just conversations dealing with alleged criminal activity.

Congress acted on wiretapping in 1934, and included in the Federal Communications Act a provision that forbade the interception of phone messages by persons not authorized by the sender of such messages. The Court held that the provision of the Act forbade interception by federal agents and that wiretap evidence was not admissible in a Federal trial.[42]

In later cases involving electronic surveillance, the Court adhered to the doctrine of *Olmstead* that an unreasonable search must involve some trespass, but appeared to reject the notion that conversations did not enjoy the protection of the Fourth Amendment. In two cases involving eavesdropping —one involving a listening device outside a room[43] and the other a hidden transmitter carried by a government agent while conversing with a suspect[44]—the Court upheld the introduction of evidence. In both, though, the majority opinion appeared to rely upon the lack of trespass by officers rather than on the fact that the evidence obtained was a conversation. In 1961, the Court ruled inadmissible evidence obtained by use of a so-called "spike mike"—a listening

---

[42]*Nardone* v. *United States*, 302 U.S. 379 (1937).

[43]*Goldman* v. *United States*, 316 U.S. 129 (1942).

[44]*On Lee* v. *United States*, 343 U.S. 727 (1952).

device which was driven through a wall and into an air shaft—by police agents. The Court ruled that though this might not constitute a technical trespass under the law, it did involve an "actual intrusion into a constitutionally protected area."[45]

Thus, the doctrine developed by the Court in the area of wiretapping seemed to undermine the *Olmstead* holding that conversations were not protected by the Fourth Amendment. What appeared to be the touchstone of the application of the Fourth Amendment was the existence of some physical intrusion.

The Court further developed doctrine dealing with electronic surveillance in two crucial cases in 1967, one involving the issuance of warrants and the other the physical intrusion doctrine.

In *Berger* v. *New York*,[46] the Court overturned a New York statute dealing with electronic surveillance by law enforcement officials. The New York statute authorized judges to issue orders permitting such surveillance upon receiving an oath from various law enforcement officials stating there "was reasonable ground to believe that evidence of crime may thus be obtained, and particularly describing the person or persons whose communications . . . are to be overheard or recorded and the purpose thereof."[47] The statute thus met the Fourth Amendment requirement that an independent magistrate make the decision. The majority of the Court, however, found the New York statute deficient in terms of the standards developed for the issuance of search warrants:

> The Fourth Amendment commands that a warrant issue not only upon probable cause supported by oath or affirmation,

[45]*Silverman* v. *United States*, 365 U.S. 505 (1961), at 512.
[46]388 U.S. 41 (1967).
[47]388 U.S. 43.

but also, 'particularly describing the place to be searched, and persons or things to be seized.' New York's statute lacks this particularization. It merely says that a warrant may issue on reasonable ground to believe that evidence of crime may be obtained by the eavesdrop. It lays down no requirement for particularity in the warrant as to what specific crime has been or is being committed, nor 'the place to be searched,' or 'the persons or things to be seized' as specifically required by the Fourth Amendment. The need for particularity and evidence of reliability in the showing required when judicial authorization of a search is sought is especially great in the case of eavesdropping.[48]

The *Berger* opinion thus made it clear that electronic surveillance fell within the purview of the Fourth Amendment. It further implied that it was permissible, if narrowly drawn statutes dealing with the issuance of warrants were developed. The difficulties in drawing such warrants and engaging in permissible surveillance were manifest, though, since it was not clear what constituted "the place to be searched" or "the things to be seized" that might be specified in a valid search warrant. In the next important surveillance case, *Katz* v. *United States*,[49] the Court not only gave an example of what it felt might be permissible surveillance, but also abandoned the doctrine of physical intrusion developed in previous cases.

Katz had been convicted of transmitting betting information in violation of a federal statute. The crucial evidence against him, admitted at trial over his objections, was a series of recordings of his voice in several telephone conversations. The material had been obtained by a listening device attached to the outside of a public phone booth from which he had made calls. The FBI had been careful not to record the conversations of others, and had overheard and recorded only the voice of the defendant. The Court of Appeals had

[48]388 U.S. 55-56.
[49]389 U.S. 347 (1967).

rejected the defendant's move to exclude the recordings, reasoning that there was no Fourth Amendment violation because "there was no physical entrance into the area occupied by [the petitioner]."[50]

The Court overturned the conviction, and with it the general doctrine that a Fourth Amendment claim turned on the existence of a physical intrusion: " . . . the Fourth Amendment protects people, not places."[51] Admitting that the absence of some physical penetration was "at one time thought to foreclose further Fourth Amendment inquiry,"[52] the Court held that this test had been eroded and was no longer controlling. Thus, both lines of the *Olmstead* opinion—the argument that conversations were not subject to the Fourth Amendment protection, and the test of physical intrusion in determining the applicability of the Fourth Amendment—were rejected by the majority:

> . . . the reach of that Amendment cannot turn upon the presence or absence of a physical intrusion into any given enclosure. . . . The Government's activities in electronically listening to and recording the petitioner's words violated the privacy upon which he justifiably relied while using the telephone booth and thus constituted a 'search and seizure' within the meaning of the Fourth Amendment. The fact that the electronic device employed to achieve that end did not happen to penetrate the wall of the booth can have no constitutional significance.[53]

Was this search, conducted without a warrant, permissible under the provisions of the Fourth Amendment? The Court said no. The absence of a warrant, issued by a judicial officer on the basis of evidence justifying the search and delimiting the scope of the search, made the activities an unreasonable

[50]389 U.S. 349.
[51]389 U.S. 351.
[52]389 U.S. 352.
[53]389 U.S. 353.

search under the terms of the Fourth Amendment. But the majority opinion granted that the activities of this search—limited to listening to only the petitioner's words, based upon prior investigation that gave the officers probable cause to believe that the defendant was engaged in unlawful conduct—might have been permissible had they obtained a warrant. Thus, though in this case the search was unreasonable because the officers did not obtain a warrant the Court intimated that there was proper ground for the issuance of a warrant and had they obtained it, apparently the evidence would have been admissible. Further, the Court argued, this type of search did not qualify for the usual exceptions to the requirement for a warrant—e.g., searches incident to a lawful arrest. Thus, the Court appeared to argue that electronic surveillance almost always requires the prior permission of magistrate, but that such permission could be granted if probable cause were shown, the crime specified, the surveillance reasonably restricted to the activities of the person named in the warrant. The Court indicated in a footnote that it was not in this case passing upon nor necessarily requiring prior permission from a magistrate in cases involving "the national security."[54]

Justice Harlan concurred in the result, agreeing that the intrusion rule should be rejected because this test for Fourth Amendment protection was "in the present day, bad physics as well as bad law, for reasonable expectations of privacy may be defeated by electronic as well as physical invasions."[55] Harlan went on to say he did not read the majority opinion to require that *any* interception of a conversation in a public telephone booth was unreasonable in the absence of a war-

[54] Footnote 23, 389 U.S. 358.

[55] 389 U.S. 362. Justice Black responded to this statement in his dissent, saying: "Such an assertion simply illustrates the propensity of some members of the Court to rely on their limited understanding of modern scientific subjects in order to fit the Constitution to the times and give its language a meaning that it will not tolerate." 389 U.S. 372.

rant, and that he would decide this question when he had to.

Justice Black was the lone dissenter in *Katz*. Adhering to his literal reading of the command of the Fourth Amendment, he argued that conversations were not protected by the language of the Amendment:

A conversation overheard by eavesdropping whether by plain snooping or wiretapping, is not tangible and, under the normally accepted meanings of the words, can neither be searched nor seized. . . . Rather than using language in a completely artificial way, I must conclude that the Fourth Amendment simply does not apply to eavesdropping.[56]

Black then articulated his own brand of "strict construction":

Since I see no way in which the words of the Fourth Amendment can be construed to apply to eavesdropping, that closes the matter for me. In interpreting the Bill of Rights, I willingly go as far as a liberal construction of the language takes me, but I simply cannot in good conscience give a meaning to words which they have never before been thought to have and which they certainly do not have in common ordinary usage. I will not distort the words of the Amendment in order to "keep the Constitution up to date," or "to bring it into harmony with the times." It was never meant for this Court to have such power, which in effect would make us a continuously functioning constitutional convention.[57]

Black's view has, on its own terms, a kind of appealing consistency to it. But he does not really come to terms with his own position in *Mapp*—that the combination of the Fourth and Fifth Amendment protections produces results that the Fourth itself might not. Black's dissent in *Katz* quotes approvingly the following view expressed by Chief Justice Taft in *Olmstead:*

[56]389 U.S. 365.
[57]389 U.S. 373.

Justice Bradley in the Boyd case . . . said that the Fifth Amendment and the Fourth Amendment were to be liberally construed to effect the purpose of the framers of the Constitution in the interest of liberty. But that cannot justify enlargement of the language employed beyond the possible practical meaning of houses, persons, papers, and effects, or so to apply the words search and seizure as to forbid hearing or sight.[58]

Yet recall that in the *Mapp* case, Black chose to combine the Fourth and Fifth to find a constitutional basis for the exclusionary rule. In *Mapp*, Black had quoted the portion of *Boyd* which said that the Court was "unable to perceive that the seizure of a man's private books and papers to be used in evidence against him is substantially different from compelling him to be a witness against himself."[59] Is not the seizure of a man's own words even more directly compelling him to be a witness against himself? Black does not answer this question in *Katz*, rather preferring to fall back on the exact words of the Fourth alone. In *Mapp* he adopted the *Boyd* combination of the Fourth and the Fifth, even though it was "perhaps not required by the express language of the Constitution strictly construed"; in *Katz* he was unwilling to do so. Thus, as suggested before, strict construction, even in the hands of one of its most consistent proponents, is an elusive concept.

The legal status of wiretapping is still somewhat unclear, and depends not only upon the Court but upon what legislation the Congress chooses to pass and what practices the executive branch attempts to utilize.[60] What the Court has

[58] 389 U.S. 368.

[59] 367 U.S. 662.

[60] For example, members of the Department of Justice have recently urged that the government possesses extensive powers to engage in surveillance of domestic radical groups without prior judicial scrutiny. Protection of national security is proposed as the justification for such power.

apparently achieved, however, is to bring electronic surveillance under the ambit of the Fourth Amendment, something that appears on the surface obvious, yet took a long time in coming. The majority opinion in *Katz* appeared to suggest that warrants are generally, if not invariably, required for such surveillance, at least in the absence of a consideration of "national security." The reservations expressed by Justice Harlan and changes in Court personnel since *Katz* leave the future course of wiretapping under the Fourth Amendment somewhat unclear. But the growth of technology and use of surveillance devices indicates that the problem is one that will increasingly occupy the attention of the Court and of our society generally.

THE PRIVILEGE AGAINST SELF-INCRIMINATION

Another important cornerstone of the system of due process is the privilege against self-incrimination. The Fifth Amendment provides that no person "shall be compelled in any criminal case to be a witness against himself." As with the closely related protection against searches and seizures, the self-incrimination provision grew out of practices in England in which individuals were put under oath and asked incriminating questions. Since oaths were taken quite seriously, such practices involved strong pressures upon the individual to make incriminating statements, even when no physical coercion was involved. The protection against such compulsion developed in England before the American revolution and was, as indicated, incorporated in our Bill of Rights.

Justifications for the privilege

Why should those accused of crime not be asked questions about their guilt or innocence? Why should they not be required to give their version of the alleged crime and have their testimony subjected to cross-examination and available to the judge or jury in determining guilt or innocence? To many, it appears that the innocent have nothing to fear from such testimony, and that only the guilty will potentially suffer. Recent developments dealing with the application of the Fifth Amendment protection to police interrogation of suspects give these questions special importance, for it is often claimed that the implementation of this privilege seriously interferes with law enforcement. What, then, are the justifications for a protection that, at least arguably, makes it harder to convict the guilty?

Two somewhat independent justifications have been offered for the protection. One deals with the question of reliability of statements; the other with the protection of the dignity of the individual from incursions by the state. The issue of reliability provides the clearest and most plausible justification for the protection. Techniques used by law enforcement officers to obtain damaging admissions from suspects are sometimes rather coercive. Ranging from the third-degree method—which involved such tactics as beating, whipping and other physical abuse of suspects in the attempt to induce them to admit to criminal activity—to somewhat more subtle tactics of extended interrogation, isolation from friends, relatives, and legal advice, and threats of dire consequences if the suspect failed to admit guilt, police interrogation tactics may subject the suspect to rather intense pressures to admit his guilt. Since admissions made as a result of coercion are potentially unreliable—the defendant may admit to activities in which he did not engage simply to end his ordeal—the privilege against self-incrimination under these circumstances appears soundly based upon factual premises, upon the desire to avoid "mistakes" in the administration of criminal justice.

The other justification for the privilege is somewhat more openly normative, broader in scope, more diffuse and perhaps harder to defend. The American criminal justice system is, at least in theory, an adversary system. The individual is presumed to be innocent until proven guilty; the burden of proof is upon the state; a man's freedom is not to be deprived upon the whim of the state, but only upon a compelling demonstration of guilt; absent such demonstration, he is presumed innocent and not to be subjected to punishment. And, the argument goes, a cornerstone of the presumption of innocence and the burden of proof upon the state is the notion that the individual not be compelled to give testimony against himself, that the state must assume the burden of developing the independent evidence of guilt. The root of this notion of an adversary system lies in the value placed upon the dignity of the individual, upon fear of tyranny of the state and consequently, the placing of restrictions upon its ability to invoke the criminal sanction, upon the notion that a free society depends upon such preservation of the integrity and dignity of the individual. As Chief Justice Warren observed in a discussion of the privilege against self-incrimination:

> ... As a 'noble privilege often transcends its origins,' the privilege has come rightfully to be recognized in part as an individual's substantive right, a 'right to a private enclave where he may lead a private life. That right is the hallmark of our democracy'.... We have recently noted that the privilege against self-incrimination—the essential mainstay of our adversary system—is founded on a complex of values. ... All these policies point to one overriding thought: the constitutional foundation underlying the privilege is the respect a government—state or federal—must accord to the dignity and integrity of its citizens. To maintain a 'fair state-individual balance,' to require the government 'to shoulder the entire load,' ... to respect the inviolability of the human personality, our accusatory system of criminal justice demands that the government seeking to punish an individual produce the evidence against him by its own independent labors, rather than by the cruel, simple expedient of compelling it from his own mouth.[61]

It is clear that the two justifications operate on different premises. That is, the question of whether testimony or a

[61]*Miranda* v. *Arizona*, 384 U.S. 460.

confession is "reliable," or true, is quite a different matter from whether *any* self-incriminating testimony violates an individual's dignity or his privacy. Presumably, if reliability were the sole concern, many incriminating statements that were coerced would still be permissible, for not all statements made under coercion are untrue, and independent, coroborative evidence could be used to test the reliability of such statements. The Court, as indicated in Warren's remarks above, has taken a much broader view of the nature, justification, and extent of the privilege. The Court has concentrated upon the issue of whether the individual was coerced into testifying against himself, and held that if coercion was applied, fundamental fairness was denied. The first confession cases dealing with coercion involved physical coercion—torture of suspects—but the Court gradually moved to include other forms of coercion more subtle but nonetheless intimidating. In developing the scope of the privilege, though, both strands suggested above—the substantive issue of reliability and the procedural issue dealing with the integrity of the adversary system—have been present.

The privilege against self-incrimination is both a powerful tool restricting the powers of the government in moving against individuals and a very complex provision, for, like most of the Bill of Rights, its bare language covers a variety of issues. Among the questions that the privilege has presented are: (1) In what sorts of proceedings by the government does the privilege apply? The language of the amendment refers to "any criminal case," but what of administrative hearings, legislative investigations, statutes requiring the keeping and production of records or registration, interrogation by law-enforcement officers? The Court has generally construed the amendment liberally to protect the rights of individuals in many contexts in which the government might seek incriminating information.[62] (2) What

---

[62] See, for example, *Blau* v. *United States*, 340 U.S. 159 (1950), affirming the applicability of the privilege to congressional investigations; *Albertson* v. *Subversive Activities Control Board*, 382 U.S. 70

constitutes a waiver of the privilege?[63] (3) Can the state grant the individual immunity from prosecution, and thereby compel testimony?[64] (4) Does the privilege extend to state proceedings: That is, is it incorporated into the Due Process Clause of the Fourteenth Amendment? (5) What constitutes "being compelled": That is, what constitutes coercion in violation of the privilege?

We shall concentrate here upon aspects of the latter two questions presented by the privilege: the incorporation issue and the application of the privilege to police interrogation of suspects. As indicated above, these are by no means the only issues raised by the privilege, but they are among the most significant. The problem of interrogation and confessions is not precisely coterminous with the privilege, for, until very recently, the Court treated the confession issue in the context of the "fundamental fairness" doctrine of the Fourteenth Amendment rather than in the specific context of the privilege. But the Court recently has moved to utilize the privilege against self-incrimination as a means to deal with the problem of police interrogation and confessions, and this development has been among the most significant and controversial recent doctrinal developments dealing with criminal justice.

Incorporation of the privilege

In previous sections and chapters, I referred to the debate that has long raged on the Court over the relationship between the provisions of the Bill of Rights and the Due Process Clause of the Fourteenth Amendment. One wing of

---

(1965), dealing with the registration provisions of the McCarran Act; *Marchetti* v. *United States*, 390 U.S. 39 (1968) and *Grosso* v. *United States*, 390 U.S. 62 (1968), dealing with the federal gambling tax statute; *Haynes* v. *United States*, 390 U.S. 85 (1968), dealing with the federal firearms registration law; *Leary* v. *United States*, 395 U.S. 6 (1969), dealing with the marijuana tax statute.

[63] See, for example, *Rogers* v. *United States*, 340 U.S. 367 (1951).

[64] See, for example, *United States* v. *Murdock*, 284 U.S. 141 (1931) and *Murphy* v. *Waterfront Commission of New York*, 378 U.S. 52 (1964).

the Court, led by Justice Black, has contended that the Due Process Clause incorporates, and makes applicable to states, all of the provisions of the Bill of Rights. The predominant view of the Court, though, has been that the Due Process Clause merely incorporates those rights that are essential to fundamental fairness or are "implicit in a concept of ordered liberty."

The history of the privilege against self-incrimination in this incorporation process is complicated, but may be briefly summarized as follows: The Court twice in this century refused to incorporate the privilege against states[65]; during the period after its second refusal (1947) the Court did incorporate other provisions of the Bill of Rights and developed more demanding standards dealing with the relationship of interrogation and confessions to the concept of a "fair" trial; finally, in 1964, the Court explicitly incorporated the Fifth Amendment privilege into the Fourteenth Amendment.

In 1964, when the Court incorporated the privilege into the Due Process Clause,[66] the majority Court referred to the incorporation of other provisions of the Bill of Rights (e.g., the protection against searches and seizures in *Wolf* and *Mapp*; the holding in *Gideon* that states were required to provide counsel to indigent defendants) and to a line of cases, discussed in the next section, that had begun to limit the admissibility of confessions in criminal trials if there was evidence of coercion. This latter line of cases had not been based upon the privilege (since it was not yet incorporated) but had indicated a movement toward implementation of the accusatorial system in state as well as federal prosecutions. The Court concluded in *Malloy* v. *Hogan*:

> We hold today that the Fifth Amendment's exception from compulsory self-incrimination is also protected by the Fourteenth

[65]*Twining* v. *New Jersey*, 211 U.S. 78 (1908); *Adamson* v. *California*, 331 U.S. 46 (1947).

[66]*Malloy* v. *Hogan*, 378 U.S. 1 (1964).

Amendment against abridgement by the States. . . . The Fourteenth Amendment secures against state invasion the same privilege that the Fifth Amendment guarantees against federal infringement—the right of a person to remain silent unless he chooses to speak in the unfettered exercise of his own will, and to suffer no penalty, as held in *Twining*, for such silence.[67]

As suggested above, the developments of the coerced confession cases and the incorporation of the privilege against state action were related. The coerced confession cases became an important justification for incorporation of the privilege; the privilege against self-incrimination then became a powerful tool in the further development of standards governing interrogation and admissibility of confessions.

Coerced confessions

Though the Court did not hold until 1964 that defendants in state proceedings enjoyed the privilege against self-incrimination protected by the Fifth Amendment, doctrinal developments since the 1930s placed limitations upon interrogation techniques used by police officers and the admissibility of confessions obtained by such interrogation. These decisions relied primarily upon the notion of "fundamental fairness" protected by the Due Process Clause. In discussing this line of cases, David Fellman points out that the Court used two types of justification for banning coerced confessions, which parallel the justifications for the privilege against self-incrimination discussed at the opening of this section:

On the one hand, a confession is bad if it is untrustworthy in the light of the confessor's power to resist the methods used to induce him to confess. On the other hand, a confession may be regarded as inadmissible if it was obtained by methods offensive to due process, without regard to the question of the probable falsity of the confession. The first test is concerned with the danger of erroneous

[67]378 U.S. 6, 8.

convictions, the second with the danger of tolerating uncivilized police methods.[68]

The first important confession case was *Brown* v. *Mississippi*.[69] Mississippi police had tortured the defendants in order to extort a confession. The Supreme Court overturned the conviction, making it clear that the use of such confession in a state proceeding violated the Due Process Clause of the Fourteenth Amendment. The Court clearly eschewed reliance upon the self-incrimination clause of the Fifth Amendment.

In 1940,[70] the Court again threw out a state conviction, this time involving somewhat less blatantly physical methods of coercion, but including arrest on suspicion without a warrant, denial of contact with friends or attorneys, and long periods of questioning by different squads of police officers.

A long line of cases dealing with the admissibility of confessions followed. As in the right-to-counsel cases, the Court adopted an *ad hoc* approach for evaluating the admissibility of confessions in state proceedings. Often called the "totality of circumstances" rule, it involved an evaluation by the Court (or, at the trial level, by the judge or jury) in each case of the circumstances surrounding the obtaining of a particular confession—the age and maturity of the defendant, the nature of the charge, the degree of pressure put upon the defendant, the length of interrogation, etc.—and of whether the confession was coerced, its admission thereby rendering the trial unfair. During the late 1950s and early 1960s, the Court evinced an increasing tendency to reverse convictions using this test, though they continued to adhere to it. The Court ruled inadmissible confessions involving a variety of forms of coercion, some quite blatant, some more subtle— including long periods of questioning and attempts at gaining

[68] Fellman, *op. cit.*, p. 181.

[69] 297 U.S. 278 (1936).

[70] *Chambers* v. *Florida*, 309 U.S. 227 (1940).

the sympathy of a defendant via an old friend on the police force[71]; threats to bring in a defendant's wife for questioning[72]; threats to place a suspect's children in the custody of welfare officials[73]; an admission by a wounded defendant while under the influence of a so-called "truth serum"[74]; and refusal to permit a defendant to call his wife or lawyer during an extensive period of interrogation.[75]

In 1964, three different developments converged in doctrine concerning the rights of defendants during interrogation. First, as suggested above, the Court had been sharpening its totality-of-circumstances test, using it to overturn increasingly subtle techniques for inducing suspects to make damaging admissions. Second, the right-to-counsel cases (discussed in Chapter Four), culminating in the *Gideon* decision of 1963, pointed to the possibility of combining the right to counsel with the protection of the suspect's rights while undergoing custodial interrogation. Finally, 1964 saw the incorporation of the privilege against self-incrimination into the Due Process Clause of the Fourteenth Amendment.

In the celebrated *Escobedo* case,[76] the Court faced the problem of a defendant who had made damaging admissions while being interrogated, after he had asked for and been refused an opportunity to consult with his attorney. The Court overturned Escobedo's conviction, saying:

> We hold, therefore, that where, as here, the investigation is no longer a general inquiry into an unsolved crime but has begun to focus on a particular suspect, the suspect has been taken into police custody, the police carry out a process of interrogation that lends itself to eliciting incriminating statements, the suspect has requested and

[71]*Spano* v. *New York*, 360 U.S. 315 (1959).

[72]*Rogers* v. *Richmond*, 365 U.S. 534 (1961).

[73]*Lynumn* v. *Illinois*, 372 U.S. 528 (1963).

[74]*Townsend* v. *Sain*, 372 U.S. 293 (1963).

[75]*Haynes* v. *Washington*, 373 U.S. 503 (1963).

[76]*Escobedo* v. *Illinois*, 378 U.S. 478 (1964).

been denied an opportunity to consult his lawyer, and the police have not effectively warned him of his absolute constitutional right to remain silent, the accused has been denied the 'Assistance of Counsel' in violation of the Sixth Amendment to the Constitution as made obligatory upon the states by the Fourteenth Amendment, *Gideon* v. *Wainwright*, and that no statement elicited by the police during the interrogation may be used against him at a criminal trial.[77]

Though a big step, the *Escobedo* ruling, as indicated in Justice Goldberg's remarks above, was still couched somewhat in the particularized language of the totality-of-circumstances rule. Soon thereafter, though, the Court drew the lines of development I have alluded to here to their logical conclusion in the highly controversial *Miranda* decision.[78]

Miranda was actually four cases—from New York, Arizona, California, and a federal case from the Ninth Circuit Court of Appeals—which the Court grouped together for argument and decision. In the *Miranda* opinion, the Court attempted to answer some of the questions *Escobedo* had raised but not resolved: Exactly what rights did the defendant have? Was it a constitutional requirement that he be informed of them? Was the state obligated to provide an attorney if an indigent suspect undergoing interrogation desired but could not afford one?

The *Miranda* rules, based upon the Fifth Amendment privilege against self-incrimination (*Escobedo* had been based upon the Sixth Amendment right to counsel), were a distinct break from past cases, for the Court rejected the ad hoc totality-of-circumstances rule. In place of this approach, the Court spelled out some behavioral guidelines for law-enforcement officials and held that if these procedures were not followed, any statement elicited would be inadmissible. The *Miranda* rules were as follows:

[77]378 U.S. 490-491.

[78]*Miranda* v. *Arizona*, 384 U.S. 436 (1966).

To summarize, we hold that when an individual is taken into custody or otherwise deprived of his freedom by the authorities in any significant way and is subjected to questioning, the privilege against self-incrimination is jeopardized. Procedural safeguards must be employed to protect the privilege, and unless other fully effective means are adopted to notify the person of his right of silence and to assure that the exercise of the right will be scrupulously honored, the following measures are required. He must be warned prior to any questioning that he has the right to remain silent, that anything he says can be used against him in a court of law, that he has the right to the presence of any attorney, and that if he cannot afford an attorney one will be appointed for him prior to any questioning if he so desires. Opportunity to exercise the rights must be afforded to him throughout the interrogation. After such warnings have been given, and such opportunity afforded him, the individual may knowingly and intelligently waive these rights and agree to answer questions or make a statement. But unless and until such warnings and waiver are demonstrated by the prosecution at trial, no evidence obtained as a result of interrogation can be used against him.[79]

The *Miranda* decision met with a storm of resistance both from the law-enforcement community and from those concerned with "crime in the streets." The decision was said to hamstring law enforcement officers. Such criticism was based upon two explicit premises: that confessions are an essential tool of effective apprehension and conviction of law violators; and that informing a suspect of his rights would greatly reduce the incidence of confessions. The third, usually unarticulated, premise of this critical view of *Miranda* was that the police would follow the Court's ruling and give warnings.

The impact of Miranda

A substantial amount of research dealing with police behavior following the *Miranda* ruling suggests, as in the case of the

[79]384 U.S. 478-479.

search and seizure rulings, that doctrinal change was not automatically followed by behavioral change, and, furthermore, that the apocalyptic view of the impact of the *Miranda* decision was perhaps misguided. Though the research discussed here is not definitive, and is subject to modification should contrary evidence be adduced, it does suggest that *Miranda* had none of the consequences that the Court or its critics suggested would follow from the enunciation of the rules for custodial interrogation.[80]

Both the New Haven and Washington studies first challenge the hidden premise in the critics' view: that the police would follow the ruling and give the warnings. The authors of the Washington study conclude:

> In contrast to the first premise underlying the Court's decision in *Miranda* that the police would give adequate and effective warnings of legal rights and honor the accused's exercise of those rights, the police in fact were reported to have failed to observe the spirit and often the letter of *Miranda*.[81]

The New Haven study comes to essentially the same conclusion: Police officers did not provide the warnings to all defendants. The authors of the New Haven study indicate that the absence or presence of warnings was not random:

> The suspect of a serious crime was most likely to get a more adequate warning in the cases where the police had enough evidence to go to trial, but not enough for a conviction. Thus, the police seemed most careful to insure the admissibility of the suspect's

[80] For studies of the impact of the *Miranda* decision on police behavior, see Michael Wald, et al., "Interrogations in New Haven," *Yale Law Journal*, 76 (1967), 1521-1648; Albert Reiss and Donald Black, "Interrogation and the Criminal Process," *Annals of the American Academy of Political and Social Science* (1967), pp. 47-57; Medalie, et al., *op. cit.*

[81] Medalie, et al., *ibid.*, p. 1394.

statement when they had a case against the suspect but when it was not clear that he could be convicted without an incriminating statement as evidence. The detectives apparently worried less about the admissibility of the statement if the case seemed open and shut. They were also apparently more willing, from sheer necessity, to take a chance of admissibility when they did not have enough evidence to get to trial unless the suspect incriminated himself.[82]

The difficulties surrounding effective compliance included not only the ostensibly simple procedure of informing the suspect of his rights. Both studies suggest that when officers did give the warnings, they would often do so in a fashion not designed to make it likely that the suspect would exercise his rights: giving the warnings in a flat bureacratic tone which indicated that the words were simply a ritual; or in a manner which implied that though the rights were available, it would not be in the interest of the suspect to exercise them. Moreover, the D.C. study suggests that a good deal of field interrogation took place prior to the offering of the warnings once the suspect reached the stationhouse.

Both studies suggest that many suspects either did not understand the warnings, or felt they were some form of trickery (e.g., that the lawyer offered was a police agent). The D.C. study indicates:

> In contrast to the second premise that the defendants would be able to have a sufficient basis from the warnings to decide in their own best interest whether to remain silent and to choose counsel, the defendants were loathe to use attorneys and frequently gave statements to the police because of their inability to apply *Miranda* to their own circumstances. Over nine-tenths of those arrested for felonies and serious misdemeanors did not request counsel . . . nor did . . . over one-third of those who reported having been given the [stationhouse counsel] warning.[83]

[82] Wald, et al., *op. cit.*, p. 1554.
[83] Medalie, et al., *op. cit.*, p. 1385.

Finally, the New Haven study suggests that, contrary to many of the statements made by critics of the *Miranda*, perhaps confessions are not as crucial to law enforcement as expected:

> ... interrogations play but a secondary role in solving the crimes of this middle-sized city, both because serious offenses are relatively infrequent and because the police rarely arrest suspects without substantial evidence. ... The reason is simple: unless the criminal is caught red-handed or unless witnesses are available, the police with their limited resources for scientific investigation cannot amass enough evidence to arrest a suspect. And since such evidence when available is all but conclusive, by the time the police have a suspect the crime is solved, conviction is assured and interrogation unnecessary.[84]

Thus, for a variety of reasons—noncompliance by police officers, lack of understanding or trust on the part of suspects, the overemphasis upon confessions as essential to crime solution, etc.—*Miranda* did not prove the disaster many predicted it would. But for some of the same reasons—noncompliance during field and stationhouse interrogation, the difficulties in developing schemes to effectively provide counsel to indigent suspects, distrust and misunderstanding on the part of suspects—neither was *Miranda* the boon that the Court and its defenders suggested it might be. The Court spoke in its *Miranda* opinion of redressing the balance between law enforcement officials and the suspect, of permitting him to make intelligent choices about how to proceed without coercion and with the advice of competent counsel should he so desire it. The studies on the impact of *Miranda* suggest that this goal has not been reached.[85] The

[84] Wald, et al., *op. cit.*, p. 1613.

[85] We have discussed here some of the difficulties that typical defendants seem to encounter in understanding and utilizing the warnings the Court ordered they be given. Similar difficulties were encountered by much more highly educated and sophisticated indi-

decision was no doubt a movement toward this goal, but the dynamics of the legal system—the gap between the "ought" of doctrine and the "is" of behavior—again demonstrate that the protection of the civil liberties depends upon much more than the words of the Court.[86]

OTHER DEVELOPMENTS IN CRIMINAL JUSTICE

The areas of doctrinal development in the administration of the criminal justice system discussed thus far—the right to counsel, the rights of defendants in interrogation, and searches and seizures—are, I believe, the most significant in recent litigation dealing with this area of civil liberties. But they by no means exhaust the Court's treatment of criminal justice. In the past ten years especially, the Court has dealt with almost all of the procedural protections in the Bill of Rights and has incorporated almost all of them against state proceedings. The Court has been emphasizing the Due Process Model of the criminal system, attempting to judicialize the process, to protect the rights of defendants against the application of the criminal sanction. In making these doctrinal innovations, the Court has been running against strong currents, both in public opinion and in the structure of the criminal justice system. Proponents of the slogan "law

---

viduals undergoing questioning in connection with draft law offenses. See John Griffiths and Richard E. Ayres, "A Postscript to the Miranda Project: Interrogation of Draft Protestors," *Yale Law Journal*, 77 (1967), pp. 300-319.

[86]In addition to the difficulties encountered in implementing Miranda, a recent Court decision has somewhat undercut the holding of the Miranda case. In *Harris* v. *New York* 401 U.S. 222 (1971), the Court held that a defendant's prior statements to police officers which were inconsistent with his trial testimony were admissible to impeach his credibility, even when police had obtained the statements without giving the Miranda warnings. This opinion, written by Chief Justice Burger, is perhaps another indication of the interaction of doctrine and activities in the broader political system. The five-justice majority included two justices appointed by President Nixon whose presidential campaign had stressed the "law and order" issue.

and order" have not been pleased by the Court's attempts to judicialize the criminal justice system and to protect the rights of defendants—for as suggested before, many of the procedural protections the Court has been moving to vouchsafe appear to make it more difficult to efficiently capture, process, convict, and punish those who break the law. Moreover, the structure of the criminal justice system itself relies heavily upon informal mechanisms, upon fact-finding outside the rigorous safeguards of the courtroom, upon an informal system of negotiation—called plea-bargaining—by which the vast bulk of defendants in criminal cases are induced to plead guilty in return for considerations offered by the state (e.g., reduced sentences, charges reduced or dropped, etc.). The emphasis upon formalizing the criminal justice system, then, has not been popular, and has not—as suggested in the previous discussions of search and seizure and custodial interrogation—been self-executing, but has encountered quite intense countercurrents. At this point, I am going to briefly sketch some of the other doctrinal developments in the area of criminal justice, and then return to their behavioral context.

Jury trials

The Sixth Amendment provides that "in all criminal prosecutions, the accused shall enjoy the right to a speedy and public trial, by an impartial jury of the State and district wherein the crime shall have been committed. . . ." As with most provisions of the Bill of Rights, the bare language of the amendment leaves many questions unanswered: For example, what is a criminal prosecution? What is an impartial jury? Is this right applicable to state prosecutions? The Court has dealt with all these questions, though, for some, the answers are still developing and the doctrine is in a state of flux. The Court did not hold that defendants in state proceedings enjoyed the right to a jury trial until 1968. In the leading case of *Maxwell* v. *Dow*[87] the Court held, in line with other

[87]176 U.S. 581 (1900).

incorporation cases of the period, that the right to trial by jury was not incorporated against the states by the Due Process Clause of the Fourteenth Amendment. In 1968, however, the Court held that, as with other provisions of the Bill or Rights, the right to a jury trial did apply to state proceedings.[88]

In what types of proceedings is a defendant entitled to a jury trial? The Court has never held that *all* defendants are entitled to a jury trial, but only that those charged with serious crimes possess this right, and the Court is still developing doctrine which differentiates serious from petty crimes. The standard is based upon the penalty that the law authorizes a judge to impose for a violation. The current standard—both for federal and state courts—appears to be six months' imprisonment. This test is not completely definitive, but the general state of the law today appears to suggest that regardless of whether a crime is called a felony or a misdemeanor, if the law authorizes penalties of more than six months the defendant is entitled to a jury trial; if less, he is not.[89]

If a defendant is entitled to a jury trial, what is an impartial jury? Again, the Court has approached this issue rather gradually, and the doctrine at this stage is not completely clear. For example, is racial discrimination in the selection of the jury a violation of the right to an impartial jury? The formal exclusion of blacks from juries was declared unconstitutional in 1880.[90] But the Court has also held that the Constitution does *not* require that each black defendant is entitled to a jury made up entirely or in part of blacks.[91]

---

[88] *Duncan* v. *Louisiana*, 391 U.S. 145 (1968).

[89] The most recent pronouncement on this subject was *Baldwin* v. *New York*, 399 U.S. 66 (1970).

[90] *Strauder* v. *West Virginia*, 100 U.S. 303 (1880).

[91] *Virginia* v. *Rives*, 100 U.S. 313 (1880); "Fairness in selection has never been held to require proportional representation of races upon a jury." *Akins* v. *Texas*, 325 U.S. 398 (1945) at 403.

The response in the South to the striking down of formal barriers to blacks was to abandon open, legally imposed discrimination and rather to fail to place the names of blacks on jury lists. The Court moved to strike this practice down, beginning with the 1935 decision in *Norris* v. *Alabama*.[92] Here, and in later cases, the Court examined the racial composition of communities and the representation of whites and blacks on grand and petit juries. When there was a marked disparity between the number of black citizens and their representation upon juries in the locality[93] the Court treated this as a *prima facie* demonstration of unconstitutional discrimination (if past legal discrimination had been practiced) and overturned convictions. The Court has held that when a *prima facie* case of discrimination is presented (either through testimony about discrimination or a statistical demonstration of substantial variance from the distribution of blacks within the population), the burden of proof falls upon the state to demonstrate there has been no discrimination.[94]

If an impartial jury cannot be selected by a system that excludes certain racial or ethnic groups from membership, what about other characteristics, for example socioeconomic status or attitudes toward the law? The Court upheld the New York scheme for so-called "blue ribbon" juries—juries used for especially important or complex cases made up of more affluent, highly educated members of the community. In upholding the blue-ribbon jury scheme, the Court held (in

[92] 294 U.S. 587 (1935).

[93] For an analysis of the jury discrimination cases suggesting that the Court—in evaluating disparities between representation of blacks in the community and on juries—was implicitly using a test similar to that of statistical significance, see S. Sidney Ulmer, "Supreme Court Behavior in Racial Exclusion Cases: 1935-1960," *American Political Science Review*, 56 (1962), pp. 1325-1330.

[94] See, for example, *Hill* v. *Texas*, 316 U.S. 400 (1942); *Avery* v. *Georgia*, 345 U.S. 559 (1953); and *Hernandez* v. *Texas*, 347 U.S. 475 (1954), which applied the discrimination rule to the exclusion of Chicanos from jury service.

an opinion by Justice Jackson) that for a successful constitutional attack on a jury selection procedure, the petitioner must show both systematic exclusion of a class of citizens and some indication that this exclusion affects the outcome of cases before such a jury.[95] Justice Murphy, in a dissent joined by three other justices, took a somewhat different position:

> But there is a constitutional right to a jury drawn from a group that represents a cross-section of the community. And a cross-section of the community includes persons with varying degrees of training and intelligence and with varying economic and social positions. Under our Constitution, the jury is not to be made the representative of the most intelligent, the most wealthy or the most successful, nor of the least intelligent, the least wealthy or the least successful. It is a democratic institution, representative of all qualified classes of people.[96]

Thus, the status of socioeconomic discrimination in jury selection is somewhat unclear. Presumably a demonstration that individuals of a certain socioeconomic class (e.g., poor people) were consciously and systematically excluded from all jury service would be held unconstitutional. It is somewhat less clear what the Court would do with a demonstration that, in a given locality, the poor did not serve on juries in proportion to their numbers in the population. Whether the Court would hold that substantial deviation from population proportion creates a presumption that discrimination exists is a moot question.

What of the opinions of the jury? The prosecution or defense is entitled to challenge jurors who express bias for or against either side, who indicate that they cannot exercise impartiality in the matter before them. The Court has not spoken out more generally on the nature of "impartiality"

[95]*Fay* v. *New York*, 332 U.S. 261 (1947).

[96]332 U.S. 299-300.

except in a few cases, the most recent of which dealt with the so-called "death qualified" jury. Many jurisdictions, including Illinois, from which *Witherspoon* v. *Illinois* arose,[97] permitted the prosecution in capital cases to excuse for cause jurors who indicated either opposition to the death penalty or conscientious scruples against it. Though schemes varied from state to state, the general principle was the same: to eliminate from juries in cases involving the death penalty jurors who had objections to the penalty; hence the term "death qualified" for juries that were "qualified" or willing to impose the penalty. The Court held that this scheme was unconstitutional, and indicated in its opinion something of its recent notions of what constitutes an impartial jury:

> ... a jury that must choose between life imprisonment and capital punishment can do little more—and must do nothing less—than express the conscience of the community on the ultimate question of life or death. Yet, in a nation less than half of whose people believe in the death penalty, a jury composed exclusively of such people cannot speak for the community. Culled of all who harbor doubts about the wisdom of capital punishment—of all who would be reluctant to pronounce the extreme penalty—such a jury can speak only for a distinct and dwindling minority ... Specifically, we hold that a sentence of death cannot be carried out if the jury that imposed or recommended it was chosen by excluding veniremen for cause simply because they voice general objections to the death penalty or expressed conscientious or religious scruples against its infliction. No defendant can be put to death at the hands of a tribunal so selected. Whatever else might be said of capital punishment, it is at least clear that its imposition by a hanging jury cannot be squared with the Constitution.[98]

The Court did not hold, as Justice Douglas urged in his concurring opinion, that the Constitution requires that even

[97] *Witherspoon* v. *Illinois*, 391 U.S. 510 (1968).
[98] 391 U.S., 519-520, 521-523.

jurors who are opposed to the death penalty may not be challenged for cause. The majority in *Witherspoon* indicated that if the state permitted challenge for cause of all jurors who said they automatically would not vote for conviction if it involved the death penalty, this question would be resolved when it came up and was not involved in this case. Justices Black, Harlan, and White dissented, arguing that in the Illinois scheme selection of "death qualified" juries was permissible since it simply sought to eliminate jurors who could not be impartial as to the guilt or innocence of the defendant.

The import of the majority opinion in *Witherspoon* is somewhat unclear. The reference in the opinion to the state of public opinion, and the apparent importance the majority attached to the fact that a substantial part of the population had opinions about an issue relevant in a case—here the death penalty—has potentially very great implications. For example, laws on drug control are a matter of dispute in this country today. Suppose the state were permitted to challenge, in a case involving a prosecution for possession of marijuana, all potential jurors who thought that there should be no laws forbidding the use of possession of marijuana. Would a jury so constituted be in a position to "express the conscience" of the community? The point raised by *Witherspoon*—that when there is dispute over the propriety of certain laws or penalities the state may not load the dice in favor of those of one view or the other—could be applied quite consistently, I think, to change drastically the notion of what constitutes an "impartial" jury. Whether the Court will, in the future, choose to do so, is of course an open question.[99]

[99]The issue of jury composition is becoming more salient as various groups of political dissidents (e.g., Black Panthers, the Chicago Eight, draft resistors) are increasingly challenging jury selection procedures and memberships. The bias against the young, the poor and the black that seems to characterize many American juries is thus becoming the subject of controversy and perhaps will result in further doctrinal development dealing with jury composition.

Justice for juveniles

One of the most striking manifestations of the recent trend of the Supreme Court in pursuing the Due Process Model and judicializing the criminal justice system came in the area of juvenile justice. The juvenile court systems developed in this country during the twentieth century consciously eschewed the adversary model of normal criminal courts. In an effort to treat juveniles with greater compassion and individual attention, the juvenile court system abandoned the adversary model and its procedural protections and put in its place an informal system in which a paternalistic judge was to act as a father would in judging and punishing wayward children. The child was not to be treated as "guilty" or "innocent," as adults were, but rather his conduct was to be evaluated and the most effective means to induce him to become a better member of the community were to be chosen by the judge as representative of society. Thus, the juvenile court system has been characterized by the informality and lack of regard for constitutional safeguards that also long characterized the criminal justice system generally—but in the juvenile court system, this procedure was a matter of conscious legislative choice rather than informally developed expedient.

The Supreme Court set out to reform the juvenile system in the latter part of the 1960s, to make the system conform more closely to the Due Process Model that the Court was also pursuing in the criminal justice system for adults. In part, this choice was informed by a growing realization that the informal and putatively paternalistic system of juvenile justice had too often in practice become a means by which young offenders were quickly and often carelessly processed and punished. As the Court observed in its first major foray into the juvenile justice system:

> ... the highest motives and most enlightened impulses led to a peculiar system for juveniles unknown to our law in any comparable context ... And in practice ... the results have not been entirely satisfactory. Juvenile court history has again demonstrated

that unbridled discretion, however benevolently motivated, is frequently a poor substitute for principle and procedure. In 1937, Dean Pound wrote: 'The powers of the Star Chamber were a trifle in comparison with those of our juvenile courts. . . . ' The absence of substantive standards has not necessarily meant that children receive careful, compassionate, individualized treatment. The absence of procedural rules based upon constitutional principle has not always produced fair, efficient, and effective procedures. Departure from established principles of due process have frequently resulted not in enlightened procedure, but in arbitrariness.[100]

Thus, the Court moved to make the juvenile justice process, at the doctrinal level at least, more like the criminal justice process for adults. In *In re Gault*, the Court held that juvenile defendants were entitled to the right to effective and specific notice of charges, to representation by counsel (and appointment of counsel if the defendant were indigent), to the right to confront and cross-examine witnesses, and to exercise the privilege against self-incrimination. In *Re Winship*,[101] the Court held that the defendant is entitled to the same presumption of innocence enjoyed by an adult offender. In *Winship*, the defendant, a juvenile, had been judged to have committed a robbery under a New York law that provided for the judge to make his decision upon the "preponderance of the evidence." The Supreme Court held that juvenile defendants, like others, should not be convicted unless guilt were proven beyond a reasonable doubt.

The *Gault* decision encountered many of the same difficulties discussed in the implementation of the interrogation cases. The extension of rights to defendants did not result in immediate or complete compliance. The leading study on *Gault* indicated that, in the three cities studied, there was extensive noncompliance with the doctrine set forth in *Gault*:

[100]In Re Gault, 387 U.S. 1 (1967) at 17, 18, 19.
[101]Re Winship, 397 U.S. 358 (1970).

If there is one central conclusion which emerges from our study, it is that total compliance with the word and spirit of the pronouncements in *Gault* will come gradually. . . . the fact remains that in the Metro and Gotham juvenile courts—and in courts like Metro and Gotham—children are frequently and sometimes flagrantly denied their constitutional rights. . . . In many courts the need undoubtedly is for new juvenile court judges, less oriented to a traditional juvenile court philosophy and more disposed to a 'legalistic' approach in their courtroom procedure.[102]

Thus, the juvenile court decisions illustrate once more two of the basic themes of this chapter and the book as a whole. First, that there has been distinctive and important doctrinal development aimed at more vigorously protecting the civil liberties and rights of citizens in our society (in the context of the criminal justice system, toward emphases upon the adversary model and the rights of defendants). Second, and equally important, such doctrinal trends are in many ways not the end of consideration of the rights that our citizens enjoy, but often just the beginning.

Double jeopardy and confrontation of witnesses

In addition to dealing with the areas of criminal justice discussed thus far, the Court also moved to incorporate other provisions of the Bill of Rights against state proceedings, and to amplify their meanings. The provision of the Fifth Amendment which forbids placing a defendant twice in jeopardy for the same offense was incorporated against states in *Benton* v. *Maryland*,[103] reversing a contrary holding of 1937.[104] The Court also incorporated into the Due Process Clause of the Fourteenth Amendment and made applicable

---

[102]Norman Lefstein, et al., "In Search of Juvenile Justice: Gault and its Implementation," *Law and Society Review*, III (1969), pp. 491-562, at 559, 561.

[103]395 U.S. 784 (1969).

[104]*Palko* v. *Connecticut*, 302 U.S. 319 (1937).

to state proceedings the right of defendants to confront their accusers.[105] This development was designed in part to eliminate the practice of using statements made against defendants by witnesses not available to testify at the defendant's trial.

In addition to incorporating the confrontation right to state proceedings, the Court has very recently dealt with another aspect of confrontation that is likely to become a salient legal issue in the future. This issue involves the defendant who attempts to disrupt his own trial. The leading case, *Illinois* v. *Allen*,[106] involved a defendant in a robbery case who made threats against the judge and generally disrupted his trial. The trial court responded by excluding him from the courtroom for a period at his trial. The Supreme Court upheld this procedure as a proper means of dealing with disruptive defendants, as well as suggesting that other remedies might be used—e.g., holding the defendant in contempt, binding and gagging—without contravening the defendant's right to confront his accusers. This case is important, and the general issue is crucial, because of the problems raised by defendants who feel they are being persecuted for their political beliefs (e.g., Panthers, the Chicago Eight, draft resistors) and who respond to this perceived persecution by disrupting the proceeding. If there is an increase in the number of trials of political dissidents, the problem of courtroom disruption will probably grow. The *Allen* opinion, countenancing remedies even though they do some violence to the defendant's right to confront his accusers, appeared aimed at this more general problem, though it arose in the context of the trial of an apparently nonideological defendant.

Retroactivity

The decisions dealing with criminal justice dealt with most aspects of the treatment of criminal defendants. A perplexing

---

[105]*Pointer* v. *Texas*, 380 U.S. 400 (1965); *Douglas* v. *Alabama*, 380 U.S. 415 (1965).

[106]397 U.S. 337 (1970).

problem raised by these decisions involved their potential application to defendants still in custody but whose cases had been decided finally before the new Supreme Court rulings. Many still serving sentences had been tried under procedures (e.g., admission of illegally obtained evidence, stationhouse interrogation, lack of jury) that the Court subsequently declared to be invalid. Were these individuals entitled to have their cases reopened? The Court generally held that its decisions were not retroactive, and that individuals whose cases had been finally decided before a Supreme Court decision was handed down were not entitled to reopen their cases. Thus, the Court spared itself and the legal system generally the enormous potential burden of retrying all those who had been convicted under previously valid practices.[107]

THE POLITICS OF THE CRIMINAL JUSTICE SYSTEM

In the course of this chapter we have discussed developments in the protection of rights of individuals accused of crime. Several observations may be made about this process by which procedural rights are developed, protected, and extended to citizens. The first observation, which should be manifest in light of the discussion of cases, is that recent years have seen extensive doctrinal development of protec-

---

[107]The major exception was the *Gideon* decision dealing with the right to counsel. This decision was given full retroactive effect. See *Linkletter* v. *Walker*, 381 U.S. 618 (1965) and *Burgett* v. *Texas*, 389 U.S. 109 (1967). The exclusionary rule of *Mapp* v. *Ohio* was held not retroactive in *Linkletter* v. *Walker*, 381 U.S. 618 (1965); the *Griffin* rule outlawing comment by prosecutors on a defendant's failure to testify was held not retroactive in *Tehan* v. *Shott*, 382 U.S. 406 (1966); the *Miranda* rules were held to be prospective only in *Johnson* v. *New Jersey*, 384 U.S. 719 (1966) but the Court did hold that the traditional tests for voluntariness of confessions were available to defendants whose cases were still under appeal; the Katz doctrine dealing with the inadmissibility of evidence derived from electronic surveillance was held prospective and applicable only to cases in which the prosecution attempted to introduce evidence gathered after the date of the *Katz* decision—see *Desist* v. *United States*, 394 U.S. 244 (1969).

tions of the rights of defendants. The Court has been moving toward implementation of the due process values that have putatively characterized our criminal justice system, but that have been generally ignored in practice.

This doctrinal movement has not operated in a broader social or political climate that has been particularly receptive to protection of the rights of criminals. Some of the survey data presented in this and preceding chapters suggests that most Americans are somewhat skeptical about, if not hostile to, the procedural safeguards the Court has been attempting to implement. Moreover, the slogan "law and order," a salient symbol in current American society, both in its rhetoric and legislative manifestations, quite often runs contrary to the trend being pursued by the Court. The reasons for public hostility toward the extension of rights to criminals are complex, and perhaps somewhat obscure.

The general feeling that our society is becoming less law-abiding and that crime rates are rising probably accounts for doubts about the advisability of legal doctrine that makes it appear harder rather than easier to apprehend and punish criminals. In addition, social offenders are very much outside of the mainstream of American life. They are somewhat hard to view as an oppressed minority in the sense that blacks or poor people are (though people accused of crime are themselves often black or poor). They are not likely to develop their own interest groups or to participate in the political process in an attempt to develop legislation and litigation protective of their rights. Thus, criminal suspects are relatively powerless both personally and as a group. They are not in a position to come together and mobilize resources in their own behalf. Much of the organizational support they can muster has lately come from groups (e.g., the NAACP Legal Defense Fund, the ACLU) that attempt to stand in as their representatives in the judicial and legislative forums. In fact, the most active "representative" and "advocate" of the rights of social offenders has been the Supreme Court itself. Even more than in the areas of freedom of expression or equality, the Court itself has taken up the cause of due process and become its most salient proponent.

Thus, in many of the milestone cases of recent years the impetus for development of rights of defendants appears to have come from the Court itself. Many of the lawyers who took these milestone cases up to the Court were themselves not so much interested in developing general legal doctrine protective of the rights of defendants as they were simply in winning the cases for their particular clients. In a study of lawyers who argued civil liberties cases before the Supreme Court, this point was suggested as follows: "The outcomes in [criminal justice] cases, often involving sweeping changes in legal and social policy, were to a large extent the unintended by-products of the activities of the attorneys [who argued these cases before the Supreme Court]. There were quite noticeable discontinuities between the kinds of outcomes pursued by the lawyers and those that eventually emerged from judicial decision."[108]

Unlike some of the other areas of civil liberties discussed here, the doctrinal developments in the area of criminal justice have frequently resulted from the Court's taking what appeared to be rather run-of-the-mill cases and using them as vehicles for the enunciation of broad policy. In part, one can view the current issue of "law and order" as a product of the Court's decisions. By moving to protect the rights of defendants, the Court has helped to place this issue on the agenda of our society. We had been indifferent about the disjunction between the "ought" of the principles upon which our criminal justice system was supposed to rest and the "is" of its operation. The Court has attempted to close the gap to some extent. The decisions in this area have not been self-executing, and we have not suddenly moved from the Crime Control Model to the Due Process Model. But the

---

[108]Jonathan D. Casper, "Lawyers Before the Supreme Court: Civil Liberties and Civil Rights, 1957-1966," *Stanford Law Review*, 22 (1970), 487-509, at 485.

Court's decisions have made citizens and political institutions face more squarely the issue of what rights alleged criminals ought to enjoy. The outcome of the interaction between the Court and the broader society is as yet quite unclear. But the Court has, in a sense, made manifest a latent conflict in the society, made us face up more squarely to the process by which we deal with those accused of violating the criminal law. The outcome may be that we will come to reject some of the values we are supposed to embrace, or we may move to implement these values. In any event, the decisions have raised the issues, not resolved them. They have been met with often intense resistance, and we have currently by no means reached the full and effective implementation of due process values. The complexity of the process by which decisions are translated into changes in behavior—or, more often, modified or ignored—is crucial to understanding the politics of civil liberties.

The implementation of criminal justice decisions

In the discussion in the preceding chapter of the implementation of doctrinal changes aimed at eliminating racial discrimination, it was suggested that difficulties were encountered both within and outside of the court system itself. That is, in order to translate doctrinal changes enunciated by the Court into behavioral changes in the society at large, a variety of individuals, groups, and institutions must cooperate. The cooperation of public officials is a product of a variety of factors, including their own attitudes toward the proposed change, the constituency which they feel themselves to be serving, the nature and strength of their role perception, and the system of rewards and sanctions in which they find themselves to be operating. In the school desegregation cases discussed before, one of the difficulties in obtaining compliance was the unwillingness of many lower court judges to cooperate, both because many were personally unsympathetic to integration and because of the intense social pressure to which they were subjected in their communities.

Given the Supreme Court's unwillingness to intervene often or effectively in the pace of integration for a long period, the lower courts and school officials were presented with a situation in which there were strong rewards and few penalties attached to noncompliance.

In the criminal justice cases, the crucial participants in the process by which the doctrinal reforms of the Court are translated into behavioral change are lower court judges, police officers, prosecutors, and defense attorneys. As with southern judges and school boards dealing with integration, many law enforcement personnel (e.g., police, judges, prosecutors) have not been particularly sympathetic to the policies being pursued by the Court. Many of them, especially policemen, see themselves as the first line of defense against lawnessness and their primary concern is that of apprehending and punishing criminals. Due process values often seem to interfere with these goals, and many law enforcement officials view them with distaste, if not contempt. This is not particularly surprising, for their role tends to produce greater concern with crime control than with the protection of the rights of defendants. Using the concepts discussed earlier, most lower-level law enforcement personnel, especially police officers, are more concerned with factual guilt than with legal guilt. The due process values being emphasized by the Court—which have the effect of tightening up the standard of legal guilt and, perhaps, widening the gap between factual and legal guilt by making the latter more difficult to demonstrate—thus encounter hostility on the part of many of the officials whose behavior must be modified if the doctrinal change is to be translated into behavioral change.

Given the hostility on the part of many members of the law enforcement community to some of the policies pursued by the Supreme Court, the implementation of such decisions becomes difficult. In the sections dealing with search and seizure, custodial interrogation, and juvenile justice, we looked briefly at some empirical research into the effects of doctrinal change, suggesting that such decisions have often met with resistance and noncompliance. Effective compliance, given the hostility of many of those whose behavior must be changed, would appear to depend upon two crucial variables—role and sanctions. Role—self-expectations and expectations of others about the behavior of an individual who is a member of a social system—is crucial in that it can induce occupants of positions in the legal community to behave in ways that they would not behave if given the opportunity to exercise their own preferences. Thus, a lower court judge may not like a decision like *Miranda* or *Mapp*, but may obey it because his conception of his role as a judge—as a subordinate of the Supreme Court in the legal system—requires that he follow the orders of his superiors. By the same token, prosecutors and police officials may, by virtue of their perceptions of their role as members of the legal community, modify their behavior to conform to the rules promulgated by what is perceived to be the most legitimate authority in the legal system.[109]

The notion of role is probably crucial in the compliance of many law enforcement officials who would not otherwise obey. A related and perhaps more potent variable in the compliance process is the application of sanctions—punishment that occurs if compliance is not forthcoming. The lower court judge is punished by having his decisions reversed by appeals courts; the prosecutor is punished by having his case thrown out, or crucial evidence excluded; the policeman is punished by a dismissal of his case or the prosecutor's refusal to prosecute a case in which evidence has been obtained through means that offend the law.

The defense lawyer is crucial in this model of the compliance process. He raises the new defenses that are provided by doctrinal change emerging from the Supreme Court (e.g., moves to have evidence or a confession

---

[109]An alternative response is to deny the legitimacy of the Court, to assert that it has so far overstepped its bounds that it has lost its legitimate authority to establish rules.

excluded). The lower court judge either complies by following the doctrine and granting the defense request, or refuses to do so and is reversed by an appeals court. Once the trial court has indicated a willingness to comply with the doctrinal change, the prosecutor must comply as well, for if he refuses, he will lose cases. His willingness to comply is then communicated to police officers, who find that the prosecutor is refusing to prosecute cases brought to them.

This model is neat, and appears quite plausible. Granted that it may take time (for example if the local judge refuses to comply until reversed several times), it looks as though it will work, producing changes in behavior and procedures that are desired by the Supreme Court. The compliance process may be even simpler, for local prosecutors or police officials may themselves read new Court decisions and decide to comply voluntarily, without waiting for the local judges to begin to sanction them.

There are two major difficulties with the model of compliance suggested above, and these contribute greatly to the degree to which doctrinal changes emerging from the Supreme Court can be effectively modified or ignored. The first is that the model depends upon the assumption that prosecutors and police are primarily interested in convictions—for the model suggests that this is what they lose by noncompliance. As students of police behavior have suggested, however, often the police are not solely interested in convictions. They may be interested in developing informants and information about other offenders. As suggested in Skolnick's discussion of search and seizure, the upper echelons of police departments may be concerned with vigilance and effective intervention in suspicious activity as well as with convictions; hence an officer who searches a suspect without probable cause on the basis of a furtive movement may gain the approval of his superiors even though the evidence obtained is not admissible. Of course, in the long run, police officers and their superiors *are* interested in convicting law violators. But the analysis above suggests that this is not their *only* goal, and the pursuit of other goals may lead them to ignore doctrinal rules in some instances simply because they are not so concerned with bringing the suspect to trial as they are in pursuing some of their other goals.

Plea-bargaining

The second deficiency in the compliance model suggested above is even more important. The model is based upon the assumption that defendants will *exercise* the doctrinal rights that they are granted by the Court, that their attorneys will raise defenses offered them by doctrinal innovation. However, the reality of the American criminal justice system to a large extent disputes this assumption. Though estimates vary, the vast majority of all defendants convicted in criminal cases in this country plead guilty to the charges placed against them. The reasons for the defendants' choice to do so involve, among other things, simply an acknowledgement of their guilt and willingness to take their medicine; the choice of the relative anonymity of the "cop-out" ceremony (the court proceeding in which the guilty plea is accepted by the judge) over the potential publicity of a trial; knowledge that juries and judges are prone to convict if a trial occurs; and, perhaps most important, considerations offered them by the state in return for their guilty plea.

Thus, the typical defendant in the American system does not, as television drama so often suggests, go to trial with a wily attorney attempting to pick holes in the prosecution case, taking advantage of every possible defense. Rather he appears before a judge, enters his guilty plea, goes through a litany of questions about his guilty plea (e.g., are you pleading guilty because you are guilty? were you coerced into pleading guilty? were you promised anything in return for a plea of guilty? etc.), gives the acceptable answers (which are often simply a charade since in fact the plea is the result of a bargain) and is judged guilty. Thus, ours is what has been called a system of "bargain justice" more than it is truly an adversary system.[110]

Defendants plead guilty because, often, they receive something in return for it—a reduction of charge (e.g., from assault to disorderly conduct, from armed robbery to robbery, from first degree murder to manslaughter), a deal about the length of sentence to be imposed, a promise of probation, etc. Prosecutors bargain for a variety of reasons, the most important of which is that guilty pleas avoid time-consuming trials. The major resource the prosecutor has to bargain with is the ability to modify the charge and affect the penalty. In addition to avoiding trials and saving time, plea bargaining, from the perspective of the prosecutor, has another important advantage—it suppresses legal issues and potentially embarrassing or damaging challenges to the state's case.

Police officers, though they often complain about plea-bargaining, also gain from it. They save the time spent waiting around and testifying in trials. Perhaps more important, the plea-bargaining process is useful in clearing cases, "solving" crimes, and the clearance rate is one of the most commonly used indicators in evaluating police performance by superiors, political figures, and the public at large. In many situations, a defendant charged with a particular offense will admit that he has committed a number of other crimes—with an agreement that he will be charged with, plead guilty to, and be punished for, his most recent arrest. Thus, in the process of plea-bargaining the police may be able to clear several other cases on the basis of admissions by the defendant.

Some students of the plea-bargaining process have sug-

[110]For an introduction to the plea-bargaining process, see Abraham Blumberg, *Criminal Justice* (Chicago: *Quadrangle*, 1967); Donald J. Newman, *Conviction: The Determination of Guilt or Innocence Without Trial* (Boston: Little, Brown and Company, 1966); Arnold S. Trebach, *The Rationing of Justice* (New Brunswick, N.J.: Rutgers University Press, 1964).

gested that the defense attorney is often the crucial participant, acting in what one scholar has called the role of "double agent." The defense attorney, bargaining for his client, is often pursuing not only the goal of getting the best possible deal for his client; he is also, some research suggests, pursuing personal goals and acting as a representative of the system and perhaps the prosecution as well.[111] Thus, many lawyers specializing in criminal work in trial courts may depend for their incomes upon turning over a relatively large number of cases representing clients paying small fees. Plea-bargaining is a relatively efficient and quick means of turning over large numbers of cases. Some research suggests that sometimes lawyers will trade one client for another—in large-scale bargaining sessions with prosecutors and judges in which the fates of several clients are determined. Not only is plea-bargaining efficient for the defense attorney, but he develops—especially if he is a court regular, practicing most of the time in the same court system—interpersonal relationships and dependencies in his dealings with prosecutors and judges. The lawyer's contact with his client will usually be brief and short-lived; he "lives" with the prosecutors and judges who are members of the social system of which he is a member. Of course, by no means all (or perhaps even most) criminal defense lawyers are solely pursuing the kinds of personal goals suggested in the last few sentences. Most defendants probably are guilty, and the plea-bargaining process offers them a way of potentially mitigating their punishment. Thus even the most devoted and noble defense attorney will often find that it simply appears in the interest of his client to plead guilty in return for some consideration.

The criminal justice system is, to a large extent, a

---

[111] See Abraham S. Blumberg, "The Practice of Law as a Confidence Game: Organizational Cooptation of a Profession," *Law and Society Review*, 1 (1967), pp. 15-40. For a discussion of defendants' perceptions of their attorneys—especially public defenders—see Jonathan D. Casper, *American Criminal Justice: The Defendant's Perspective* (Englewood Cliffs, N.J.: Prentice-Hall, 1972), ch. 4.

bargaining process in which each participant (defendant, prosecutor, judge, defense attorney) has resources and goals, and the outcome is the product of the application of these resources in a bargaining game.

Plea-bargaining does not look much like our conception of the adversary system: the formal battle in the courtroom, the strictly controlled contest most of us think of when we conceive of what it is like to be charged with a crime and to put the state to the test of demonstrating its case. Rather it more resembles a game, though the stakes are terribly high. Moreover, it has developed and flourished for a reason. It is much more efficient than going to trial, and, one might hypothesize, it produces results with which the participants are satisfied. Whether the gap between the "is" of plea-bargaining and the "ought" of the adversary model is a good or a bad thing, the system does exist, it is the predominant mode in American criminal justice, and it has crucial consequences for the implementation of Supreme Court decisions attempting to judicialize the administration of criminal justice and to move towards the protection of due process rights.

For, as suggested above, plea-bargaining *suppresses* legal issues. A guilty plea obviates the necessity of (or, from another perspective, prevents) raising defenses about the character of the evidence against the defendant, the activities of the police in their treatment of him, the right to a jury trial, or whatever. A defendant who agrees to a bargain generally forgoes his ability to raise issues about his procedural rights (though, the existence of potential defenses is a resource to be used by the defendant and his attorney in bargaining with the prosecution).

From the perspective of police officers, then, following procedural rules (e.g., about searches and seizures, interrogation, etc.) is not the overwhelming concern it would be if it were likely that each defendant would use every procedural imperfection as a weapon in his defense. Rather, much police conduct not conforming to legal doctrine will be buried in the process which eventually results in a guilty plea.

Recall that the New Haven study on the impact of *Miranda* suggested that police were most conscientious about following the *Miranda* rules when they had enough evidence to go to trial but not enough for a conviction. They were less careful when they had an open-and-shut case even without a confession or when they had insufficient evidence to go to trial without some incriminating statement. One might suggest that it is the plea-bargaining process which is behind this finding. The police were willing to fish for incriminating statements in the absence of evidence in hopes that a confession would produce a guilty plea; by the same token, the strength of their case, even in the absence of a confession, made them lax in following the rules, for, again, a guilty plea was likely. It is in the case where a trial was most likely that they followed the *Miranda* rules most closely.

CONCLUSION

Thus, the Supreme Court rulings not only encounter difficulty in implementation because preferences of law enforcement officials often are hostile to the goals pursued by the Court. Implementation runs into difficulties because of the absence, to a large extent, of an effective mechanism for sanctioning conduct that does not follow doctrinal rules. The reality of the system, plea-bargaining, tends to suppress doctrinal issues, to make behavior not in compliance with doctrinal innovation less likely to produce sanctioning that will reduce future noncompliance. This is not to say by any means that law enforcement officials will never obey new doctrinal rules promulgated by the Court, nor that most willfully disobey. What it does argue is that the translation of doctrine into behavior involves a number of participants with different preferences, goals, and resources, and that this fact produces a wide gap between the doctrine enunciated by the Court and the behavioral changes that must occur if that doctrine is to become reality.

In the area of criminal justice, as we have seen, there are forces at work that make implementation difficult and slow, but the future will probably bring increased compliance. Especially important may be the Supreme Court decisions dealing with the provision of counsel. For if more and more defendants are provided with counsel, they will be in a position to assert their rights more effectively. Research dealing with the activities of defense counsel—some of which has been discussed briefly above—suggests that defense counsel may not in all cases be expected to carry out singlemindedly the function of protecting the rights of their clients, for they have personal goals and interpersonal relations to maintain that may affect their performance. And, it appears quite unlikely that plea-bargaining will in the foreseeable future disappear as the predominant mode of the operation of the criminal justice system.[112] But perhaps the provision of attorneys to defendants will make the sanctioning necessary to compliance by police officers more effective. More defendants may choose to go to trial if police misbehavior occurs; more defendants may threaten to go to trial and use this resource to garner better deals from prosecutors. In either case, sanctioning will occur, and compliance will presumably increase.

Thus, the translation of doctrinal change into behavioral change will, no doubt, increase in the area of criminal justice. It seems unlikely, given the efficiencies of plea-bargaining, that we shall move towards a true adversary system. But the provision of rights to defendants by the Court will affect police practices, resulting in a growing respect for the rights of defendants. The gap between doctrine and behavior,

---

[112] In *North Carolina* v. *Alford*, 400 U.S. 20 (1970), the Supreme Court held that it was permissible for a trial court to accept a guilty plea of a defendant who maintained his innocence, so long as there was evidence of his guilt and no indication that he had been coerced. The Court thus recognized that a defendant might find it in his interest to plead guilty to a crime he claimed he did not commit in order to lessen his possible punishment.

though, will continue to exist, regardless of what the Court does. This is an inevitable and perhaps defining characteristic by which civil liberties and civil rights operate in our society.

SIX
THE POLITICS OF
CIVIL LIBERTIES

THIS study has stressed two themes in recent civil liberties litigation: the expansion of these liberties in the past fifteen years and the importance of viewing Supreme Court decisions in a perspective that includes activities in the broader political system of which the Court is a part.

In all of the issue areas discussed, recent years have seen extensive and often quite rapid expansion of civil liberties at the doctrinal level. This expansion has come as a result of increasingly broad interpretation of the protections of the Constitution (especially the process of incorporation of such protections against state action), and a movement toward vouchsafing the rights of minorities not fully enjoying the liberties putatively extended to other groups in our society.

In the area of expression, the Court, after a period of repression during the 1950s, moved to expand the protections of the First Amendment. Striking down vestiges of the loyalty-security program and often dealing tolerantly with forms of expression going beyond writing or speaking, the Court has helped open our political system to new forms of expression. Granted that the Court has moved in fits and starts, showing more zeal at some times than at others in the protection of freedom, the general trend has been towards increasing the amount of political expression protected from governmental infringement.

In dealing with the value of equality, the Court has pursued the goal of equality of opportunity, often somewhat beyond the preferences of the public, especially in the area of racial discrimination. In dealing with substantive equality, the Court has been somewhat less innovative, dealing quite sympathetically with governmental programs designed to produce more material equality in the society but not attempting to develop new forms of material redistribution in the society. Thus, the Court has been quite protective of the rights of individuals to participate in the marketplace of social and political life, pursuing the goal of equality of opportunity. Though we may regret the fact that the marketplace has not produced the substantive equality which would seem just, the doctrinal developments pursued by the Court have helped to point up these inequalities and have helped to place more saliently on the agenda of our society the inequities that our system has produced.

The activism and expansive mood of the Court has nowhere been more manifest than in the area of criminal justice. The suspect and defendant in our criminal system are far outside the mainstream of American social and political life. Because many of these individuals lack the resources for effective participation in the political system and because their acts are often viewed as rendering them justifiably vulnerable to whatever ills may befall them, they have lacked an effective advocate in our society. The result has been a criminal justice system characterized by procedures and practices that seem simply unjust. The Court took upon itself the burden of becoming the advocate for defendants in our society. In one sense, this might be viewed as simply its natural role: The Court is the highest authority in the legal system and hence should pay particular attention to its own machinery, including the criminal justice system. But previous Courts refused to play this role and countenanced, indeed legitimated, many practices that today seem odious. Thus, the activity of the Warren Court in attempting to reform the criminal justice system was no mean feat. Moreover, the combination of a rising fear of crime and Supreme Court decisions dealing with the treatment of offenders produced a new political issue. The Court's work in this area really was only a beginning, not an end, for the criminal justice system has not been completely reformed by Court decisions; rather, the administration of justice has become a more salient political issue. Thus, in this area, as in the others discussed here, doctrinal developments have been protective of civil liberties, often in innovative fashion, but have not produced the revolution in behavior that one might imagine if he simply read the cases and paid attention only to the developments in doctrine emerging from the Court.

This suggests the second theme emphasized here: the importance of the political context in which the Court does its work and doctrinal change emerges. Most of us are ambivalent about the political role that the Court plays in our society. Survey research suggests that most Americans believe that the Court's major function is interpreting the law or the Constitution, that the issues it deals with and the method by which it reaches decisions are peculiarly legal. By the same token, though, the decisions of the Court constantly touch issues that Americans care about, making policy that meets with support and opposition. The often cynical dictum that the Court follows the election returns exemplifies this ambivalence about the Court. The statement recognizes that the choices the Court makes are related to developments in the broader political system, but bespeaks a dislike of this fact and a longing for the Court to stick to its own business and decide legal questions on legal grounds.

As I've tried to argue, such a hope is futile. The questions that face the Court, particularly when dealing with Constitutional issues, are political, involving the allocation of values in our society. Though forms of legal reasoning—*stare decisis*, argument by analogy, neutral principles, etc.—are tools to be used by the Court, they do not typically provide unambiguous answers to the questions that come to the Court for resolution. Moreover, because these questions are highly political, there would be something amiss, if the Court proceeded to decide them on the basis of criteria that failed to take account of the state of opinion and activities in the political system.

To say that the Court is a political institution, that the doctrine emerging from it is related to activities in the broader political system, is not to say that there is always a neat congruence between doctrine and attitudes and behavior in the society. Many of the issue areas discussed here have produced marked disparities between the policies being pursued by the Court and preferences of other institutions and the people at large. The Court can be "ahead" of and "behind" the dominant political trends in our society. The developments in recent years in the areas of criminal justice, racial equality, schoolhouse religion, and pornography are probably examples of the Court's being "ahead" of the bulk of the polity. The reactionary protection of *laissez-faire* by the Court during the 1930s is an example of a Court lagging "behind" changes in preferences in the larger political system.

If there is not always a neat congruence between doctrine and attitudes and behavior, neither does everything always "work out" in the end. There is in fact no "end," for the issues that the Court deals with are recurring questions that are never resolved, but are constantly being considered and about which tentative decisions are made. The doctrinal shifts we have seen in the area of freedom of expression, for example, have not by any means arrived at a fixed "answer" to the question of how much speech shall be protected in our society. We see today questions being raised that have been dealt with extensively in the past. The "answers" to the question of what speech is protected and what is not that have been developed in the past—clear and present danger, balancing, absolutism, etc.—are still available and can be brought forth in particular cases. But two crucial points remain. Almost none of the tests provides unambiguous answers to decide specific cases, and which of these "answers" the Court will choose in any particular case during any particular era depends greatly upon the currents abroad in the political system.

This lack of congruence between doctrine emerging from the Court and developments in the political system, as well as the often tortuous path that the Court follows in applying doctrine to various issues at different times suggests a further point. In discussing doctrinal developments here—especially in the areas of racial equality and criminal justice—we have alluded to research indicating that often doctrinal development is not met with immediate or complete compliance. Rather, behavior lags being doctrine; the policy being pursued by the Court is not always embraced by those who are putatively the "subordinates" of the Court, but is often met with indifference if not hostility. If we view this process from a hierarchical perspective, looking at the legal system as though the Court were the ultimate arbiter of certain issues, it would appear that there is something wrong with noncompliance, that noncompliance is an indication that the system is not functioning properly. But the relationship between the Court, other government institutions, and the people at large is in an important sense not a hierarchy at all. Sometimes the Court will be at the top of the hierarchy issuing orders and making policy that will produce immediate compliance by those whose behavior must be affected if its policy is to be effective. In the vast bulk of cases that come before the Court this is in fact the way the system operates, for the Court can issue reasonably unambiguous orders to lower courts and expect them to be obeyed.

But many of the issues discussed here, because they are allocative and touch upon behavior that is important to people in the society, do not have this character. The Court can order that John Smith be released from jail or given a new trial, with a reasonable expectation that this order will be followed by the behavior necessary to carry it out. The Court cannot order that every police officer in the nation inform a suspect of his rights during custodial interrogation with the same expectation of compliance. The Court can order that the convictions of a group of civil rights demonstrators be overturned and they be released and expect that they will be freed. It cannot order that southerners be more tolerant toward advocates of racial equality and cease harassing them for their activities.

Thus, when making broad social and political policy, the Court can expect to and does encounter a good deal of resistance and noncompliance. And such noncompliance is not a symptom of something "wrong"; it is simply a defining characteristic of a system in which legal doctrine interacts with preference and prejudice. Noncompliance may be an essential element of the role that the Court plays in our political system. We have given the Court the power to "decide" questions that are basically political. The system has characteristics that tend to make doctrine promulgated by the Court congruent with the decisions made by other institutions and with the preferences of the polity (e.g., the appointment process). But such mechanisms are not infallible: Neither can the Court invariably gauge correctly the preferences of "the people" nor do "the people" in fact have identical, or sometimes even any, preferences about the issues that come before the Court. In this sense, noncompliance can be an essential element in the interaction between the Court, other institutions of government and the people at large. For noncompliance is a kind of safety-valve, permitting accommodations to occur when the "correct" policy—defined by that which will permit the system to continue to function, by what is "right," or in whatever way one chooses—is unclear and must emerge gradually. Thus, noncompliance is part of a colloquy between the Court and the society that it serves, a defining characteristic of our system, not a defect in it.

The protection of civil liberties and civil rights in American society involves the Court and other institutions, as well as doctrine, attitudes, and behavior. The nature of the issues, the equivocal support that civil liberties enjoy in our society, the ambiguity of the doctrinal tools with which the Court must deal all make this process complicated and often controversial. A reading of the cases, or attention to the doctrine, sometimes gives the impression that the issues in dispute are in some sense *sui generis* and "legal"—that there are right and wrong answers. More careful reading of the cases should dispel this impression. This is not to say that there are no criteria for judging the doctrinal work of a judge or a court, nor that the opinions are irrelevant and that only the preference of the judge and the outcome of the case matter. Members of the legal community do have standards for what is "good" and "sound" judicial reasoning and result and what is not. The role of "judge" places constraints upon an individual, forcing him to pay attention to logic and continuity, and the judge is not in the same position as a legislator or a private citizen asked his preference about a question.

But the tracing of cases here and other exposure to case material suggests that the cases and the opinions—the doctrine of the Court—are by no means the end of consideration of civil liberties and rights in American society. The cases, when they reach the Court, are often the product of social and political activity—lobbying, mobilizing resources, etc.—and present important and divisive issues. The Supreme Court, in making choices—developing doctrine, applying tests, coming out on one side rather than another—is playing a role in the broader political system and is by no means entirely insulated from the currents abroad in the society.

Moreover, the emergence of a doctrine—whether it deals with equality, freedom of expression, or ciminal justice—is by no means the end of the matter. Rather it is a beginning, for the doctrine and the policy implicit in it will then move back into the political system, the environment of attitudes and behavior surrounding the Court, and its outcome is an open question. The doctrinal development—itself to some extent a product of the environment—may meet with easy acquiescence and be implemented without change or modification. Or, it may meet with intense resistance and modification by those whom it is supposed to control. This reaction to doctrine becomes itself a factor affecting further doctrinal development, change, or modification. Such interplay between the Court and its doctrine and the broader political system is the essence of the politics of civil liberties in our society.

In considering the issues of civil liberties and civil rights discussed here, it is clear that there are no definitive "answers" to the questions that are presented to the society and its Court. Rather there are many answers, many doctrines, many tests, all of which compete within the Court and the broader society for acceptance. At any particular time, one doctrine may emerge to deal with an issue involving freedom of expression, equality, or fair procedure. But as the character of the society changes, so may the answer change. In this fashion we continue to face questions about what rights our citizens shall enjoy, responding differently at various times, sometimes choosing the path of increased freedom, sometimes the path of repression. The law, the Constitution, the Court are all sources of answers to these questions, but they never provide simple, final, and unambiguous resolutions to the issues they present. Instead, they interact with attitudes and behavior in the political system to produce approximations of answers, always subject to change. Both in the Court and the society at large, today's dissent often becomes tomorrow's majority opinion.

INDEX

TABLE OF CASES

73 74 75 76   9 8 7 6 5 4 3 2